Samuel Beckett's Theatre

SAMUEL BECKETT'S THEATRE

Life Journeys

KATHARINE WORTH

CLARENDON PRESS • OXFORD

OXFORD
UNIVERSITY PRESS

Great Clarendon Street, Oxford OX2 6DP

Oxford University Press is a department of the University of Oxford and furthers the University's aim of excellence in research, scholarship, and education by publishing worldwide in

Oxford New York

Athens Auckland Bangkok Bogotá Buenos Aires Cape Town Chennai Dar es Salaam Delhi Florence Hong Kong Istanbul Karachi Kolkata Kuala Lumpur Madrid Melbourne Mexico City Mumbai Nairobi Paris São Paulo Singapore Taipei Tokyo Toronto Warsaw

with associated companies in Berlin Ibadan

Oxford is a trade mark of Oxford University Press in the UK and in certain other countries

Published in the United States by Oxford University Press Inc., New York

First published 1999
First published in paperback 2001

British Library Cataloguing in Publication Data
Data available

Library of Congress Cataloging in Publication Data
Worth, Katherine, 1922–
Samuel Beckett's theatre: life journeys / Katherine Worth.
Includes bibliographical references and index.
1. Beckett, Samuel, 1906– —Dramatic production. 2. Beckett, Samuel, 1906– —Dramatic works. 3. Beckett, Samuel, 1906– —Stage history. 4. Drama—Psychological aspects. I. Title.
PR6003.E282Z965 1999 792.9'5—dc21 99–20891
ISBN 0–19–811745–0

ISBN 0–19–818779–3 (pbk.)

3 5 7 9 10 8 6 4 2

Typeset in Sabon
by Alliance Phototypesetters, Pondicherry, India
Printed in Great Britain
on acid-free paper by
Bookcraft Ltd,
Midsomer Norton, Somerset

For George
and for the Family

Acknowledgements

I wish to thank the Leverhulme Trust for the award of a Leverhulme Emeritus Fellowship, 1987–9, to assist my research for a book on Samuel Beckett's drama.

I quote from Beckett's writings with permission from: The Beckett Estate, the Literary Executor, Faber & Faber, Les Editions de Minuit, the Beckett Manuscript Collection at the University of Reading, John Calder Publications, and, in the USA and Canada, Grove/Atlantic Inc., and Foxrock Inc.

My warm thanks go to Edward Beckett for his kind interest in my work.

I have pleasure in thanking all those who have enriched my appreciation of Samuel Beckett's art through their writings, productions, and in many other ways. The gratitude is no less real for my being unable to mention each by name. Special thanks to the friendly Beckett Archive at Reading University Library and to Ellie Roper for the efficiency and good humour she maintained in the typing process.

For the support they have given me throughout the writing of this book I wish to thank above all George Worth, without whom it would scarcely have been completed, and Barbara Hardy, who made much-valued suggestions on those parts of it she read. I am most grateful also for the help, advice, or information provided by Mary Bryden, Julie Campbell, Richard Cave, Ruby Cohn, Michael Fry, Alice Griffin, Joan Grundy, James Knowlson, Mary Lynch, Anthony Roche, and Christopher Worth.

Of my debt to Samuel Beckett and his light-giving art my book itself must speak.

Contents

List of Illustrations

(between pages 116 and 117)

Note to the Reader

Quotations from Beckett's plays, unless otherwise stated, are taken from *Samuel Beckett: The Complete Dramatic Works* (London: Faber & Faber, 1986).

Reference is also made to the revised texts, incorporating changes made by Beckett in directing his plays. For these, see the following series:

The Theatrical Notebooks of Samuel Beckett, general editor James Knowlson (London: Faber & Faber):

vol. i: *Waiting for Godot*, ed. Dougald McMillan and James Knowlson (1993)
vol. ii: *Endgame*, ed. S. E. Gontarski (1992)
vol. iii: *Krapp's Last Tape*, ed. James Knowlson (1992)
vol. iv: *The Shorter Plays*, ed. S. E. Gontarski (1999)

Also in the series:

Happy Days: The Production Notebook of Samuel Beckett, ed. James Knowlson (1985).

Dates in brackets following the first mention of a play refer to its first production, in English unless otherwise indicated. Dates of non-dramatic works refer to first publication.

Square brackets indicate ellipses of my own rather than those in Beckett's text. Their use in some *TN* references indicates Part 1.

For useful quick-reference bibliographies, see James Knowlson, *Damned to Fame: The Life of Samuel Beckett* (London: Bloomsbury, 1996), *The Cambridge Companion to Beckett*, ed. John Pilling (Cambridge: Cambridge University Press, 1994), and Beryl S. Fletcher and John Fletcher, *A Student's Guide to the Plays of Samuel Beckett* (London: Faber & Faber, rev. edn., 1985).

ABBREVIATIONS

TN	*The Theatrical Notebooks of Samuel Beckett*, general editor James Knowlson, 4 vols. (London: Faber & Faber, 1992–5), as above
MF	Dougald McMillan and Martha Fehsenfeld, *Beckett in the Theatre* (London: John Calder; New York, Riverrun Press, 1988)

Our Life Journeys in Beckett's Theatre: An Introduction

THERE are as many ways in to Samuel Beckett's art as individual imaginations to respond to it. The route I aim to follow is that described by Coleridge as 'the high road of human feelings'. It is, I believe, the way travelled by Beckett's characters. Though so strange and rare, it is still recognizable at every step and stumble as the road we are all taking through life towards that almost unimaginable 'end'.

Since starting on this book some years ago I have changed my approach to the extent of allowing in a little of my personal experience, including meetings with Beckett from the mid-1970s onward. It seems fitting now as it wouldn't have been while we were still talking.

The popular idea of Beckett as reclusive and remote has some obvious truth in it. No one who met him could fail to sense the deep reserves he had, and the capacity for withdrawal. But neither could be missed the interest in others, the courteous considerateness, the humorous or reflective observations on people and things which gave a strong impression of understanding and sympathy. In the theatre it is well known that he tended to disappear from the scene once the play was ready for performance. Such retreats, and his uncompromising pursuit of his vision, undeflected by critical reactions, may have suggested to some that he cared little about the response of audiences or readers.

However, he did care. He told me in a letter written early in our acquaintance: 'It is the nearest an author gets to sense when someone feels about his work as you about mine.'[1]

I felt this accorded with the wish to be heard, to make sense, which often drives his characters. Despite its emphasis on the solitary, his drama seems above all concerned with company, the company of the living and of the dead: 'All the dead voices'. Beckett protected his privacy fiercely. But countless people could testify how generously he opened his mind, to strangers as well as friends. While still in the thick of his writing life he was ready to make drafts or working notes available to those seriously concerned with his work, and his donations to archives were liberal.

Much that he made available was unfinished (like the fragmentary *Human Wishes*, given to Ruby Cohn) or unedited: jottings, heavily revised drafts, personal notebooks. That he would allow these telling glimpses into the workings of his mind suggests a certain friendliness towards readers. His commonplace book known now as the 'Whoroscope' Notebook[2] is great company; a gallimaufry of snatches of *Murphy*, learned notes, quirky sayings, Rabelaisian jokes, quotations, and 'wild thoughts'. Conscientious, student-like notes on authors are enlivened by jocose marginal comments: 'How would you like to have been Thespius's 50th daughter?' or 'Not only did he know nothing, but he was ignorant of the fact'. Lists abound: of Greek playwrights, Irish agrarian fraternities like the 'Peep o' Day boys', the vital statistics of the Venus de Milo, names of legendary Irish lovers. Odd words, comical sayings, squeeze into corners ('Making the worst of a good job'; 'He'd go through the eye of a needle for a bottle of stout') along with quotations from Spinoza and Sheridan, Pascal and *The Beggar's Opera*. At one point one or two pages of the score for *The Marriage of Figaro* are carefully copied out by hand.

It was said of Oliver Goldsmith by Dr Johnson that, although inveterately convivial, 'he never exchanged mind with you'. It could not be said of Beckett, to judge by his readiness to share his unbuttoned mind with us in the ways I've mentioned.

It is well known that Beckett makes close and continual use of his own life in his art. James Knowlson provides telling evidence of this in his richly documented biography, *Damned to Fame*,[3] and one critic, H. Porter Abbott, has written a study entirely focused on the extraordinary alchemy involved in Beckett's 'self-writing'. He has coined the term 'autography' to distinguish his own critical approach from the type of 'autobiographical' criticism which risks shrinking the art into the 'epiphenomenal residue of a single life's contingencies'.[4]

It is an important distinction. Beckett's fictions, full of personal detail as they are, can lead us into our own lives with great ease. They move with a sense of inevitability into the mythic realm where we may perceive their affinity with other great, universal journeys of the imagination, *The Divine Comedy*, *The Pilgrim's Progress*, and *Don Quixote* among them (a hostile reviewer of the first English production of *Godot* described it as a nursery version of *The Pilgrim's Progress*, getting one half of the equation right, at least). The light Beckett's fictions cast on our lives seems to stream out from that mysterious dimension. There is a religious element in this, though not in any doctrinal sense. Beckett is usually described as an agnostic, which seems right, as that simply means 'not knowing', and 'not knowing' was the condition he set himself to plumb to its depths in his art. Going into those depths was itself an arduous spiritual quest.

It is one that people have understood and maybe shared without knowing quite why. The enormous impact of *Waiting for Godot* tells us that. Crucial to its effect is Beckett's wry, humorous understanding of people and things: his sympathy with small upsets as well as great traumas, his enjoyment of the absurd as well as his use of it for profound musings on the meaning of life. 'Never neglect the little things of life', says Vladimir. Beckett never does. He opens his theatre buoyantly (though less spectacularly than his fiction) to mundane concerns with bodily matters and sordid little habits like Willie's trick of blowing his nose without the aid of a handkerchief. In a biography which stresses the bohemian side of the younger Beckett Anthony Cronin suggests that his work has had a profoundly cathartic effect by exposing the gap between the heroic/romantic standards set for us in literature and the unheroic state of mind 'in which most of us actually live most of the time'.[5]

It is still the ordinary stuff of life Beckett gives us even when the imagery is as fantastic as in *Happy Days*, with its chattering woman buried up to her waist in earth. Madeleine Renaud in the role was every inch the highly proper French lady of the old school, working at being well groomed as long as she had the use of her hands—and making the best of a bad job when she had not. With the prospect of playing Winnie in mind, Billie Whitelaw asked herself, 'how on earth could this man have written the story of my life so long before he knew me?'[6] Many have felt like this. It's the commonest thing to hear lovers of Beckett's work cheering themselves up in hard straits by recalling Beckett's disabled beings and applying to themselves the kind of bracing humour that helps Hamm and Clov to keep going:

CLOV. I can't sit
HAMM. True. And I can't stand.
CLOV. So it is.
HAMM. Every man his speciality.

Beckett speaks of the artist as bound to fail, repeatedly: 'Fail again. Fail better.' Yet he succeeds, astonishingly, in reflecting our lives for us and perhaps changing them too. The playwright Maria Irene Fornes is only one of many who have told of the impact his art has made on their attitude to life. When she saw Roger Blin's production of *En attendant Godot* she felt her life had been turned round, that she saw 'clarity', though 'If you'd asked me then what it was I'd understood, I couldn't have told you.'[7]

It is often the plays which have this radical effect and it is on those, in their English texts and performances, that I will be focusing (with occasional glances out to the prose fiction and the French texts and performances). Drama is the genre which provides the acid test of a writer's ability to reach out to all kinds and conditions of folk. No play ever survived in the theatre for decades, as *Waiting for Godot* has done, without possessing the common touch. Enoch Brater quotes Arthur Miller, not a leading admirer of Beckett, admitting 'if somewhat grudgingly', says Brater, that in *Godot* 'that playwright was up to something universal'.[8] Beckett consciously adapted his literary style for the theatre, as anyone acquainted with the fiction will recognize. In turning from the solitary reader (dictionary to hand, like Krapp) he sharply pruned his luxuriant pedantry, those recondite allusions and arcane words which are part and parcel of the *Molloy* trilogy and shout at us in byzantine works like *Watt* and the verbally intoxicated, youthful extravaganza, *Dream of Fair to Middling Women*. Just enough remains in the plays to thicken the mental world round the characters and give us companionable entry to it as we pick up their quotations and allusions (generally not too obscure in this domain).

It is from this perspective that I will look at Beckett's use of quotation, not attempting to chart it (an entire book would be needed for that) but to speak of the camaraderie he offers through 'shared words'; a snatch of Yeats or Shakespeare, a resonant biblical or Miltonic phrase, a comical Dickensian one. It is, in the Japanese phrase, a kind of 'borrowed scenery' within the mental landscape he unrolls for us. The sense of it is bound to vary from one individual to another and everyone will miss something (the biblical echoes presumably won't be heard by the young American actress who had to ask what *were* these ten commandments that cropped up in the play she was rehearsing). But enough common ground will remain for enough people, I believe, to allow for discussion along the lines I have set for myself. It is only part of what Beckett offers, but important for those who can receive it.

The journeys traced in the plays, as those in life, go through some dark and formidable spaces. Chapter 1 is given to the scenic imagery through which Beckett communicates the strangeness of the seemingly indifferent, inscrutable universe we inhabit. Theatre space in his hands becomes the cosmic space in which we are together and yet alone. It is this imagery above all which has seized the communal imagination. People have evidently recognized something true to their own mental experience in the iconic scenes: the leafless tree on the bare stage, the claustrophobic room with its remote, high windows, the human bodies trapped in earth or urns, the severed head or mouth continuing to function in a void of darkness. Delicately and subtly Beckett has generated scenes with the sort of power to haunt that popular horror fables like *Frankenstein* have. A thoroughly visceral unease is created, making us aware of the black holes that may gape for us (including the Sartrean God-shaped hole in the universe) and prompting questions about meaning which can't be avoided even when they are mocked as Winnie mocks the passer-by who gazes incredulously at her: 'What's the idea? he says—stuck up to her diddies in the bleeding ground—coarse fellow—What does it mean? he says—What's it meant to mean? . . .'.

Though Beckett's scenic images are unique, there are pointers to them in his dramatic background, in the plays of W. B. Yeats, for instance, and of Ibsen and Strindberg. I will touch on these, in particular on the model for an existential 'outdoor' drama offered by W. B. Yeats's *Where There is Nothing*, before considering the response to *Waiting for Godot* in the first English production by the scene designer, Peter Snow. The focus will be on scenic images recurring in Beckett's theatre and on how he recreates each main type from one medium to another. The road of *Godot* becomes the 'roads' of *. . . but the clouds . . .*, one of many fascinating metamorphoses.

Beckett's characters have their own ideas about the nature of the daunting universe they find themselves in. This is the theme of my second chapter. Doubt or uncertainty prevail. 'The key word in my plays is "perhaps" ', Beckett said, in an early interview.[9] But through the uncertainty run yearnings for a spiritual good as well as bitter scepticism and angry rejections of God, if God there be, who could allow the terrible suffering humans endure. Maddy and Dan Rooney in *All That Fall* scream with laughter when she tells him what the lesson for the coming Sunday will be—that God 'upholdeth all that fall'—and Hamm, having ordained a prayer session, growls sardonically when it leads nowhere, 'The bastard! He doesn't exist!' But the Rooneys go to church all the same and Hamm continues to call for prayers (we know that everything that happens in *Endgame* is part of a daily ritual). Beckett's characters often long for an end to it all: 'Why this farce, day after day?' But they also long to 'be again', as Krapp does, looking back on his life. These are contradictions and divisions of feeling which many if not most of Beckett's audiences will recognize and perhaps share. Christopher Ricks sees Beckett as especially true to life in his treatment of death and the tangled human reactions to it. We want to 'go on being', but 'most people some of the time, and some people most of the time, do not want to live forever'.[10]

The religious note isn't struck only as a Christian response to life, though there's no doubt that Christian imagery predominates: it was what he knew best, having been brought up in the Protestant faith, Beckett once pointed out. But some have sensed other faiths finding their way in too; perhaps faintly, as a breath of thought, a verbal echo, like the emphasis on 'nothing' (central in *Eleutheria*) which has been linked with the Nirvana of Buddhism. Though a non-doctrinal 'way', Buddhism nevertheless emphasizes the virtue of compassion and the desire for enlightenment, both strong impulses in Beckett's dramatic world. They coexist with what one commentator has called the Beckettian dilemma: 'the need to know God and the conviction that there is no God'.[11] These same virtues are lights in the darkness for many people nowadays who can't subscribe to a more comprehensive faith. 'If there were only darkness', Beckett said, 'all would be clear. It is because there is not only darkness but also light that our situation becomes inexplicable.'[12] His novella, *Stirrings Still*, written shortly before his death, movingly describes the departure from life of a narrator who has attained a state of transcendent calm but is still deeply affected by the strokes of a clock and distant 'cries' (faint echo of Vladimir's 'The air is full of our cries'). He has no wish or sorrow left, we are told: 'save that he wished the strokes would cease and the cries for good and was sorry that they did not'.

No doubt there of the speaker's pity for the suffering of humanity, but running through it all is the stirring of some profound intuition which opens up almost unimaginable horizons into the unknown. In the plays, as in modern life, scepticism or refusal of religious belief doesn't necessarily extinguish spiritual longings—or terrors, such as the fear of hell. Traditional imagery of hell looms large in the plays, and echoes from Dante are strong. *Endgame* probably ventures as close to the repetitive rituals which characterize the *Inferno* as any play could go without losing its audience. It might well have lost them, in the early years at least, had there been two acts, as originally planned.

Those bitter repetitions and recyclings of Dante's hell surely had to find a place in Beckett's theatre. We can't but recognize, if only from daily news bulletins and charity appeals, the sad vein of truth in the view that human life is a kind of hell. An eternity of afterlife pain may be rejected by most people now, but 'hell' as a term for the worst horrors of real life surfaces continually, as in media accounts of the Holocaust, or of atrocities in Bosnia and Rwanda, or of murders of peculiar depravity. Plays derived from the grim real-life experiences of Beirut hostages—notably Frank McGuinness's *Someone Who 'll Watch Over Me*—have inspired comparisons with Beckett's theatre, reminding us how he has placed his finger on an uneasy pulse of our time. The point was made in 1993 by Susan Sontag when she directed *Waiting for Godot* in Sarajevo. Peace there, at that time, seemed as remote a prospect as the arrival of Godot himself. Whether the production (an eccentric one) raised the spirits of the audience may have been debatable, but Sontag argued that the poverty of their theatrical means put all the participants in closer touch with Beckett and helped the healing spirits to flow.

Torments within the individual psyche—schizophrenic breakdowns, compulsive disorders, depressions—have been seen as the hell of our time. Beckett drew on his own neuroses and experience of analysis to reach into this dark region, but we all have access to it, if only through ordinary anxieties, glooms, and nightmares. Sombre imaginings are a natural feature of the high road, not a perverse turn-off from it; so Beckett can make us feel. He sheds a light of wisdom and humour on that hard truth, helping us through perils of the way; sloughs of despond, night terrors, painful retracing of the same old ground. The word 'sin', once the pivot of hell imagery, isn't much in use today, but notions of sin and punishment haven't gone away. They survive comically in a popular idiom of the 1990s, 'the so-and-so from hell'. 'Everything on TV is from hell these days', says a reviewer as *Nannies from Hell* succeeds the previous week's *Neighbours from Hell* (*Times*, 15 January 1998). Humour makes its way in when it can, as it does into Beckett's abysses of the self: another reason for trusting his view of things.

In 1929, writing on Joyce and Dante, Beckett dismissed hell and heaven as too 'static' to be interesting to a writer. Purgatory was the dynamic region, where change was possible. When he turned to writing for the theatre the need for dynamism was obvious, but more than artistic necessity was involved. Dante's hell is an unforgiving place: the sufferers in its horribly descending circles are fixed there forever; by God's will, it is said, but also, we can see, because they can't bear to give up the passions that cause their torment. So, revengeful Ugolino chews avidly on the flesh of the man who starved him and his sons to death, the two fitting together with awful neatness: 'the one head was a cap to the other'.

The notion of a divinely decreed hell as a place of perpetual punishment could only be repugnant to the Beckett who wrote *Waiting for Godot*. By the 1950s he had experienced the trauma of the German occupation of France and such emotional shocks as the death of his friend, Alfred Péron, from ill treatment in a concentration camp. James Knowlson suggests that his wartime experience changed him from the 'arrogant, closed-in young man of the 1930s' to the considerate, almost saintly character of the later years. There had to be a place in Beckett's art for the blackness of life, but he tilts it away from hell to a kind of Protestant purgatory where a redeeming truth may be sought. Ideas of a divine harrowing remain, as in the punishing spotlight of *Play*. But we are enabled to see reason in this, to sense the need for change within the egotistical psyches that are being probed. 'Change' is a key word. Whether it can be achieved is one of those questions we answer according to individual temperament. What is certain, I agree with Richard Coe, is that Beckett clings to the relative hopefulness of purgatory (his own version): it 'is the residence of every different manifestation of Beckett's *moi*: it is the home of Man'.[13]

What of the other locale in the worn, old, tripartite map of the human mind taken over by Beckett? 'Heaven' is not a concept many would think of in connection with his writings. But it is there in the plays, in the only way, perhaps, it could be; as a transient vision, a flood of memory, transcendent moments of truth. There is a hint of it in Beckett's affecting comment made in 1983 about a consoling thought he had carried through from his youth: there might be in later age, 'now; the true words at last, from the mind in ruins'.[14]

Against a background of illusion (continually brought to our notice) these moments stand out like landmarks of some intimate though infinitely elusive truth. Paradise may be always lost, but gleams of heavenly light visit the characters even when they are *in extremis*. Mouth in her agonizing void envisages a field of flowers on an April morning; Winnie in her hellish heat turns her mind to the 'holy light'. The longings she expresses could not be felt by the doomed egotists in the *Inferno*.

The heavenly elements in the Beckettian world are closely linked to the human quality of compassion, as when Vladimir tenderly lays his coat over the sleeping Estragon or reflects, 'Was I sleeping while the others suffered? Am I sleeping now?' The mystical dimension which gathers around these meditations intensifies in later plays like *Rockaby* and *A Piece of Monologue*.

It is natural to shrink from getting too close to purgatorial ordeals. Some seek to distance them by assuming a neurotic state of mind in the writer. Reviewers have sometimes seized with relief on terms like 'clinical pessimism' to account for *Endgame*, the play which especially draws out reactions of dislike. Beckett amusingly measured in terms of hard wood the resistance of early audiences to the French original, *Fin de partie* (Royal Court Theatre, London, 3 April 1957): it was 'like playing to mahogany, or rather teak'. Later in the smaller Studio des Champs-Élysées, he thought 'the hooks went in' (letter to Alan Schneider, 12 August 1959). His use of the word 'hooks' suggests that something violent and unpleasant in the experience was intended.

It is a special mark of his dramatic genius, in fact, that he can draw his audiences with astonishing directness into the physicality of interior events. We are made to feel on our pulses the awful threat of boredom in *Godot* and *Endgame*, the hallucinatory effect of concentration on a fixed point in *Not I* or *That Time*. Intentness seems to gather strength from the communal sense of being gripped in this way, whether or not the play is understood. After a lunch-hour performance of *Footfalls* at the Gate Theatre, Dublin, during the Beckett Festival of 1991, I heard a young woman who clearly hadn't known what she was in for saying to her friend on leaving: 'Didn't it give you the willies?' A raw reaction to something real and raw which Beckett had succeeded in conveying through his most delicate, ghostly play.

Beckett's humour is a strong lifeline for his audiences as for his characters. Ruby Cohn, doyenne of Beckett scholars, went straight to the mark when she called the first of her many books on him, in 1962,

The Comic Gamut. Beckett's humour often seems the breath of life itself, keeping human sympathy flowing, reminding us of sanity and the light of dawn. Humour is so ingrained in the work that it is hard to separate as a topic on its own, but I do so in Chapter 3 to the extent of looking at the companionable element in the comedy of the earlier plays and the survival in the later ones, where company has quitted the stage, of a lonely humour which can't be lost. A habit of mind, it comes out in a gesture, a droll aside, an ironical joke against the brooding self. In a separate part of this discussion I look at the piquant connection between the homely, often humorous, sayings that Beckett loved and the fantastic imagery he draws from them.

Humour often comes in slyly with a change in tone of voice, that instrument on which Beckett plays subtle tunes. Some dry remark can change the mood disconcertingly, as with Winnie's 'mondaine' greeting of Willie on his startling reappearance after a whole act's absence. 'Well this is an unexpected pleasure! (*Pause.*) Reminds me of the day you came whining for my hand.' Huge demands are made on actors for these changes of register, as Billie Whitelaw and many others have testified. But Beckett knew what he wanted: his own vocal tones could be very expressive in that way. I remember once describing to him a play of Edward Bond's, *Restoration*, which I admired, and commenting that Bond wanted to change the world. His reply—'Let it burn'—lost its death-wish effect when spoken as he spoke, with wry good humour, the tone of one aware that the world would refuse to change—and probably wouldn't burn.

There are deep connections between the humane humour and the intimations of a mystical dimension which run through the plays. James Knowlson has suggested that Beckett saw life as tragedy and Andrew Kennedy has argued, apropos *Endgame*, that the play's lack of final reconciliation ties it to the Absurd, and is in tune with the 'universalising pessimism, the nihilistic strand' in Beckett's work.[15] It was natural that Beckett's formidable technique for rendering the 'mess' of life, with pungent mockery and anguished protest, should have led Martin Esslin to make him the starting-point in his influential *The Theatre of the Absurd*.[16] But the term itself doesn't quite fit. The arch Absurdist, Ionesco, explained the Absurd as a theatre which shows man 'cut off from his religious, metaphysical and transcendental roots', so that all his actions become 'senseless and absurd, useless'. Fear of that fate may haunt Beckett's characters but it is not the medium in which they exist. On the contrary they pursue enlightenment in the teeth of absurdity—and experience it too, if only partially and intermittently.

Beckett himself described *Godot* in its English edition as 'tragicomedy' and it's a term that can be applied to most of the plays (though not, to my mind, to the 'cruel' investigations conducted in *Rough for Radio 2* or *What Where*). A Divine Comedy of some inscrutable kind comes and goes in the mind of his questioning, doubting, rebelling characters. It is a fragile compound of emotion, imagination—and humour. The hard-won, ambiguous reconciliations of Shakespeare's late plays must often have been in Beckett's mind, as critics have observed. Hamm has been seen as a 'toppled Prospero,' echoes from *The Winter's Tale* have been noted in the 'sad tale' of *Ohio Impromptu*, and *The Tempest* sends out further echoes into Beckett's world through the name Miranda, she who was able to suffer 'with those that I saw suffer'; the authentic Beckettian note.

From cosmic spaces and the characters' speculations about the 'void' and its meaning my discussion moves to the journey they and we are taking through this universe. It is one that has to be not only taken but told, not only told but sifted: separating the grain from the husks is how Krapp puts it. When he picks his way to his cubby-hole over the tapes spilt on the floor, he is 'treading on his life', Beckett told Pierre Chabert.[17] The sense of life as a journey whose value and purpose is found in the taking of it lies at the heart of Beckett's theatre. He writes in a long-continuing and universally understood tradition which takes in at one end *A la recherche du temps perdu* and at the other innumerable fleeting comments about their day-to-day experience made by people writing memoirs or being interviewed about their careers: one such came from Tim Waterstone, the bookseller: 'As I look back on my life, it does feel like a constant journey' (*Sunday Telegraph*, 10 August 1997).

From the moment when Estragon struggles to shed his painful boots, Beckett's theatre is alive with the physical effort of journeying. Characters limp, puff and pant, stumble, fall, pull themselves up, and with difficulty push the body forward. Mostly they have been on the road a long time, often retracing familiar tracks. 'I have lived on it . . . till I'm old', muses Opener in *Cascando*, while Mouth shocks herself by remembering that when the light 'went out' for her she was 'coming up to sixty when—. . . what? . . . seventy? . . . good God!'

The same intense physical effort goes into pushing forward the mind through its endless recall and revaluing of the journey so far as it has gone. A resonant common chord is struck in those 'retrospects'. People do feel the need to keep their life journey fresh in mind by telling it to others as well as themselves, with the aid of letters (including circular ones summarizing a year's events), diaries, photograph albums, cassettes, camcorders. Beckett's travellers are sometimes, like Krapp, professional writers. But they tell of their strange journeys through life with the aid of the common touch; it links their stories to the universal activity heard in snatches on buses or at parties or glimpsed in letters. Laurence Olivier's letters, according to his official biographer, were 'like a tireless commentary on his own existence' (*Times*, 4 January 1996). The line between professional and amateur is not rigid. As Barbara Hardy comments in her *Tellers and Listeners*, the man in the street who says he could write a novel if only he had the time isn't necessarily a laughing-stock. He might not produce a readable narrative, but 'Like everyone else, he is telling stories and scraps of stories every day of his life, assembling and revising the stories of his days into an informal autobiography'.[18]

The tales of the life journeys on Beckett's stage record just such a process; subtle and refined far beyond the common capacity, but keeping company with it all the same, on the high road of human feeling.

Sometimes Beckett's travellers may seem doomed to remain on the same track forever like the doomed souls in the *Inferno*, who waste the moment of reprieve offered by the arrival of Dante and Virgil in simply reliving past traumas. Beckett's travellers, even those seemingly most hopeless, like Mouth, are still travelling, could still change track, as I see it. This part of my discussion has links with Chapter 2, which goes into those imagined zones of hell and purgatory.

Often we can sense the wrong notes in the fictionalized accounts characters or people we meet in life give of their journey. Hamm's false starts in his compulsive story ('the one you've been telling yourself all your . . . days') signal some kind of deceit, like the stagy monologues of the trio in the first round of *Play*. But for all the 'play' Beckett's story-tellers make with their material, they are also driven to get it right. There is a powerful sense of a need to satisfy some recording angel, whether situated within or without the private consciousness. The angel's eye might be the shadow-self, the 'other' hinted at in Beckett's complementary pairs (Didi and Gogo, Hamm and Clov) or heard as a voice outside the listening self, as in *That Time*, or given shape in the dimly lit Auditor of *Not I* or the startlingly identical old white-haired men of *Ohio Impromptu* who share one black hat between them. This sense of a divided or multiple self, though potentially lethal, in its less extreme form is also part of the common experience, as common speech testifies with familiar metaphors: 'I told myself', 'I just stopped myself', and so forth. We all have a reader and a listener within.

Beckett touches the springs of our sympathy by being exceptionally ready to expose his most intimate memories. Probably no other playwright has made such bold, continuous, and self-lacerating use of his own life, not excluding Eugene O'Neill, who wrote his 'naked' play about his family, *Long Day's Journey Into Night*, in 'tears and blood'. Or James Joyce, whose one play, *Exiles*, testifies in a quiet way to what his fiction demonstrates flamboyantly, that, as Brenda Maddox comments, quoting *Finnegans Wake*, like Shem the Penman, he 'wrote with the ink of himself over the skin of his body'.[19] In his manuscript drafts Beckett can be seen perfecting a technique—'Vaguen', he calls it—which deliberately obscures the real-life sources of his drama. S. E. Gontarski has closely charted this fascinating process.[20]

Yet Beckett does exactly the opposite too, offering autobiographical signposts, including place-names (Croker's Acres, Ballyogan Road) and family names. He gave the pacing woman in *Footfalls* the name of his own mother, May, around which painful memories clustered. Beckett knew when writing the play in 1975 that his difficult, close relationship with his mother was no secret. Only a year or two later Deirdre Bair was to describe in her biography May Beckett's insomniac habit of walking the house at night during her son's impressionable youth. She quoted too Beckett's sad comment on the feeling between them: 'I am what her savage loving has made me'.[21] In his play he impresses on his audience the haunting persistence of this deeply incised name.

His memories were, he said himself, 'obsessional' but in his theatre they take on a wonderfully vivid, independent life which allows them to seem everybody's. He was uneasy about the way his fictional 'places' were increasingly pinned down to the actuality they sprang from. It happened especially after his Irishness was seized on, which was surprisingly late in the day. An evocative account of Irish places in Beckett's writings by Terence Brown, of Trinity College, Dublin, redeemed a noticeable paucity of Irish speakers at the great conference in Paris, Beckett dans le Siècle, in 1986. In that same year, at a private view in the Olivier Gallery in London's National Theatre, of the photographs in Eoin O'Brien's book, *The Beckett Country* (1986), I heard the Irish Ambassador, in his opening remarks, say that he hadn't till then fully realized that Beckett was Irish. A complimentary exaggeration, no doubt, but for many, at least in the 1960s and 1970s, it was no more than the truth. Michael Colgan, Director of the Gate Theatre, Dublin, commented to this effect in a radio interview (on BBC's *Five Live*, 16 March 1997): 'People used to think Beckett was French and Bernard Shaw English. But we're taking it all back now.' True indeed, Beckett appears on the tourist T-shirts, along with Yeats, Joyce, and the rest of the pantheon: the 'back roads' round Ballyogan may attract visitors of the future as Joyce's tower or Yeats's do now.

Eoin O'Brien himself expressed some uneasiness about contributing to this process: perhaps 'obsessional diligence in identifying realities could blight the creative beauty of Beckett's imagination—the "soul-landscape" '.[22] He concluded that everything turned on the approach, and most would no doubt agree with this. I found it a rather melancholy part of reading James Knowlson's absorbing biography when Beckett's memories of place and event were recalled for the benefit of his biographer in the flatter, more fatigued tones of the writer near the end of his life, no longer wielding inspired words. Yet there was a reminder in this gap of just how magical the art is, how it can carry the imagination far beyond material reality, into our own 'soul-landscape'.

It is this theme I pursue above all. The weaving of his life-material into his *œuvre* is a fascinating story, of course. New biographical material or stimulating new points of view on it add extra layers of interest to our thinking about the plays. But the work remains itself, working with its own power to touch the springs of imagination in us all, allowing the events and places that belonged to the writer to belong to us. It was certainly interesting to learn from Knowlson's biography that a real-life affair with Barbara Bray lay behind the half-comic, half-deadly torments of the trio in *Play*. But the play still challenges us to see into it as an experience freed from specific facts and circumstances. From this point of view the jewel in the biographical revelation was the review of the play by Barbara Bray herself. She struck the general, human note when she described the ravaged heads as 'people in all their funny, disgraceful, pitiable fragility and all the touchingness, in spite of everything, of their efforts to love one another, and endure'.[23]

Is there too much missing from the journeys taken in Beckett's theatre to let us have a sense of life's fullness? Some have thought so. The reviewer John Peter has argued that Beckett's is a 'closed' world and that the social and psychological density of his characters is 'almost nil'.[24] Kenneth Tynan had his doubts about *Endgame*, but said of *Godot* that it showed the theatre what it could do without and exist: 'It arrives at the custom-house, as it were, with no luggage, no passport and nothing to declare; yet it gets through as might a pilgrim from Mars.'[25] He had formal elements in mind, but his remark could be applied to subject-matter and to the *œuvre* as a whole.

It does have many apparent gaps. With rare exceptions, young adults do not appear on Beckett's stage, and there are no scenes of youthful love nor sexual passion: sex in *Godot* is fuel for gallows humour about the interesting connection between hanging, erections, and mandrakes. So many seemingly crucial 'omissions' might have been expected to deter young audiences, as too the preponderance of middle-aged and elderly characters in the plays (often roughly corresponding with Beckett's age at the time he wrote them). That has been far from the case, however. Students, young actors, young people in general can be the most excited and fascinated by Beckett's plays, as anyone who has discussed Beckett much with them will know. They can perceive, with their fresh imaginations, that youth, sex, and love are not absent from Beckett's theatre but on the contrary intensely there, in longings, dreams, memories, visitations. Krapp relives the lyrical moment with the girl who narrowed her eyes against the light. Nagg and Nell attempt to kiss, stretching between their dustbins: a grotesque and touching flicker of old love.

Memory figures inevitably in my discussion of the life journey, but the vast theme spills over into separate discussion of two of its component parts which are related, though one is to do with forgetting, the other with tenacious remembering. Forgetting or half-forgetting is mysteriously connected in Beckett's world with creative acts of evocation. It is also, whether painfully or comically, instantly recognizable as an ordinary part of every life. Who hasn't sympathized with Winnie's unforgettable 'What is that unforgettable line?' Beckett had a stupendous memory, but had to work a little to recall favourite lines in his last year or two, in the way of most people as they age. It was a phase he seemed already to have captured in imagination in *Happy Days*, written many years before.

Ghostly encounters on the other hand might not be thought part of the common experience. Yet we all have our ghosts and we do meet them at times on the road of the mind. Beckett shows them taking shape at the place where memory, dream, and imagination meet. A composite ghost grows in *Footfalls* from imagery of ancient use; in *Ghost Trio* a man waits in vain for a presence to appear. The repeated word 'ghost' draws *A Piece of Monologue* to a transcendent consummation. Here and in . . . *but the clouds* . . . and *Eh Joe*, the ghosts are deeply inward, close cousins to the one who walks 'in the waning dusk' in T. S. Eliot's 'Little Gidding'; the 'familiar compound ghost | Both intimate and unidentifiable'. That disconcerting mix is what Beckett gives us supremely, taking us into the most unknown by way of the most known.

Even in the tenuous atmosphere of the later plays the visionary is 'earthed' in day-to-day reality. Nostalgia is not facile in Beckett's characters. The past has to be experienced in full, with its pain sometimes dominating, as in the torments of Mouth. In the atmosphere of sad calm that characterizes *Ohio Impromptu* the 'old terror of night' retains its power to strike. Like all of us Beckett's characters sometimes look back with rose-coloured spectacles: 'rosy' is a term used with gentle irony by the reminiscing voice in *Company*. But Beckett alerts us to keep our distance from soft nostalgia. He used to say drily when people asked him whether Krapp missed his real chance of happiness in parting from the girl in the punt, that if she had become Mrs Krapp he would probably have been listening to her nagging rather than dreaming about her. The play itself implicitly tells us that it could be so: and that such is life.

Yet there is a place for pleasurable dwelling on time past. Beckett touches another of the great common chords in the attachment his characters have to 'the old style', as Winnie puts it, only half-ironically. I used to enjoy the picture postcards he sometimes sent, with views of bygone Paris, amusing and poignant in one. There was the horse-drawn double-decker bus, crammed with young girls in veils, looking like under-age brides but presumably *en route* to a first communion. An entertaining fashion picture of ladies in Edwardian hats, some in tantalizing profile, set up thoughts of the hatted trio in *Come and Go* (hats make their way into these pages). And a park scene with smart, white-aproned nursemaids (also in hats) wheeling smart prams could not but recall Krapp brooding fondly on such: 'One dark young beauty I recollect particularly, all white and starch, incomparable bosom, with a big black hooded perambulator, most funereal thing.' The Paris of a later period had a nostalgic glow too: Beckett told me he liked the novels of Jean Rhys for the atmosphere of Paris in the 1920s evoked in them. I sent him a copy of the posthumously published, unfinished autobiography, *Smile Please* (1979) which he had been doubtful about: this too he enjoyed, it seemed, for its evocative Paris sequences.

Like most of us on reaching a certain age, Beckett's speakers often feel the need expressed by Henry in *Embers* for 'someone who . . . knew me, in the old days, anyone, to be with me, imagine he hears me, what I am, now'. It is close to the note Shakespeare strikes, only half-comically, when Justice Shallow reminisces about high times in the Clement's Inn of his youth, then asks sadly, 'And is old Double dead?' Irish playwrights have made this domain their special province ever since Oliver Goldsmith's Mr Hardcastle defended to his wife his love of 'everything that's old: old friends, old times, old manners, old books, old wine. . . .', ending with the tactless coda, to his disgruntled wife: 'and, I believe, Dorothy (*taking her hand*), you'll own I have been pretty fond of an old wife'. Her tart response changes the mood just in time to ward off sentimentality.

Beckett's fondness for Goldsmith could be deduced almost from this scene alone. He shared with him an exceptionally strong affection for scenes and places of childhood and early youth; unaccountable 'maladie du Pays' Goldsmith called it. Another admired predecessor, W. B. Yeats, had a passion for the bare Irish countryside and made it a shaping force in his drama. A younger contemporary, Brian Friel, charmed audiences everywhere with the music crackling out of the old wireless in *Dancing at Lughnasa*. Beckett satisfies the same sort of yearning for the time just gone by: for old films, old tunes, Laurel and Hardy, sounds of steam trains entering a country railway station, quiet roads where a car was an event.

This theatre of his, so bare and stark from a distance, reveals itself on closer approach as exceptionally rich in allusions and echoes—from the arts, as from real life. I will be looking especially at verbal echoes (in some detail in Chapter 6), but other kinds will make their way into the discussion here and there, as they must: our life is lived to a great extent in our aesthetic experience, after all. The road Beckett's travellers tread, like Prospero's island, is full of music and artistic visions. Paintings by Caspar David Friedrich and Jack Yeats (an artist close to Beckett's heart, as friend and painter) hover in the background of *Godot*, and many other transferences from the world of art have struck lovers of the plays. Music occurs intermittently in the theatrical *œuvre* from first to last, sometimes drawn from classical stock, as in *Ghost Trio*, sometimes newly composed for the occasion.

Beckett gave me permission to find new music for the productions of *Words and Music* and *Cascando* which he allowed me to make as teaching material. I will refer briefly to this experience in discussing in Chapter 7 some of the many different rhythms—of performers and of writers as unlike as Yeats, Maeterlinck, and Dickens—that have entered into my appreciation of Beckett's art.

Beckett struck those who met him as someone who was not a performer but always himself to a remarkable degree: 'consistent to his flinty core', says Mel Gussow, speaking of the way any extract from his work seems to contain his 'essence'.[26] Many have commented on this and on the significant fact that Beckett never lost his Dublin accent after many years of living in Paris. Yet of course those familiar with his writings knew that he had many selves inside him: it's a critical commonplace that the four unlike characters in *Godot* can be seen, from one angle, as aspects of a single, though complex and divided, personality, a state Beckett understood from within. He impressed actors with his ability as a director to convey just what nuance or posture he required in a role. I was amused to hear from Peggy Ashcroft that when preparing to play Winnie she had told him she knew how the character must sound—'Like you'—and got the reply, 'I don't know about that.' Easy to imagine the words, said in his driest tone, expressing a personality as far as could be from the voluble Winnie or the outgoing actress. Yet it was he who produced Winnie, this 'other', out of himself.

Reflections of the kind I have been venturing can only be personal: there's no legislating for taste nor the camaraderie of 'sharing'. But Beckett's art inspires shared responses by its magical ability to communicate the special aura of the well loved. Lehar's Merry Widow waltz has surely acquired that aura by the end of *Happy Days*, even if we don't already have the tune tucked away in some dusty corner of consciousness—or not so dusty for those of us who heard the production of *The Merry Widow* at the Royal Opera House in 1997. In the midst of the extrovert bonhomie there was something slightly but charmingly inward in the scene when the lovers who have such difficulty in speaking of love sing to the tune of 'Winnie's' waltz, 'We can choose to let the music say it all'. Banal words, haunting tune, giving the illusion of true feeling. The classical works heard in the plays can always hold their own. It is Beckett's kindness to lesser music that is so endearing. I recall the slight shock of disappointment I felt at Stirling in 1986 when Pierre Chabert gave the first performance I had seen of *Krapp's Last Tape* minus the hymn 'Now the day is over | Night is drawing nigh' (Beckett had cut it out). It was like losing a friend.

The old-fashioned songs and hymns Beckett loved are drawn into a more ironic framework in his plays but they are not there to be mocked. I thought of this when seeing on video Jonathan Burrows's piquant postmodern dance piece *Hymns* (1988, televised for a documentary by BBC Television and Arts Council Films, 1991). His style was also ironic, playful, and slightly mocking but could change, as when the rousing opening hymn, 'Onward Christian Soldiers' (appropriately danced to what sounded like a harmonium), slid into 'Father, hear the prayer we offer' and the two male dancers slowed down, the debonair feet becoming reflective, old. Burrows's clergyman father, who had watched the performance, was surely right when he commented, as the quiet, closing tableau faded out to the strains of 'The day Thou gavest, Lord, is ended', 'Oh, it isn't a send-up at all. No, it's just life.'

The test for Beckett is always 'just life': it is one of the great sources of joy in the plays that he can convey so much of it through little scraps of music and art, from sources quite as heterogeneous as those most of us carry around in our heads.

One great proof of Beckett's importance for us all is the power his work has to attract creative interest from actors, directors, adapters, and audiences of all kinds, from the San Quentin prisoners who turned themselves into a dramatic company in order to perform his plays to the innumerable groups of students fired by reading the work into bold stabs at producing it. The fiction has almost from the start been a magnet for performers. Spoken Beckett anthologies have flourished since Jack MacGowran created 'Beckett Man', the stick-like figure in the dilapidated boots and 'tattered, ankle-length coat' described by Jordan R. Young, who moved in and out of scenes from the novels, stories and plays.[27] The MacGowran vein has been tapped more recently by Barry McGovern's virtuoso solo rendering of the *Molloy* trilogy, adapted by him and Gerry Dukes as *I'll Go On*, and in many different ways the work has been much heard.

The analogy with Joyce is obvious. It has been said that to hear *Finnegans Wake* well spoken by an Irish voice is the best of all ways to 'read' that intricate piece of sound. John Calder set up a Theatre of Literature which met a genuine need for close listening, as I discovered when filling in for him once at the Cheltenham Festival of Literature as commentator in the Beckett programme he had devised for three actors. There was an instant response from a large, ordinarily mixed audience. Admittedly the enthusiasm of some young schoolboys in the front row for a passage from *The Unnamable* ('there's a story for you . . . well well, so that's emotion, that's love, and trains') owed something to the fact that the reader, Sylvester McCoy, was the current Dr Who: they sported the badge of his fan club. But who can say that Beckett didn't make his way into their minds too?

The plays were at one time strictly guarded by Beckett from free treatment by directors and adapters. He relaxed his rule somewhat in later years but no one could be quite sure what he would allow: this no doubt adds to the difficulties experienced since his death by his Literary Executor and the Beckett Estate. The problems are real, but my focus will be less on these than on their cause: the amazing magnetism of the *œuvre*. A mythology of performance has been created under our eyes, expressing Beckett for many who might never read the fiction nor even see the plays.

I conclude with a brief account of my own involvement in this scene through my adaptation of *Company*, with Julian Curry in the solo role and Tim Pigott-Smith directing. The word 'company' seems the right one to end a study such as this which aims to bring out how closely to everyday living Beckett works; how his feeling for the common, 'little' experiences of life and art warms and upholds us as we enter various kinds of depths and darkness; how our own life journeys are returned to us with a mythic dimension, a rich bloom on them, from the strange, remote regions where his characters enact theirs. He invests with new significance the familiar processes of life: looking back, looking forward, suffering from bad feet or some other trouble ('blind next', says Winnie), feeling oneself get old, or, if young, trying to imagine it, pursuing dreams, struggling to look into the 'abyss' of the self or confront unpalatable truths like the certainty of death.

There is a moment in *Godot* when the pair who routinely separate and come together again confront the idea of a more permanent parting and Gogo says:

That would be too bad, really too bad. (*Pause.*) Wouldn't it, Didi, be really too bad? (*Pause.*) When you think of the beauty of the way. (*Pause.*) And the goodness of the wayfarers . . .

We can't but sense the weight in this little word, 'way', linked as it is with pointed, if faintly ironic, allusions to 'beauty' and 'goodness'. In the context of the whole *œuvre* we can recognize it as the road we see from many perspectives as we accompany Beckett's travellers on their journeys. Shadow and light have fallen across it from other mental travellers, as when it takes a dark Dantesque turn, or a Proustian one (we might recall that *Du côté de chez Swann* was translated by Scott Moncrieff as *Swann's Way*). Various mystic ways might come to mind: the negative way of Buddhism, the spirals of reincarnation, or the way of Christ which Estragon says he has been seeking to follow all his life. It is also and above all the common way, the 'high road of human feelings' which everyone alive has to take, from birth to death—and perhaps, who knows, beyond it. At the fearful end of *King Lear* the faithful Kent sees death as a strange continuance of travelling: 'I have a journey, sir, shortly to go; | My master calls me, I must not say no'. The light shed on this awe-inspiring 'way' in Beckett's theatre is the theme of my book.

I
Cosmic Scenery

ALL the scenic spaces Beckett creates become cosmic spaces where we find ourselves, in the Maeterlinckian phrase, face to face with 'the vast unknown that surrounds us'. It is on this aspect of his scenic techniques that I focus.

THE ROAD

Looking back now, it may seem inevitable that the first of his scenic images to be realized in the theatre was the empty open road of *Waiting for Godot* where a cryptic moon rises on cue at the end of each act, harbinger of a longed-for night. Not so long ago before the first production of the French original in 1953 Beckett had travelled with Suzanne Deschevaux-Dumesnil on a painfully real road, travelling by night and sleeping by day, escaping from the Gestapo into Vichy France: a time of trauma. Behind that, in sharpest contrast, lay the beloved roads of childhood, winding up into the Dublin hills. The road in the play is fraught with these memories. It was chance that brought *Godot* to the stage before *Eleutheria*, a quintessential play of the 'room' which Suzanne had also tried to place in 1949. But how inevitable it seems now that audiences should first meet Beckett through a play which has turned its back on rooms, where there is nothing to break the emptiness but a single tree, nowhere to sit down but a mound of earth (later to become a stone).

The utter bareness and openness of the scene retains its power to shock even today when it is so familiar, perhaps because television keeps audiences habituated to the idea of conversational plays being set indoors. In the 1950s that was true of stage plays in general: typical was Terence Rattigan's *Separate Tables* which opened in London in the same year as *Godot*. And in Paris Jean-Paul Sartre had set his play about hell, *No Exit* (*Huis Clos*, 1944) in a hotel room elaborately decorated in Second Empire style. Open-air settings had come to seem an aberration by then. What the theatre had taken over from the great scene-setter, Ibsen, was the claustrophobic domestic space of *A Doll's House* or *Hedda Gabler* rather than the vast, bleak mountain landscapes of *Peer Gynt* or *Brand*; or *John Gabriel Borkman*, where the damaged hero is kept pent up in airless rooms before being sent in the final act to climb a wintry mountain track, confront his soul, and die of an icy hand gripping at his heart. Munch described this as 'the mightiest winter landscape in Scandinavian art'. Such landscapes were not easily appreciated by European audiences more at home in the heavily furnished theatre room.

Strindberg became more noted for his oppressive middle-class rooms where the deadly marital battles of *The Father* or *The Dance of Death* were fought than for the daunting scenic spaces of an expressionist work like *A Dream Play*. It opens astonishingly with an astronomical/metaphysical vision as the daughter of Indra slowly descends into the stifling air of Earth through a space adorned with constellations: Leo, Virgo, and Libra and the planet Jupiter shining with a bright light. Unsurprisingly, Beckett was interested in Strindberg. He saw Roger Blin's production of *The Ghost Sonata* in Paris in 1949, and in *Eleutheria* he presented a character reminiscent of Strindberg's Glazier in *A Dream Play*, he who opens the door behind which supposedly lies the solution to the riddle of the universe and finds—'nothing'.[1]

Beckett might have thought too of Maeterlinck who in his 'little' plays of the 1890s invested with cosmic significance any stage space he touched, whether an ordinary bourgeois interior like the room with many doors in *The Intruder* (*L'Intruse*, 1891) or a limitless exterior like the ancient forest of *The Blind Ones* (*Les Aveugles*, 1891) where the lost blind people sit on tree stumps. *Pelléas and Mélisande* (1893), which Beckett admired, also opens in a lonely forest with Mélisande sitting by a well, unable to tell Golaud anything about herself or where she has come from. Her meetings with Pelléas too are mostly in the open: on a terrace looking out to sea; by (another) well; on the seashore itself, or in the garden where Golaud's long shadow finally extinguishes the light the lovers create around themselves.

Aurélien Lugné-Poe, director of Maeterlinck's earliest symbolist plays, devised a whole new stage strategy to give theatrical life to their ambivalent scenic images: toy-like, nursery-style castle turrets, reversible painted sets, gauzes drawn between audience and actors to create mesmeric dream effects. The art of painters entered significantly into these dramatic structures, creating such effects as the scene which closes *Interior* (*Intérieur*, 1895), when the stage doors at the back are flung open, the family rush out through them, and we see in the background a night sky blazing with stars. It is a scene, as usual in these early plays of Maeterlinck, which points outward to the mystery of the universe. In this way above all the Maeterlinckian images have a flavour suggestive of things to be in Beckett's theatre.

The cosmic scenic imagery of these great innovators entered the bloodstream of the European theatre slowly, almost imperceptibly, until Beckett reinvented it for the 1950s in *Godot*. There were some obvious, practical reasons for the delayed reception. Ibsen himself originally thought of *Brand* as a 'dramatic poem', not a piece for performance. It wasn't produced until twenty years after its publication, and he saw it for the first time a few years before his death, in 1898. It took still longer to visit the capitals of Europe, interestingly reaching Dublin relatively early, at the Gate Theatre (8 December 1936) with Micheál MacLiammóir playing Brand. This was a time when Beckett was taking a close interest in Dublin's theatre activities: he had helped a friend, Mary Manning, to revise her play, *Youth's the Season?*, for production by the Gate and would have known about *Brand*, though he was in Germany at the time of its production.

He did have opportunities, however, to see open-air settings on the Dublin stage where a more rural tradition was still in force, one which allowed for subtly inward effects in the hands of someone like Synge. His *The Well of the Saints* is a play about the mind's inner workings set entirely in the open air. Yeats enormously admired Synge's quiet country road settings and took them over, investing them with mystical intensity in such plays as *At the Hawk's Well*, *The Cat and the Moon*, and *The Dreaming of the Bones* (the two last were produced at the Abbey in 1931). Beckett certainly received inspiration from these plays and from Yeats's *Purgatory* (1938) which offered a powerful model for *Godot* with its deceptively simple set; a country road, a ruined house (common then in Ireland), a solitary, leafless tree. From these ordinary components Yeats aimed to draw a ghostly scene, representing what he called the 'deep of the mind'. Stage directions call for a window to light up in the ruin, revealing the figure of a young girl long dead; hoofbeats are heard on gravel no longer there; at the climax, the tree glows with brilliant white light before fading back to its dead state. A disturbed state of mind is being illuminated.

Or so we should feel: stage light was meant to play the sort of role here that it has in Beckett's theatre, though I've not yet seen a production which quite managed this. The transformation effects are sometimes left entirely to the audience's imagination, which seems something of a theatrical let-down as well as a sacrifice of the ambiguity Yeats intended. At the other extreme we get too much visualization, as in the production at the Abbey Theatre which showed the dead girl with her lover in an all-too-fleshly nude flashback. We may see here how much more tightly Beckett choreographed his lighting effects. Yeats had brilliantly original ideas for exploring the mind's depth through scenic imagery but wasn't able to keep the same firm grip on later realization in the theatre as Beckett is famous for doing.

Yet the ideas are there, copious and fecund. Another play of Yeats's offered a piquant model for an open-air drama with a mystical core. *Where There is Nothing* could not but interest Beckett. He knew all Yeats's plays, though he couldn't have seen this one on the Dublin stage; it has never, so far as I know, been professionally performed in Ireland. When it had its première in London at the Royal Court Theatre (20 June 1904) directed by Granville Barker, its Nietzschean, iconoclastic hero, Paul Ruttledge, would have been too strong meat for Irish audiences. He is still an uncomfortable kind of hero with some points of likeness to Victor Krap in *Eleutheria*.

The designers for *Where There is Nothing* had a task unusual for the theatre of the time. The majority of the settings were outdoor. Act 1 gives us a tamed version of nature, a prosperous bourgeois garden with neat path, croquet lawn, and scattered symbols of domesticity (children's toys and a pram belonging to bachelor Paul's relations). The danger here, as Yeats realized on seeing the initial design by Pamela Colman Smith, was of the humdrum being only too boringly convincing. He solved the problem, so he hoped, by suggesting to his designer a curious stylizing device: bushes shaped into cocks, ducks, and so forth, with caricature suggestions of human features. A fantastic visual sub-text, it was meant to point to the ironical 'occupation' of Paul's bored leisure: 'all the people I meet are like farmyard creatures'.

The play then goes out on to the roads. The bare country road of Act 2, with its background 'wall of unmortared stone' was also humdrum on the surface, at least for Irish audiences. Yeats's designers (Edith Craig had joined Pamela Colman Smith) pleased him by recognizing its symbolic connection with the all-important roads. He observed: 'There is to be a stone wall, a gallery wall in every outdoor scene as a kind of repeated *motif*.' Visual effects were whenever possible to give a glimpse into the way Paul sees the tracks he travels on: 'As I can't leap from cloud to cloud I want to wander from road to road . . . Did you ever think that the roads are the only things that are endless . . . They are the serpent of eternity.'

In the closing scene of Act 5 Yeats imagined a set that would express something of his troubled hero's innermost vision; ecclesiastical ruins on a stretch of grass, in the background a glimpse of the River Shannon and a rocky plain. In this bleak, exposed place, where the unfrocked friars gather reeds to make a living, Paul Ruttledge was to experience the God who is to be found in 'nothing'. As he lies dying, he begs to be taken 'down' into 'that field under the earth', not to be left floating into the dark 'beyond Saturn'. Whether the visionary words were matched by the scenic imagery is something we can't know.

Perhaps unexpectedly, there was a welcome in London for *Where There Is Nothing*. A. B. Walkley wrote sympathetically of the text when it was published in 1903 ('*Lavengro* in an Irish setting'), and Granville Barker's production made William Archer think of Ibsen's *Brand*: Yeats's hero was a 'far off cousin', belonging to 'the Irish branch of the family'.

There was some slight encouragement here for a drama set in the open air—and open in other ways to mystical concepts of nothingness. But it was essentially the fresh, natural quality of Yeats's scenic effects which appealed to Londoners. His country road had believable, mundane tinkers on it and the possibility of colourful, real-life company turning up at any minute. This was still a far cry from the empty roads of *Godot*, as too, for that matter, were the essentially true-to-life lanes, rivers, and boggy wastes of Synge's plays.

In 1904 *Where There is Nothing* caused no more than a flicker of interest in an English theatre which continued to be dedicated to the drama of a solid indoors. It was still that way on 3 August 1955 when *Waiting for Godot* opened at the tiny Arts Theatre Club, London, confronting audiences with a scene that took away all the sure old landmarks and refused the relief of scenic variety. In feeling bewildered or threatened, as they often did, early audiences showed in a way true appreciation: if the play doesn't unsettle, it doesn't quite work. Scenic effects had a great deal to do with the unsettling process and presented an unusual challenge to the first London designer,

Peter Snow, which he tackled in interesting ways. I will glance briefly at these.

Being familiar with the design actually used at the Arts Theatre, from photographs and memories of the first production, I was startled, a few years ago, in a London art dealer's, to come upon a water-colour by Snow which showed what was unmistakably the set for *Godot* but a very odd one, certainly not what I had seen on the Arts stage in 1955, or later at the Criterion when the production moved there. There were the well-known icons—the two tramps, the tree, the pair of boots—but the tree had profuse foliage, reeds sprouted round the actors, and, most striking, two doors were highly visible, one on each side of the scene. The story of Snow's designs illustrates well, I think, both the formidable brief *Godot* presented to the English theatre designer of 1955 and the inventiveness it could stimulate.

I bought this water-colour, intrigued by its curious combination of familiar and odd. When, later, I met the artist, he showed me another of his paintings which accentuated the 'road within a room' effect by an electric light bulb dangling near the tree. Later again, in 1995, I bought from his exhibition at the Morley Gallery a model he had made of this surreal set, complete with working electric light.

Peter Snow's account of his various attempts at the design for the first production brought out the power of Beckett's laconic stage directions to move a designer away from naturalism. Snow was ready for the move, being young and in touch with the avant-garde art movements, which struck him as having some bearing on what Beckett was after. He thought at one stage of using screens and gauzes to produce the impression of a 'flat' tree, existing in some other dimension than the natural. Another variation centred on a Francis Bacon type of box, enclosing tree, mound, and all; hence his emphasis on incongruous doors and (in the model) surrounding curtain.

Beckett visited his studio, Snow told me, and showed interest in the 'room' concept, though not for *Godot*. Some interest wouldn't have been too surprising. His next play was to be *Endgame*, which did make many people think of Francis Bacon's oppressive rooms and 'screaming popes'. When I showed Snow's design to Sir Peter Hall in 1996 (the year before he returned as director to *Godot*) he kindly ransacked his memory for details of the long-ago set. They had faded somewhat, though he observed at once that the tree in his production was nothing like so bushy as in the design. The tree was crucial to him. Snow told me that although Hall had at one point been interested in the idea of the 'flat' tree produced by screens and gauzes he had decided against it and called on his designer for a three-dimensional object which he envisaged as 'small and stunted'.

A single stage object, a tree, gripped the imagination of the director and designer in the midst of all their bigger problems. One practical consideration that figured in Peter Snow's recollections was the needs of the actors. The reeds which remained a feature of his final design were, he said, in part a way of helping them (they were young, like the director and the designer) to meet the formidable challenge presented by a bare stage in 1955. They felt more comfortable with something around them; furniture ideally, but, at a pinch, reeds. Snow thought that perhaps something in the text had also contributed to the idea. If so, it must have been Estragon's line, replying to Vladimir's alarm at a sound which suggests Godot might be arriving: 'Pah! The wind in the reeds' (a line with powerful Yeatsian resonance).

Peter Snow was right to think of painters in connection with Beckett, though Bacon didn't provide a model in this case. The scenic image which has become an icon for the modern theatre does have paintings in its background. Jack Yeats's *Two Travellers*, and the *Two Men Contemplating the Moon* and *Man and Woman Observing the Moon* of Caspar David Friedrich were favourite pictures of Beckett's; the last is cited by Ruby Cohn as the specific source for *Godot*.[2] Both draw an extraordinary sense of cosmic space from the image of two figures in an empty landscape; in one, gazing up at the moon, in the other, appearing to meet in the middle of nowhere, totally isolated in natural yet mysteriously alien countryside.

The moon in *Godot* is one of Beckett's most playful and at the same time most poetic effects; a reminder of vast surrounding space, the backdrop to the road where his travellers make their life journey. It comes up on cue at the close of each act, sailing up the cyclorama, a theatrical object that changes the mood, speaks of night and rest, calls forth romantic lines of Shelley from Estragon (immediately undercut with an ironic twist) and suspends us momentarily in a mental space open to poetry, beauty, and spiritual expansion. Peter Snow couldn't remember how the moon was done in that first production, and I found I had no special recollection of it either. Since then, images have been created which seem likely always to remain in memory, like the pure, luminous round and elegantly sparse tree designed by Louis le Brocquy for the Gate Theatre, Dublin (1 October 1991). The moon was well captured in the sketch done by Brian Bourke, along with other evocative recordings of the production (I longed to buy it but, forestalled by the Director, Michael Colgan, acquired instead a vivid likeness of Barry McGovern as Vladimir and Johnny Murphy as Estragon). In Peter Hall's new production of *Godot* (Old Vic Theatre, 16 June 1997) the moon of Mark Henderson, his lighting designer, met Beckett's wish for playfulness, drawing amused chuckles as it rose with ostentatious deliberation. It was also affecting; a serene, pale golden orb silently speaking of transcendental space.

Peter Hall knew, he said, that his first production had too much scenery. He corrected this in 1997 with a tree whose austere starkness was remarked upon by reviewers: it stood on a stage of polished wood, arrestingly bare except for Estragon's stone. It is fascinating to observe how, over the years, the stage objects imagined by Beckett have been recreated, sometimes by major artists like Giacometti almost as the Crucifixion scene was continually recreated by Renaissance painters. The tree of *Godot* does indeed make connection with Crucifixion art. Beckett made the point when directing his play by having Vladimir (in his 'exercises') stand with arms flung out against the tree in the unmistakable, painful posture. Another tradition—the tree of life—is given impish pictorial expression with the shock appearance in Act 2 of 'four or five leaves'.

We occasionally get negative reminders that the emptiness of the *Godot* scene can still make actors or audiences uneasy. In Michael Rudman's production at the National Theatre, London (25 November 1987) with Alec McCowen and John Alderton as a piquantly contrasting pair, the emptiness was softened by the use of different levels with an embankment sloping down to the site of the tree and in the background a glimpse of what looked rather like a deserted motorway. Some saw this as an arresting scenic image, suggestive of moon craters; for others it was a distraction. The set certainly gave the actors more to do, by going up and down the embankment, for instance, as well as more places to sit down. But it tended to shield actors and audience from what they should be exposed to: the terror of nothingness.

The image of the road where a life journey is taken runs right through Beckett's theatre, taking form only perhaps as a bare stage identified as a public street by two characters who meet there, as in

Rough For Theatre I (published in 1976). Unusually in *Film* (New York Film Festival 1965) it is a commonplace New York street made eerie by its total silence. He carried the image over from *Godot* to the first play he wrote for radio, *All That Fall* (1957), or rather, perhaps, it carried him. He wrote to Nancy Cunard that he hadn't previously thought about radio play technique 'but in the dead of t'other night got a nice gruesome idea full of cartwheels and dragging feet and puffing and panting which may or may not lead to something'.[3] In the play that emerged from the strange dream, the cartwheels, panting, and the rest build up a road in two dimensions: the one travelled on weekdays by Maddy Rooney, to bring her blind husband home from the railway station, and the lonelier one they travel in their minds. The latter begins and ends with the music of mortality, the strains of Schubert's 'Death and the Maiden', played over and over, so we're told, by a poor woman, 'All alone in that ruinous old house'.

A massive accumulation of sound effects defines the road as what Beckett towards the end of his life called 'the long crooked straight':[4] it must be traversed with whatever aid comes to hand. Company abounds on the outward journey, announcing itself through robustly idiosyncratic human voices and sounds suggesting a whole history of human transport: donkey-cart wheels, bicycle, train whistles, motor car, railway carriage doors closing. On the homeward journey husband and wife are alone except for the sounds of nature (coming very unnaturally to remind us, like much else on the road, that all may be illusion: '*Brief wind . . . Brief chirp . . . Brief moo*'). Other sounds are closer to real life though the dream-like rhythm of dragging footsteps, tap of the blind man's stick, and moan of wind and rain increasingly suggest that real life is being seen *sub specie aeternitatis*. To see life that way might be the only reason for going on living, Beckett once implied.[5] The shock at the end—the news of a child killed by falling from the train Dan has travelled on—is followed by an overwhelming sound, called for twice in the text: '*Tempest of wind and rain*'. Otherwise, silence. No doubt here that this is a road running through deep inner space, a region not easy to chart but whose reality penetrates and comes through the 'nicely gruesome' sound effects Beckett heard in his dream.

There is no road to see or hear in the plays Beckett wrote for television. What we do have, very strangely in *. . . but the clouds . . .* (1977), is an immense unseen, 'the roads'. Something like Yeats's 'serpent of eternity' perhaps, they could be imagined coiling round the luminous circular space Beckett devised, a challenge to the square box. Donald McWhinnie's production achieved the right dream-like effect, following Beckett's instructions for dark shadows at the periphery, lightening towards the centre. The circle of dim, suffused light becomes a kind of 'no-place' where a mute figure, M1, face unseen, exits and re-enters at three compass points. To the eye of the viewer he makes his first entry on screen left, emerging from the shadow on the West which represents 'the roads'. Dressed for walking, in familiar Beckettian garb of hat and greatcoat, he moves slowly and gravely across the screen or stands still while an offscreen voice speaks for him in the first person, as though he himself cannot speak of what he does, only do it:

'Right. Came in, having walked the roads since break of day, brought night home, stood listening'

The complex creative rituals which ensue all involve walking: a slow walk by M1 into the centre of the screen, an exit to the East shadow which is his closet or changing-room, a reappearance dressed in long robe and skullcap, another exit to compass point North which is his 'sanctum', then again back to the West, his point of entry. There follow elaborate retracings of these routes; a process fixed, repetitive, and, to many viewers on first view, no doubt baffling or infuriatingly arcane (I have met this reaction even when showing the video to students keenly interested in Beckett's plays). But the strange distancing or alienating effects—in a medium given to warm intimacy—are a necessary part of the experience. A mesmeric grandeur is communicated through the level tones of the narrator, the slow, ritual movements of M1, the man who walks, and the intermittent glimpses of the other self, M, who sent him out to walk. The lit screen is an empty site until the figure in walking-clothes enters, bearing with him the vast, untold experience of the dark space beyond: the 'roads'.

It is the experience of a whole life expressed in an image we can all recognize. Probably memories come into play of roads in myth and poetry; those travelled by the solitary wanderers of Synge or Wordsworth; the narrow track that Bunyan's Christian diverged from at his peril; the road where Dante halted in the middle of the wood; or loved roads of childhood like those travelled in *Company* by the boy and his father. Or the familiar roads of our own life which acquire mythic potency as the ruthless passage of time makes ghosts of them. I felt a surge of the feeling engendered by the play when taken by an Irish friend, Anthony Roche, at the time living in the Ballyogan area, along a road dear to Beckett: the quiet, country almost-lane running past the now unused, overgrown railway station which he had in mind when writing *All That Fall*. Among the austere ceremonies and invocations of . . . *but the clouds* . . . there is an appealing human poignancy in the look of the traveller dressed for the long walk and his terse account of being out from break of day and of bringing 'night home' with him.

THE ROOM

After the road of *Godot* the image of the imprisoning room is probably what most will think of as typifying Beckett's scenic spaces. He used the image with great brio in *Eleutheria*, the play written in French which he never saw performed and in later years didn't want to have published, though this came about in 1995.[6] It still hasn't had a full performance, so comment on the stage effectiveness of the room imagery must be speculative. The text makes clear, however, that Beckett had fun playing with that dominant scenic image of the time, the opulent bourgeois living-room.

The 'cell' to which the dissident young hero, Victor Krap, retreats in revolt against narrow, middle-class comfort gets about as near as a practical living-room could to the scenic emptiness of *Godot* and . . . *but the clouds* . . . There is nowhere to sit down except the bed or floor. Victor's room occupies only part of the stage at first, the remainder being given to the ornate, heavily furnished Krap morning-room. Then the bohemian garret takes over the whole stage space. Beckett plays great games with the relationship between the two rooms, calling in his witty stage directions for changes of angle and a 'swing of the scene on stage' which results, so he jokes, in the Krap morning-room during the interval falling into the pit. It would be fun to see a hint at this attempted in the theatre.

It's not just theatrical play, of course. Beckett's note in the text spells out the importance to him of the awkwardness and oddity of the divided set. He intends it to be seen as serious exploration of 'real space' and, as soon becomes clear, of a deep psychic divide, a 'flagrant disharmony'. The portion of the Krap morning-room the audience sees (the rest has already been eaten up by Victor's room) must look as if 'wedged' into the other room. Yet characters can't move from one room straight into the other: the partition which keeps them rigidly separated is not visible. An ingenious designer will be needed when the play is finally performed, as it surely will be before too long: Richard Hudson, who designed a dizzily tilted set for Ostrovsky's *Too Clever by Half* (Old Vic Theatre, London, 1988), could be imagined enjoying the task. It involves showing Victor's room from different angles in different acts (now to the left of the Krap room, now to the right). The designer is required to show it moving 'imperceptibly' into the Krap morning-room. Beckett offers some help with a tart textual clue as to the effect desired: the movement of 'the sullied into the clean, the sordid into the decent, breadth into clutter'. The contrast was to be maintained right down to the floor covering. Shared by the two rooms, in the Krap morning-room it should seem 'housebroken and presentable [. . .] the high seas becoming the harbour basin'.

Running through all this is a suggestion of some indefinable dimension, a space that can't be contained in either room. To read Beckett's wonderfully interesting note is to imagine great scenic possibilities, rather hard for a reader to keep continually in mind. One such is the suggested use of light. Here again one can think of designers, Jean Kalman, for instance, capable of achieving the subtle fluctuations Beckett wanted. The light emanating from the floor lamp in the Krap morning-room is charged in the text with cryptic significance, so too the light in Victor's room and the Glazier's insistence on repairing the one window which Victor breaks at the start of Act 2, by hurling his shoe through it. We might see the seemingly pointless act as an Ibsen-like letting in of fresh air or a more Strindbergian demonstration of the effort to look beyond rooms of any kind, into unknown space.

These uses of light anticipate scenic effects in later plays, as does the aggressive bareness of Victor's room. The lack of anywhere to sit down is continually brought to our attention by visitors looking in vain for seats and ending up on bed or floor. Obscure lines of thought connect this discomfort with the difficulty both M. and Mme Krap have in getting up from a sitting position. There is a touch of the 'cell' in their lives too, perhaps the prisoner's rather than the bohemian or monastic kind. Dominating all is the deliberately awkward join between the two rooms which makes it impossible for Victor to be content in either. Readers must look forward to becoming audiences and testing in the theatre the dramatic power of Beckett's ingeniously imagined sets, with their distortions and visual jokes. We will need to see rooms which are believable in ordinary terms and yet a world away from the day-to-day reality to which they are so mockingly attached.

After setting a theatrical firework under the bourgeois family room in *Eleutheria*, Beckett took the same scenic image in *Fin de partie* (1957) and turned it into one of his most haunting cosmic spaces. There were some potent models in the background here. Ibsen's interior sets, for all their convincing realism, hinted steadily at an all-enveloping, claustrophobic psychic climate. Strindberg did more than hint, investing his indoor sets with malignant oppressiveness. In *A Dream Play* the servant, Christine, circles the room where husband and wife struggle with domestic irritations, filling in every crack in walls and windows, and chanting 'I paste, I paste'. It is not too far from here to Clov hobbling round Hamm's room, announcing 'No more pain-killers'.

Maeterlinck provided a different model. His stage interior is not so much shut in on itself as terrifyingly open to the universe and its mysterious laws. Between 1891, when *The Intruder* was produced by Lugné-Poe, to 1896 when Maeterlinck published his manifesto for the modern theatre, *Le Trésor des humbles* (published in English as *The Treasure of the Humble, 1897*), the stage room took on a strange new life, became another kind of dramatic space. The Flemish living-room of *The Intruder* is unremarkable as described in the text: it wasn't too unreasonable for Stanislavsky to produce it, as he did in 1904, in a set of massive realism. But Maeterlinck's focus on the iconic figure of the old blind grandfather who listens to 'the voice of the light' and senses death entering through the closed doors of the room invests the bourgeois set with a spirit far from the external world of everyday.

Doors and windows played a key role in Maeterlinck's technique. The topography of the soul in *Pelléas and Mélisande* is plotted around them, as in the shattering scene when the jealous Golaud, desperate to 'know', holds his young son up to a window to peer in and tell him what Pelléas and Mélisande are doing, alone together in the room. 'Nothing', the boy says; they are only looking at each other. A typically Maeterlinckian window, it both offers and withholds a view from the outside of what goes on 'within'. Another window, in *Interior*, offers the audience a curious perspective. We see from outside, through three lighted windows on the ground floor of a house, into a room where a family group sits in the lamplight, engaged in commonplace activities; reading, sewing, and so on. Our viewpoint is that of two watchers in the garden, one of whom is nerving himself to enter the house and break terrible news: the third daughter has been drowned. As if drawn by some chilling intuition, each of her two sisters comes to one of the three windows to look out into the darkness. A ghost almost comes into view behind the Old Man's sad comment: 'No one comes to the middle window.'

It is, in Maeterlinck's phrase, the 'tragedy of everyday life'.[7] Not to hear the people in the room, only to see them from this strange distance, in the shadow about to be cast, would be to see them, so Maeterlinck hoped, *sub specie aeternitatis*. Their every little ordinary movement, he opined in his stage direction, would be 'spiritualized by the distance, the light, and the transparent film of the window-panes'. It seemed to work like this for some at least of the early audiences. The Old Man draws the moral for us—'You can't look into the human soul as easily as into that room'—but the scenic image speaks more powerfully.

Maeterlinck's emphasis on doors and windows seems almost bound nowadays to point us to Beckett. We might think of the windows in *Ghost Trio* (1977), or *A Piece of Monologue* (1980), or those in *Endgame*, and of the door through which Clov makes continuous exits and entrances. This door was very real to Beckett. In one of the first letters I ever had from him he said of it, replying to a query I had raised about a production in the round which allowed more than one exit point through the audience, 'There is only one door in *Endgame*, that leading to Clov's kitchen. A second door is very wrong. Clov's "door" should be a simple aperture, with no opening or shutting to bother about.'[8]

In Katie Mitchell's production (Donmar Warehouse, London, 11 April 1996) Clov entered through the audience but always through the one door. It met Beckett's criterion of simplicity 'with no opening or shutting to bother about' by being a kind of screen of shells which made a faint tinkling sound if Clov brushed against them. Sitting as I was on 'his' side of the action I felt this worked subtly to indicate the crucial line of demarcation between servant and master while allowing for the equally crucial easy transit between them. The invisible kitchen became its own place, where Stephen Dillane's gaunt, saturnine Clov could more easily be imagined experiencing real visions such as Hamm attributes to him ('Have you had your visions?'). Less convincing were the windows, set lower down and larger than Beckett indicates. Admittedly, as some thought, this increased the intended absurdity of Clov's climbing up and down the ladder, and Beckett had used low windows in his production of 1980 at the Riverside Studios.[9] But it lost the sense of the painful, audacious effort involved for the lame man in getting a view of the world beyond the room; that universe so far off that he has to use a telescope, so all-encompassing that two windows are needed, one for the 'earth', one for the 'sea'.

All he can report to the blind man on first viewing is 'Zero' which tunes with the visual statement the room itself makes; there isn't much of anything left, almost 'nothing'. The set is a strong piece of action. There is an oppressive impact from the unvarying grey light and the refusal of ordinary comfort. No chairs: that recurring visual motif. Hamm has his wheelchair, Nagg and Nell their dustbins, Clov nowhere to sit. It seems not to matter—'I can't sit down', he says—but our sense of his relationship with Hamm is obliquely affected by Clov's continual standing. Beckett said that an essential tension of the play was Clov's desire to get to his kitchen and Hamm's to prevent him.[10] The scenic imagery reinforces this idea; Clov looms over the cripple in the wheelchair, yet moves at his word; is forced at his will to stay in the family room.

It is still, if only just, recognizable as the room so well known to the modern stage. It is a family room, occupied by three generations: Hamm, his parents and, as he hints at the end, his son, Clov ('It was I was a father to you.') But it's been stripped, made more naked than the room of *Eleutheria*, opened up to become another kind of interior, reflecting an obscure region of consciousness. Critics have used metaphors like 'womb/tomb' to suggest the nature of this strange zone: Maeterlinck's would probably have been 'soul'.

Comparison with the other most celebrated 'room' play of the century, the *Huis Clos* of Sartre, brings out the expressive power of Beckett's set. The grey light, high windows, and so forth are a language, speaking directly to us, telling us something profound and real about the state we are entering. Whether we see it as hell, as the characters occasionally do, is for us to determine. The Second Empire drawing-room of *Huis Clos* has features which can easily be thought of as hellish. The light can't be turned off, there are no mirrors (and the valet in charge has unmoving eyelids). But none of this works on its own power. We learn to attach meaning to the different coloured sofas or Barbedienne ornament because the characters explain them to us. Otherwise the set could serve perfectly well for a totally naturalistic play, except perhaps for one structural feature, the door which begins to lock or open of its own accord, according to the thoughts the characters have about the unknown beyond ('even hotter than in the room', we're told). It's an effective and chilling theatre scene but one which remains rooted in boulevard tradition and, compared with Beckett's, a long way from becoming a cosmic space.

Convenience is one of the solid links with 'old earth' which Beckett maintained in constructing his deep psychic regions. It's somehow reassuring when confronted with an ambience as dauntingly bleak and grey as *Endgame* to learn that Nagg and Nell were originally to have been in wheelchairs but got dustbins instead as a practical way of dealing with the long spells when they weren't needed for the dialogue.

The cell which is both shelter and claustrophobic enclosure, the cell of a prisoner or scholar or poet, goes through many subtle metamorphoses in later plays. Immediately after *Endgame* it reappears in *Krapp's Last Tape* (Royal Court Theatre, London, 28 October 1958) in shorthand form as the 'den' where Krapp is alone with his tape recorder. The room has shrunk to its most important item of furniture, the table where he plays his tapes and records his life. The area round the table is in strong white light, the rest of the stage in darkness, though we're encouraged to imagine scenes of ordinary life within the unseen 'cagibi' or cubby-hole by the sound of corks popping when Krapp takes trips there for refreshment. In the television version (BBC2, 1972) with Patrick Magee as Krapp the camera travelled down a corridor of dark to indicate the retreat to the cubby-hole. Though a technique appropriate to the medium it made the little trips rather too momentous, I thought. The beauty of the stage journeys is their utter ordinariness, an effect which enhances—makes almost miraculous, even—the poetic transformations of the ordinary achieved at the recording table under the strong white light.

Light shapes the room too in *A Piece of Monologue*. It is faint and diffuse, shed by a standard lamp with a '*skull-sized white globe*'. Despite the pointer towards an obvious symbolism in that last stage direction, the lamp has to be seen too as a standard feature of a room which might be quite commonplace if it were shown in full. All we see, however, apart from the lamp, is the merest glimpse of the end of a white pallet bed. When preparing to direct *A Piece of Monologue* once for summer school audiences at London and Sligo,[11] I happened to mention to Beckett my worries about getting the right type of lamp. He swept them away, remarking that any lamp would do; the main thing was to follow the lighting instructions. We did this and I believe managed to convey the insidious, ghostly parallel that runs through the play between what is said by the Speaker and what is seen on stage. Thirty seconds before the closing words the lamplight begins to fail, then goes out, keeping pace with what is happening—must happen—in the 'one matter' of the story. Poignantly, the Speaker accepts with sad calm how it must be: his acceptance controls and perhaps changes our response to the sadness of things: 'such as the light going now. Beginning to go. In the room. Where else?' The room has expanded now from the thin outline sketched by a lamp and a pallet bed to be the infinite room of the universe, the place of 'the dying and the going': 'The globe alone. Not the other. The unaccountable. From nowhere. On all sides nowhere. Unutterably faint. The globe alone. Alone gone.'

There is no window in the stage setting, yet by the end of the play it would be hard to be sure we hadn't seen one, so mesmeric is the Speaker's account of groping to it and looking out into 'that black vast'. The unseen window becomes more real than the pallet bed which is actually there. So too, at times, with the lamp. When the Speaker conjures up a vision of the lamp smoking 'though wick turned low' we might well catch ourselves looking to the real lamp, uneasily checking for smoke. Do we peer into the stage dark when he says 'There in the dark that window' or try to see the 'faint hand' that appears, holding a lighted spill, when he turns from the invisible window to gaze into the half-visible darkened room? I believe we do, and see with him still further into that mysterious dark which is never without light: 'No such thing as no light.' Words and scenic image create a vision of the room ('Where else') in which we all live, and it is not a void: 'No such thing as none.'

Towards the very end of his writing for the theatre Beckett gave us in *Ohio Impromptu* (1981) a new, riveting stage image of the room; no longer in the grey mode of *Endgame* nor the faint glow of *A Piece of Monologue* but in sharp contrasts of black and white. The two white-haired old men in black coats sitting at a white table on white chairs, a broad-brimmed black hat on the table between them, make up an image like a concrete poem, with a hint of humorous self-caricature. Quite mixed audiences often chuckle gently, as the academic one at Ohio State University unsurprisingly did when the play had its première there (it was sent in response to their request for Beckett's support). The effect—nicely captured in a publicity postcard—was to shrink the familiar room to a table where a mystery is being performed.

No 'room' image of comparable power emerged from Beckett's writing for radio, a medium favouring open spaces. The scene is a road in *All That Fall*, a seashore in *Embers* (1959), an undefined 'listening' space in *Words and Music* (BBC Third Programme, 13 November 1962) and *Cascando* (in French, ORTF, 1963; in English, BBC Third Programme, 6 October 1964). We may infer some room in the background of the two *Rough for Radio* plays but it is only a sketch, like the plays themselves, which were written in French in 1960–1 and published in English in 1976. Commonplace sounds denote the room of *Rough for Radio 1*: a telephone is heard ringing, curtains are drawn with a violent clatter of heavy rings along the rods. But the focus is elsewhere, on the business of turning knobs and listening intently to the faint emerging sounds of words and music. In *Rough for Radio 2* (BBC Radio 3, 13 April 1976) the room where Fox is roughly interrogated has no presence except as site for an obscure inquisition.

Film and television on the other hand offered chances which Beckett seized on to create new, memorable images of the room. In *Film* it is a genuinely bizarre and thought-provoking place. The protagonist, O, reaches it after a journey along a road which must be Beckett's drabbest (he proposed a 'small factory district' but got something rather bigger and draughtier looking). After we've seen O hurrying uneasily home, keeping his face averted from curious eyes (including the camera's), we are ready to anticipate the room being home and shelter, but this turns out to be anything but the case. It's an uncomfortable place, despite its chair, mirror, picture on the wall, and—remarkably, in Beckett's dramatic world—domestic pets (cat, dog, and goldfish). But these are not comforting objects to O, given that they all have eyes and are looking at him; even the chair joins in, as seen through the camera's focus on the eye-shaped carving in its high wooden back.

As the director of *Film*, Alan Schneider, tells it, Beckett was charmed with this chair, which was there by chance.[12] It's a nice example of his pleasure in picking up meaningful signs from perfectly ordinary, casually encountered things. The nervy balance of the typical and alarming in O's room (the print of God the Father would be one of the latter) makes for a real sense of shock but also, I suppose, for a degree of understanding. When the film ends with the camera finally showing us O's face, with its arresting black eye-patch, then switches to the wall to reveal the same face gazing back at him, we may surmise that the room represents the impossibility of escaping from the self.

That at least is one view. *Film* is an enigmatic work even, perhaps even more so, with the exegesis provided by Beckett's notes. Access is easier to the first television play, *Eh Joe* (BBC2, 4 July 1966), which also features a room whose occupant is seen making obsessive efforts to check that he is alone. It is emptier than the room of *Film*. The production which Beckett allowed me to make for teaching material[13] was filmed by David Clark in a studio at the Royal College of Art with very modest resources, but these proved quite adequate for the play's needs: curtains and doors to be checked by Joe, for instance, and a bed for him to sit on—and to look under for intruders. It was thrilling to see this homely material fading out as the camera focused with increasing ruthlessness on the one thing that mattered most to it: the face of Patrick Magee as Joe. Finally the anguished face filled the screen, blotting out all traces of the room.

All these rooms from *Eleutheria* on have a family likeness in their bareness, their lack of customary comforts like chairs. By the time of the television play, *Ghost Trio* (1977), Beckett was referring to the room as the 'familiar chamber', one of the many only half-ironic nods to his viewers conveyed by the unseen female narrator, V (for Voice). She teases by pointing out the obvious: the 'indispensable door' and so forth. The lineaments of an almost commonplace room are there as usual: door, window, bed, mirror on the wall (an interesting extra in the screenplays), and, unusual convenience, a stool where the mute protagonist sits.

The touch of archaic rigour in the stool is felt again in the term, 'pallet', as the bed is described in the text. In the BBC production it is scarcely more than a mattress on the floor. The room is set at a distance from ordinary television reality by such hermit-like touches and, more drastically, by the use of black and white, television's equivalent of grey, to immerse the viewers in that colour. Beckett evidently expected this early silent-film effect, like the faint voice of the offscreen narrator, V, to disconcert. In regard to the faintness the voice warns us to 'tune accordingly', a highly significant instruction. As to the greyness, she leaves us in no doubt that we must adapt to it with attention to fine shades of meaning:

Colour: none. All grey. Shades of grey. (*Pause.*) The colour grey if you wish, shades of the colour grey.

The camera tracks round the room to illustrate, showing its contents with an impersonal, geometrical emphasis. When she says 'Wall', we see a smooth grey rectangle; for 'door', the same; even the pallet has a 'grey rectangular pillow'. We are not meant to forget this greyness and surely do not, though we might find it hard to say how it affects us. Greyness can seem dull or depressing to those used to colour. But here it insidiously establishes itself as perhaps the only condition in which certain kinds of fine-tuning can occur. After V falls silent and there is no further sound except snatches of Beethoven's music from the cassette held by the mute figure, F, we may find ourselves watching the ritualistic movements on the screen with more intentness because we've been so immersed in this 'colour grey'. When the inaccessible high window and the closed door of the room open, as they do of their own accord at climactic moments, we see more grey: driving rain through the window and, beyond the open door, a long, grey corridor stretching into nowhere. A disturbing visual metaphor, suggestive of some remote, infinite space, extending far beyond the single consciousness of the room's occupant. I will say more in a later chapter of this testing, curiously haunting scenic imagery.

In the companion play, *. . . but the clouds . . .* (both broadcast on BBC2, 17 April 1977) the rooms into which the mute walking figure, M1, disappears at intervals are quite excluded from our view. We may guess it is because they are, like the far, offscreen 'roads', the site of a process too intensely private to be shared except in the telling. All we see from time to time is the shadow of a hint at a room where, in the BBC production, a huddled shape in voluminous robe, one hand resting on his other arm, face indistinguishable, sits on an 'invisible stool', a nice little joke. This M, as he is named in the text, has to be imagined sending his persona out into the screen to perform acts of evocation: the begetter of M1 has almost vanished into his character. I have never been sure that viewers would get the full force of this image from the screen alone, though with the textual directions in mind it is easy to see the faceless M as the real owner of a real room from which all the real-life detail has been faded out. The invisible table then takes its place in a succession of Beckettian tables which hint that the ubiquitous room is at least partly to be thought of as the place where a writer toils in the grip of his imagination. We might think of it too as the place in the mind we all have access to, where we conjure up our own visions and memories.

THE PLAY OF THE LIGHT AND THE DARK

Stage light is one of Beckett's most potent instruments for creating cosmic spaces. He reinvents the three-tiered stage of the medieval mystery plays—heaven, earth, and hell—with the aid of electricity. Often his technique is extravagantly minimalist, 'wasting' large areas of stage to produce icons of light in surrounding dark. He shapes the dark and light around the figures on his stage, or those parts of them his explorations of the human psyche need; in the later plays it might be no more than a woman from the waist up, a mouth, a head.

Odd angles and other kinds of asymmetry contribute to the unsettling impression of being in some unearthly yet curiously recognizable dimension. Mouth and her listener are spectacularly raised above stage (or earth) level; she eight feet up, a luridly lit human feature; the Auditor, four feet up, on an invisible podium; a shadowy figure in hooded djellaba, dimly lit, whose arms we see raised and dropped to the sides again, three times, 'in a gesture of helpless compassion'. The two are at an awkward angle from each other, a fact which struck me, at the first showing of *Not I* in London (Royal Court Theatre, 16 January 1973), as planting an insidious question mark about their connection, or lack of it, making this in fact crucial to the play. The slight strain of looking from one to the other helped to fix the question and hint at some awful gap in Mouth's understanding.

I once asked Billie Whitelaw whether the deletion of Auditor from the television adaptation of the play had any effect on her performance. None at all, she said; he wasn't missed, by her, nor, she suggested by Beckett. It is true that Beckett cut the Auditor from a production in Paris (though difficulties with staging came into this). It is true too that the silent watcher can't easily be imagined on screen; the small box probably had to be given over to the writhing

Mouth, to achieve an effect comparable in intensity to the divided image for which a wide stage has room. Billie Whitelaw was totally mesmeric onscreen too. 'Billie is unbelievable' Beckett told me, using the epithet very obviously as a term of praise. Yet something crucial goes out of the play for the audience when we no longer see the shrouded figure (sex unknown) placed at that troublesome angle which forces us to think not just about Mouth alone.

When directing his plays Beckett has been reported as requesting 'off-centre' placings for objects originally placed centrally, like Winnie's mound. The later texts are sometimes specific on this point. Speaker in *A Piece of Monologue* is to stand 'well off centre', contrasting with Hamm who forces Clov to try and get him 'Bang in the centre'. 'Hell is the centre', Beckett jotted down in his *Murphy* Notebook. In his great exemplar, *The Divine Comedy*, hell isn't the structural centre; but the Inferno is a place of raging egos, determined, like Hamm, to be at the centre of the story. Suggestively, the dancers in *Quad* (Süddeutscher Rundfunk, 1982) make dramatic swerves to avoid the centre of the television screen; it is for them, Beckett's notes tell us, a 'danger zone'.

The human figures—or the parts representing them—often come close to dissolving altogether into their mysterious context of dark, light, and shadow. Jocelyn Herbert has told how the urns for the first British production of *Play* (Old Vic Theatre, 7 April 1964) were textured 'so that the actors seemed to be continuous with them'.[14] This was responding to Beckett's direction: '*Faces so lost to age and aspect as to seem almost part of urns*'. For the audience—I remember it vividly—the sense of mortality conveyed by those ravaged, peeling faces was a huge shock (a visual effect well captured in photographs of this production). Billie Whitelaw amusingly reports that bits came off when actors began to speak (she felt they were disintegrating in full view of the audience).[15] Yet the objects in the urns were—still—recognizable human faces, nakedly exposed to our view. Beckett stipulated there should be no use of masks, a deeply characteristic direction.

Beckett said of his move away from prose fiction that he turned to the theatre as to the light 'after the blackness of the novel'. There is irony here, given that blackness was the physical element he brought into the theatre as no one had done before him. *Endgame*, he said wittily, was 'dark as ink'. Very early in the *œuvre* the setting of *Krapp's Last Tape* struck the note:

Table and immediately adjacent area in strong white light. Rest of stage in darkness.

And towards the end *Ohio Impromptu* repeated it:

Light on table mid stage. Rest of stage in darkness.

In between came many sculptured arrangements of light and dark. Another piece of furniture, the rocking-chair, is picked out of surrounding dark in *Rockaby* by a 'subdued' light. The subtle coming and going of the light on the chair helps to etherealize the solid, homely object. The narrow platform at the back of the stage designed for *Act Without Words 2* (1960) was to be 'violently' lit for its length, giving the effect of a frieze, the rest of the stage blacked out. In *Footfalls* (1976) the dark is disturbed by a dim glow which makes of the narrow strip of stage where May paces a 'defined pathway of light'.[16] Light is a strong presence here, though dim; we cannot but note its every fade-out and renewal (with progressively reduced strength) till on its final return there is '*no trace of May*'. It is a ghostly effect that can be lost if the technical direction is at all failing: Beckett demands from stage lighting the same exactitude he seeks in words. A similar ghostly effect is evoked in *Come and Go* (1968; in German, 1966) where Beckett's note suggests that a soft light be 'concentrated on playing area. Rest of stage as dark as possible.' In the '*diffuse light*' of *A Piece of Monologue* the Speaker is '*barely visible*'. Arrestingly, in other plays we are made uneasily aware of the power of blackness by a narrowly focused light trained on small human objects: the heads in urns of *Play*; Mouth in *Not I*; the Listener's face, also high in the air, in *That Time* (1976).

The enveloping dark—defined as it is by the light—is a disturbing force in Beckett's theatre, though there are many hints that it could also be the source of a relief or creative renewal so deep that it would constitute a new dimension. Beckett said that it wasn't until he fully acknowledged and tapped his own darkness that he began to write as he should.

Grey tones conducive to reverie set the mood in *Endgame* and in some other plays. The phrase 'shades of grey' used by the voice in *Ghost Trio* describes what we see onscreen while hinting at the other sense of the word 'shades'—unquiet or tutelary spirits—which is omnipresent in Beckett's theatre. At the other extreme is the bright, hard, unvarying stage light of *Happy Days* (1961). Beckett called for a *trompe l'œil* backcloth '*to represent unbroken plain and sky receding to meet in far distance*', an impression captured with impressive simplicity in Peter Brook's production of *Oh les beaux jours* (Riverside Studios, London, 27 November 1997). The terror of the hard light on endless plain and sky doesn't always come through in productions, probably because audiences tend to take a brightly lit stage for granted and are in any case usually protected from discomfort by the conventional lowering of house lights. We may sit comfortably in the shade while Winnie suffers under the punishing glare.

More often, however, there is no escape from involvement of a direct, nervous, physical kind. I recall the unnerving effect of the swivelling spotlight in the first English production of *Play*. Might that normally subservient stage instrument, now seemingly a power in its own right, turn on us the audience and rake along the rows as along the urns, needling us too into facing ourselves? Though it entertains and amuses, making little mistakes like focusing on the wrong speaker, it is never less than formidable. We may think of it if we choose as an internal psychological process, which in part of course it is. But Beckett wanted an emphasis beyond this, to judge from his concern to have a mobile single spot or, when exceptionally required, a single spot branching into three. A separate spot focused on each face did not fit his idea of a 'unique inquisitor' (this too he suggested to George Devine, might be thought of as a victim, weakening somewhat as it went along). An unknown force was to be felt to be at work, operating enigmatically beyond any individual consciousness.

In other plays a similarly disturbing effect is created by a fixed rather than restless light. Narrow focusing on points of light in a dark background can play strange tricks on eyes and mind. The potentiality for hallucinogenic reactions was strong in the first production of *That Time* at the Royal Court Theatre in 1976. Everything was blotted out for the twenty minutes or so of the performance except for the old man's face with its streaming white hair high up in the stage darkness and the flow of his voice, coming from three different sources. The idiosyncratic, melodious tones of Patrick Magee heightened the hypnotic mood, but we had to be active, not passive, listening for the voices as they tracked around, catching minute changes: in Listener's breathing or the closing of the eyes at certain points; his smile at the end.

We would probably need the help of Beckett's stage direction, '*as if seen from above*'—or an unconventional auditorium—to visualize this head as he imagined it (the view into a coffin, some have thought). To look up from the stalls is to get a different, possibly more heavenly, perspective. The Magee image had a Blake-like quality in tune with such a vision.

Not I took the hallucinogenic effect to the nth degree, as anyone will know who saw Billie Whitelaw's mouth transformed into a lurid object, in Irving Wardle's words 'stretching and contracting and pulsing like the eye of a monster or the entrance to the birth canal' (*Times*, 17 January 1973). Keir Elam has brought out, with the aid of Gustave Doré's illustrations to the *Inferno*, the closeness of Beckett's visual image to Dante's vision of bodiless heads sticking out of dead seas.[17] Like the Dante persona in the poem, the Auditor can only watch, though with the pity expressed by the repeated throwing out of his arms in a 'gesture of helpless compassion'. It's a relief for the audience, I believe, to turn to him when he makes these gestures: we escape momentarily, as Mouth can't do, from the hard, unwinking light.

Light has a kindlier aspect in other plays. In *Nacht und Träume* (1983) the figure in the dream (B) sits in the same posture as the man dreaming (A), but is 'faintly lit by kinder light'. A gentle glow encircles the three women in *Come and Go*. Each in turn leaves the luminous round while the others talk of her fate. But none must leave the stage, Beckett said, only go out of view, preferably into a real stage dark. When they return to the light, sitting close on a narrow bench, Beckett's note, 'It should not be clear what they are sitting on', suggests that they have been abstracted into some space where we will see only what the light chooses to reveal: three female figures, like fading flowers in their dresses of dull violet, red, and yellow, their hats shading and concealing their faces. The play can work in any setting, with minimal lighting effects, but when Beckett's intentions are fully realized it becomes a thing of exquisite beauty. It seems then to make a mysterious promise, to do with the women restored to their fragile being in the light with their hands, intricately linked, spread in their laps to show us they are bare of rings, even as Flo speaks the closing line 'I can feel the rings.'

Like the light, the darkness has a double face. It is an ominous absence of light in *Come and Go*, so too in *Krapp's Last Tape* at the moment when Krapp looks apprehensively into the surrounding dark, as if, said Beckett, 'Old Nick's there'. He added this touch when directing Martin Held in the role in 1969: it has never been more movingly or convincingly done than by that solidly human actor. Rooted in the ordinariness of life, this Krapp could make us feel with him the unearthly presence of the 'Hain', portent of dissolution. Yet the dark can promise rest too and strange consummation, the kind dreamed of by M in *Play*—'all going down, into the dark, peace'—or conjured up through music and words out of the dark of the radio plays.

In these mind-expanding scenic spaces which seem to stretch out to infinity, particles of 'old earth' keep their place. Little homely things—a well-used rocking-chair, a tape recorder—are etherealized without being made alien. Beckett was pleased, James Knowlson has noted, when he discovered that the tiny lamp built into Krapp's tape recorder continued to glow after the stage lighting had faded. He saw it with his visionary eye, as we can deduce from entries made in his production notebooks about the 'magic eye', the 'white light of tape recorder in the darkness'.[18]

The speakers on Beckett's stage 'see' for us into another dimension, sometimes bringing before us objects that have their existence only there, like the hand holding out the cup in *Nacht und Träume* or the longed-for woman's face in . . . *but the clouds* . . . (Or the figure pacing the 'defined pathway of light' in *Footfalls* which becomes almost indistinguishable from the 'semblance' said to haunt the churchyard.) Invisible windows appear in the narratives for us to look through into the 'vast beyond'.

The light fades out at the end as it must. Beckett often dwells on the fading, making it a thing of unearthly sadness and beauty. If only for a moment, the path of light glimmers on after May goes; the lamp outlasts the Speaker in *A Piece of Monologue*, suggesting that what has been seen through the windows of imagination is not easily to be extinguished. Along with the sombreness of ending in these plays there is the sense of life ever reincarnating itself in the cosmic spaces between the light and the dark.

2

Heaven, Hell, and the Space Between

'OUT . . . into this world . . . this world'. *Not I* opens with a tormented vision of birth as ejection into an unfriendly void. In an earlier play, *Act Without Words 1* (1957), the idea takes graphical physical form in the abrupt arrival onstage of a mime player 'flung backwards' as if by an unseen hand in the wings, an act repeated each time he tries to make an exit. Whistles from above call his attention to solaces—a meagre, shade-giving tree, a tiny carafe of water—which are withdrawn as soon as he gets within reach of them. Life continues as it began: hard, unfriendly. Having failed to hang himself (means to that end are provided) he ignores the latest tantalizing offer, sits down and contemplates his fingernails, cutting short the sport someone or something is having with him.

Do we see it so, imagine the unseen manipulator amusing himself in the way of Hardy's President of the Immortals who brought poor Tess to death by hanging before he 'had finished his sport' with her? Hanging comes near in *Act Without Words 1*, but the rope offered from 'above' is withdrawn as the player reaches for it: a more benign frustration. When the solitary figure onstage sits down at the end is he simply giving up in despair, or, as some have thought, broken free of illusion (a word much emphasized in the stage directions)? We have to decide for ourselves. What Beckett does for us is register the urgent questioning, the not knowing, the contradictory possibilities; states of mind well known to people today brooding on the meaning of life, perhaps at times of crisis.

In *Act Without Words 1* it is easy to understand the mime player's attempt to end it all. The grim temptation, which many have admitted to in real life, figures insistently in Beckett's earlier plays. With one tragic exception, in *Eh Joe*, nothing comes of it, any more, fortunately, than in most lives. Winnie keeps a revolver handy (affectionately called 'Brownie') but can't be imagined using it even when she has the use of her hands. Willie might do that: the final tableau leaves the question open, freezing him half-way in his crawl up the mound so we can't tell whether he's heading for Winnie or 'Brownie'. Winnie can only put the question, not answer it: 'Is it a kiss you're after, Willie . . . or is it something else?'

Suicide draws close in *Rough for Theatre 2* (written in French, late 1950s). 'Let him jump', say the investigators, A and B, at the start of their probe into the life history of C, a mute figure standing upstage by a '*high double window open on bright night sky*', his back to the audience. He is ripe for suicide, they conclude, hunting through a pile of quirky, written testimonies which note his tendency to dwell too much on the black side of things. His own statement admits to the failing: his humour and sense of proportion have been 'swamped'. The touch of humorous self-caricature on the playwright's part is bracing; it is not as surprising for us as for A when he realizes, on looking closely at C's face (by matchlight) that the mood has changed. The question 'How end?' seems unlikely now to lead to a suicidal leap.

The same is true in *Eleutheria* where Victor abandons the idea of suicide because he wouldn't be able to see himself dead. 'That's the only thing I've got against death', he says; amusing proof of his intense interest in life. Practical difficulties continually get in the way of would-be suicides. In *Godot* there's no rope to be had and the cord holding up Gogo's trousers proves useless for the darker purpose. With jokes about trousers falling down and nothing working Beckett fixes the pair's half-attempt at ending their lives as a kind of half-farce, connected to melancholy thoughts of death but also to the warm, boisterous living world of the music hall. The clincher for them both is the realization that practicalities would prevent their going together; one would survive, alone.

To be alone in the Void (I capitalize to indicate its status) is a nightmare thought for Beckett's characters. The Void has another aspect for them, which I will return to, but in their bleaker moods it looms up as a terrifying vision of negatives: a limitless empty universe with no meaning, no God, no point; the dark side of the modern moon. Listener in *That Time* envisages it as a 'shroud billowing in all over you on top of you'.

Estragon takes an airy approach to the terror on occasion—'There's no lack of void'—but that doesn't diminish it. The Void can't be tolerated for long, by them or us; not when time is stretched out to the limit as in *Godot* and *Endgame*. Meaning has to be admitted to the scheme of things, even at the cost of bringing in with it the fear of hell.

HELL

It does do that: the Void easily fills up with troubled imaginings of hell and judgement. Right at the start of the theatrical *œuvre* in *Eleutheria*, the banal chatter in the Krap morning-room is punctuated by a sour joke on the subject. M. Krap indulges in a fantasy about a poor cow *en route* for the slaughterhouse discovering too late 'the utter absurdity of pastures', and Mme. Krap dismisses it with chilly reference to his intellectual 'circle':

MME KRAP. Pay no attention. He thinks he's in his circle.
M. KRAP. I am. In the ninth.

The ninth was the bottom circle in the *Inferno*, abode of traitors, including Bocca who continued to sin by refusing to speak of his sins. Banality torments. Henry in *Embers* recalls with loathing endless domestic chat with Ada about margarine prices: 'That's what hell will be like. Price of Blue Band now?'

Often the characters feel themselves already there: Estragon shouts in Act 1 'I'm accursed', in Act 2 'I'm in hell'. If Godot comes they'll be saved, says Vladimir, and when asked 'From what?' says 'From hell'. Hamm envisages 'the other hell' beyond the wall of his shelter; Winnie complains of the 'hellish light', warns Willie to keep out of the 'hellish sun'. *Play* has a 'hellish half light' and in *Eh Joe* the reluctant listener is mocked for believing that the voice tormenting him has no existence outside 'the penny farthing hell you call your mind'.

Dan Rooney brings the *Inferno* directly into the soundscape of *All that Fall* with his ironical suggestion to Maddy as they struggle homeward against wind and rain that they should travel backwards, 'like Dante's damned, with their faces arsy-versy' (the tears of the sorcerers in the *Inferno* run down their backs, and down their buttocks: *Inferno*, XX. 21–2). Uneducated Mouth can't credibly quote Dante, but her ghostly kinship with some of his damned souls is ominously demonstrated in her dismembered state and, for those who recognize it, her nominal connection to one particular soul, Bocca (meaning 'mouth').

We see that the fires of hell still burn in the minds of Beckett's modern characters. The smell of it hangs ominously round W2's desolate account of the end of the affair in *Play*: 'I made a bundle of his things and burnt them. It was November and the bonfire was going. All night I smelt them smouldering.' In *Happy Days* this fire gets scenic expression. There is scorched earth at the front of Winnie's mound and her parasol does actually catch fire, to be whisked away, her one fragile protection against the hot, unrelenting light. When she tries in her usual way to cheer herself up with the thought that things could be even worse, she opens up a vision of further hells: 'It might be the eternal cold. (*Pause.*) Everlasting perishing cold. (*Pause.*) Just chance, I take it, happy chance. (*Pause.*) Oh yes, great mercies, great mercies.' We might hear an echo from Shakespeare's Claudio, terrifying himself with afterlife horrors in store if sentence of execution is carried out on him: 'Aye, but to die, and go we know not where; | To lie in cold obstruction, and to rot.' The nightmares stretch back to those of antiquity.

A precise doctrinal note is sometimes struck, as it is—mockingly—by the voice tormenting Joe with thoughts of impending judgement. How will he respond when called on by his 'Lord' to answer for his sins, 'one dirty winter night'? The woman speaking hasn't much respect for the 'Lord', cheekily referring to him once as 'His Nibs'. But she is sure that the voice when it comes is one Joe won't be able to 'throttle' as he has done with so many he no longer wanted to hear: 'Till one night. . . . "Thou fool thy soul". . . . Put your thugs on that. . . . Eh Joe? . . . Ever think of that? . . . When He starts in on you . . .'. More ambiguously, the hooded dancers in *Quad* (BBC2, 16 December 1982) when drained of colour in the black and white coda, have a touch of the grimly repetitive movements in Dante's hell.

In such visionary scenes and moments Beckett expresses anxieties his audiences probably need to have released, even—or perhaps especially—in the secular, sceptical world most may know best. The trial of the serial killers, the Wests, in 1995 triggered off an explosion of hell metaphors in the popular British newspapers, some violently crude—one witness wanted to see the pair 'burn in hell'—some attempting to look deeper. A. N. Wilson, an observer at the trial, thought he detected on the face of the accused when memories struck 'a shadow of something like Hell'. Inevitably, imagery of hell is used about the devastating public atrocities of our time: the massacres in Bosnia were described by David Owen as 'scenes of hell written on the darkest pages of history'. Such events almost force us to wonder whether hell might not after all exist as an absolute state of evil somehow shadowing human life. Beckett takes this dread up into his drama. His characters respond on our behalf, with doubt, wit, and painful self-scrutiny to ancient spiritual terrors and the question, more insistent than ever in our time: 'If there is a God, why such wickedness, why such suffering of the innocent?'

Perhaps we are simply paying the price for being born. That bleak thought emerges from time to time. 'Use your head, can't you,' Hamm tells himself, 'use your head, you're on earth, there's no cure for that!' Maybe human life was a mistake. To cut life off at source is a temptation which disturbingly flickers into view in the early plays. The child's death by a fall from the train reported in *All That Fall* is presumably an accident, but uneasiness hangs over Dan Rooney's presence on the train: his dislike of the idea of children is a source of woe for Maddy, we may guess. Clov goes so far as to pick up the gaff with the intention of eliminating the young boy seen approaching the shelter: a 'potential procreator'. That it's Hamm who stops him may surprise us, given the chilly attitude to a child in need conveyed in his story and his less than kind treatment of his father. He usually draws a laugh from the audience when he addresses Nagg as 'Accursed progenitor' and jokes about the 'old folks at home' in their dustbins. But black shadows hang about this comedy: the laughs may be more nervous than sympathetic. We could be reminded of the extraordinary moment in Yeats's *Purgatory* when the terrible Old Man, who shrinks from 'Fat, greasy life' screams at his mother's ghost not to conceive him. Beckett claimed to remember his foetal existence, and it was nightmarish.[1] Who knows what influence this birth trauma might have had on the creations of his imagination?

Beckett characterized hell in his youthful essay, 'Dante. . . Bruno. Vico. . Joyce', as a place of deadly stasis:

> In the absolute absence of the Absolute, Hell is the static lifelessness of unrelieved viciousness. Paradise the static lifelessness of unrelieved immaculation. Purgatory a flood of movement and vitality released by the conjunction of these two elements . . .[2]

The threat of 'static lifelessness' hangs over the plays though it is far from being the thing itself; only the fear or sense of it. Fearfully cramped postures—paralysed Hamm, Winnie reduced to a head, the other heads in urns—mimic the grotesque fixity imposed on sinners in the *Inferno*; Ugolino frozen with his enemy in one hole; Paolo and Francesca locked in a frustrating embrace while driven in a 'hellish storm'; Bocca reduced to a head whose hair can be pulled, as Dante pulls it, under Virgil's instruction.

An alarming layer of real life—the physical suffering of the actors—intensifies these images. When playing the first English Winnie in *Happy Days*, Brenda Bruce asked Beckett why he had written the play, which 'is such torture for me'. And Billie Whitelaw said of playing Mouth, 'Every night was like falling backwards into hell'.[3] She has given hair-raising details of what she endured in the role: the concealing hood, the clamps on her head, the straps tying her to a chair: causes of damaging neck tension, hyper-ventilation, and extreme disorientation. Though one couldn't wish such agonies on any future player, I have always felt that they must have taken Whitelaw's performance to a higher power than could be generated in one less rigorously set up. Great force was generated, however, in Juliet Stevenson's performance for the Royal Shakespeare Company (The Other Place, Stratford-upon-Avon, November 1997). She was not quite so rigidly confined, nor at the great distance from the audience which made Whitelaw feel, as she told me, alone in the world. The RSC audience were in fact in one room with Mouth, standing throughout quite close. This, though different, was also a physical pressure on the performer, one which surely contributed to the intensity of the angry, disturbing torrent of sound she produced.

Is it all a question of the breakdown of a 'machine', Mouth wonders. Critics have diagnosed from the symptoms she records—the 'sudden flash', the buzzing in the ears, the 'dull roar in the skull'—various kinds of bodily malfunction that might cause a near-mute to pour out her seemingly uncontrollable flood of words. Like Hamm's blindness or Clov's lameness, it could be just one of the harsh conditions of being here 'on earth'; an accident of the Void, without meaning.

PURGATORY

Beckett's characters refuse to see it that way: they demand purpose even if it never gets beyond a wavering intuition that 'something is taking its course'. They feel themselves being 'seen', judged. 'Mene, mene', Hamm remarks, connecting Clov's habit of gazing at his kitchen wall with the writing on the wall that warned Belshazzar he had been weighed in the balance and found wanting. They will be punished, Vladimir tells Estragon, if they don't keep their appointment with Godot. Clov thinks his whole life has been a punishment, teaching him to 'suffer better'. Krapp also feels obliged to judge himself, sift the grain from the husks in his memories. It's the process that is forced upon the adulterous trio in *Play*. And a shadowy Auditor listens pityingly to the incomplete 'audit' of Mouth, who also wonders if she is being punished for 'some sin or other'.

The sense of being under questioning from an unknowable source gets steadily stronger in the *œuvre*, coming to a head in *Not I* in 1972 (Lincoln Center, New York) but with hellish aspects well to the fore in *Play* in 1963 (as *Spiel*, Ulmer Theater, Ulm-Donau). The trio in the urns think of the swivelling spotlight as a refined form of torment. W2 wonders if she can stand it, dreams of escaping into madness. 'Am I not perhaps a little unhinged already?' she says, 'hopefully'. W1 has religious anxieties, is afraid her longing for more darkness may be 'wickedness', struggles to discover what is expected of her: 'Penitence, yes, at a pinch, atonement, one was resigned.' There are no answers: she can only pray: 'Mercy, mercy, tongue still hanging out for mercy.' M has an unanswered question too: 'I know now, all that was just . . . play. And all this? When will all this . . .'. The spotlight moves on, then returns to let him finish: 'All this, when will all this have been . . . just play?' No answer, but the question itself holds a gleam of promise: there might be a way out, through some deep change of attitude. That change has already begun.

This is in Dantesque terms not hell but purgatory. The two states are very close; in *The Divine Comedy* as in Beckett's theatre they are separated not by the absence of suffering but the attitude of the sufferers. The souls in the *Purgatorio* have to endure grim conditions; they totter under heavy weights, choke in fog or fire. We hear one voice wondering if he can endure. But they accept, even welcome the 'purging', in the sure hope of redemption. With no such sure hope, Beckett's characters somehow manage to keep from falling into inertia and despair, trademarks of hell. Among the hazards which confront them in their idiosyncratic purgatory, two loom especially large: cruelty and boredom.

Cruelty is shown as a kind of spider's web, trapping the well-meaning as well as the less so. Maddy Rooney is one of the former, but it's she who advises Christy, when the donkey stalls, to 'Give her a good welt on the rump', and then tries guiltily to get out of its line of sight, uncomfortably aware of its 'great moist cleg-tormented eyes' on her. Later she laments elaborately over a hen accidentally killed by Mr Slocum's car, but ends on a very matter-of-fact note:

'They would have slit her weasand in any case.' Rueful reminders occur in other plays of the near-impossibility of avoiding the cruelty inherent in life. Complicity is widespread: Lucky mysteriously colludes in the ill treatment he receives from Pozzo, as does Clov in Hamm's tyranny. Sympathy veers wildly as victims become bullies, Lucky, for instance, taking advantage of Estragon's show of pity to deliver a sharp kick.

The element of inquisitorial cruelty in the creative process itself is a recurring theme. Battles for mastery over recalcitrant material figure vividly in Beckett's theatre, perhaps reflecting the 'fierce need' for total control over his writings which Deirdre Bair attributed to him.[4] Instruments of torture are applied or threatened, to drag out from a victim some word or truth he refuses—or is unable—to give. Victor Krap's inability to explain himself causes the Glazier to threaten him with the pincers of the Chinese torturer, Tchoutchi. In *Rough for Radio 2* the instrument of torture is a bull's pizzle, heard landing with a sickening thud on the unlucky Fox when he fails to produce what the Animator wants to hear. In *What Where* the inquisition goes round in a ritualistic circle, each torturer becoming the victim in his turn:

BAM. Take him away and give him the works until he confesses.
BEM. What must he confess?
BAM. That he said where to him.

Neither the symbolism of the rituals (however we read them) nor the jokiness of the dated gangster-style idiom ('give him the works') can quite reduce the harsh resonances from real life: this does seem to leave us in a kind of circular hell. In his chamber opera based on the play, Heinz Holliger used percussion to suggest 'sounds of torture, chains, broken glass, squeaking fingernails on metal', and so forth. Was the voice of Bam, Holliger speculated, that of God, who at the end of the performance puts out the light?[5] We may hope not; but it's harder here to see a way out such as Kay Boyle thought Beckett once offered her. They were talking about the nature of madness, and she felt 'it was almost as if we moved through purgatory together, and he was quite modestly showing me the way out for the condemned'.[6]

It's a little sad, to my mind, that the accident of chronology made *What Where* the closing piece of *Collected Plays* rather than *Catastrophe*, where the victim does not collude but against all expectation raises the head that was humiliatingly arranged in a bowed posture by a Director obsessed with artistic form. The play was tellingly related to political actuality by Beckett when he dedicated it to Václav Havel, at that time (1982) still under house arrest by the Czech Communist regime. But *Catastrophe*, like all Beckett's *œuvre*, is essentially on a vaster theme, to do with the relation of darkness and light in a spiritual universe.

In his production at the Haymarket Theatre, Leicester (5 October 1989) Antoni Libera (who had translated the text sent to Havel) brought out the metaphysical aspects, introducing playful touches of traditional hell imagery: a hint of cloven hoof for the Director; a suggestion of hell fire when the Assistant who has perched on his chair in his absence jumped up as from a very hot place indeed. In this context the Director's instructions to his unseen lighting technician—pointedly named 'Luke' and heard as an 'off, distant' voice—became part of a will to misuse the force of light. The light would not allow it, as the final stage image poignantly showed.

Boredom, that other lurking bogy of ordinary life, is taken by Beckett to an extreme where it merges with the medieval 'accidie' or sloth, the sin that kept Dante's Belacqua frustratingly in the Ante-Purgatory, a waiting-room for those late in repenting and seeking the light. *Godot* is such a waiting-room, perhaps, so too *Endgame*, where the agonies of boredom are intense. For one reviewer in 1996, the skill of Katie Mitchell's production of *Endgame* couldn't alleviate them: 'The relentless drip, drip, drip of misery is like Chinese water torture' (*Times*, 19 April 1996). It was a pity he could get no further, but the 'drip, drip, drip' is something we are meant to feel. Deadly boredom, as experienced by blindfolded, shackled hostages ('the boredom, the boredom, the bloody boredom' says the Irish hostage in *Someone Who'll Watch Over Me*), has provided a frightening image of spiritual torment for our time. Beckett trod a dangerous tightrope here as he well knew. He warned the German actors whom he directed in *Endgame* that too slow a pace would be 'dangerous' for the play.[7]

Monotony is enacted with comic inexorability in *Act Without Words 2* when A and B respond to jabs from a goad on wheels emerging from the wings and act out a humdrum routine (touches of Winnie here, including tooth-brushing). In laughably opposite styles, one slow and clumsy, one brisk, they do the same things and come to the same end, miming their prayers and crawling back into their sacks. Probably the 'violently lit' frieze effect designed by Beckett is needed to bring out the cosmic implications in this dour comedy.

Winnie is the classic example of determination to cope with the boredom of the long day: hers stretches before her 'with hours still to run, before the bell for sleep, and nothing more to say, nothing more to do'. Natasha Parry's exquisitely controlled performance in the role (Riverside Studios, London, 27 November 1997) should stand as the last word in contradiction of those who see Winnie as a brave but rather silly optimist. Parry's Winnie understood her fate and met it with the weapons at her command: humour, importantly, but also imagination and grace. She took us with her beyond the bell for waking and the bell for sleep into some other dimension which was free, spacious, and welcoming to the spirit. The actress told me that she had not before felt quite so strongly the sensation of something 'beyond' or 'the importance of being like an empty vessel through which the life of the words passes'.[8]

Winnie was 'air and fire' Beckett said; Willie, an 'old turtle'. Both are subject, like characters in other plays, to whiffs of hell's 'static lifelessness' issuing from inexorable daily rhythms and routines: time for 'pap', for a story, for a pain-killer (it is 'too soon', says V. in *Footfalls*, on a note of sad realism). These are conditions of life 'on this earth that is Purgatory', as Beckett said in that youthful essay:

> On this earth that is Purgatory, Vice and Virtue—which you may take to mean any pair of large contrary human factors—must in turn be purged down to spirits of rebelliousness.[9]

Though far from being an orthodox purgatory of a Dantesque, Catholic, or any other formal theological kind, in common with most of these it makes stern demands for spiritual refining. Repetition and variation are linked in a cumulative process which has this end in view. Repetition is there, we might say, for the sake of the variations. It's well known that Beckett often required of his actors a level tone, denuded of emphasis; within its bounds actors had to make room for the subtle nuances that would tell of changes deep within. Audiences must listen as to music to capture these fine shades. Natasha Parry, in Peter Brook's production, gave a virtuoso demonstration of the technique, conveying a seemingly inexhaustible range of feeling in the changes she rang on two words, 'Et maintenant?' French proved better here for the purpose than the English 'And now?' There will be a fascinating chance for comparisons when Parry plays Winnie in English which she is preparing to do at the time of writing; as she has told me (letter, 27 October, 1998), enduring the agony of relearning a text that is the same 'and yet totally different'.

Beckett's method bears hard on actors. Peggy Ashcroft told me how she once cut five pages from *Happy Days* by taking the wrong turn at one point of repeat and had somehow to find her way back.[10] Faced with such minute, demanding variations simple repetition can come to seem friendly. We all understand Hamm's feeling: 'Ah the old questions, the old answers, there's nothing like them!'

The repetition may have to be extreme before it forces change: we see this in *Play*. The astonishing repeat of the whole play, word for word the same, has been taken by some as a metaphor for hell, in the style of Sartre: 'Hell is other people.' Of the reasons for not seeing it so, two stand out, one to do with the characters, the other with the audience. Both have to experience the shock of change and are not left as they were at first. Between the 'Narrative', the unregenerate version of the trio's tangled lives, and the 'Meditation' which forces them to think differently about it there is a vast divide:

> When first this change I actually thanked God. I thought, It is done, it is said, now all is going out—

It is M speaking but the trio all know that deep psychic changes are occurring. They are signalled to us not just in the obvious terror and confusion but in movements towards kinder feeling, shown in no more than a change of tone or word. We hear W2, the mistress, tormenting herself by imagining her rival speaking patronizingly about her to the husband: 'That poor creature who tried to seduce you, whatever became of her, do you suppose?—I can hear her. Poor thing.' 'Poor creature', is what W1 does say when the spotlight moves to her later, but then, surely in changed tone, she amends to: 'Poor creatures'. It is of them all she speaks now, becoming, like the others, 'just a shade' less egotistical. We don't know how many repetitions were needed to bring them to this stage nor how long the process will have to continue. It can't but be slow, as such changes usually are in life.

The other reason for not seeing *Play* as an endless hell of repetition is the effect it has on us, the audience, on its second round. The posturing Narrative hasn't changed—but we have. We hear it differently, can't quite laugh as before. Admittedly, I have heard a few laughs sometimes: people don't like giving up comedy, especially in a situation seeming to promise none. But more often an atmosphere of stillness descends, allowing us to see further into both Narrative and

Meditation and perceive more sharply changes of feeling. M's comic 'pardon' for his recurring hiccups takes on another sense when the spotlight first breaks up the word—'Par'—then allows it to be completed. Heard again, it becomes 'Pardon', a plea for mercy. This sense of seeing further and deeper should be exhilarating, not lowering. I still remember vividly feeling it so on emerging from the first British production at the Old Vic in 1964.

Whether the same could be said of *Not I* may be questionable: Mouth's situation is more harrowing, suggestive of an inescapable hell. Yet she is an energetically questioning spirit too: her monologue is structured round a question whose meaning we deduce only from her answer, the 'what? . . who? . . no! . . she!' (glossed by Beckett as a 'vehement refusal to relinquish third person'). What we make of this probably depends on our whole attitude to life. We are clearly invited by the Auditor's gestures of compassion to see her repeated pushing away of the question as a stumbling-block of some kind. Yet she does return to it: it bothers her, reminds her that something is wrong in the way she tells her story.

Keir Elam has speculated that Beckett intended to place the audience in the position of the Dante persona in the *Inferno*, instructed by Virgil not to pity Bocca because he won't acknowledge his sins.[11] Do we feel like this? Only partly, I think. Reactions to Mouth and her plight vary enormously. She has been admired as someone who has broken free of the devouring ego and pitied as a victim of social 'exclusion' or illness or horrific breakdown ('half-demented', Anthony Cronin calls her). And she has been respected as a witness against defunct ideas of God. 'God is love', she pants, neither believing nor, so she says, wanting it: 'no love . . . spared that'. Her story as she tells it could well seem to support her sardonic view. God's 'tender mercies' have not been much in evidence for the unwanted child brought up in cold charity, never listened to, frozen into painful inarticulacy.

Yet if we're listening hard we realize that her repetition of the religious mantras she despises result in variations that move her on towards a hazy intuition of not having rendered the truth about this life she speaks of. She wouldn't know, if she heard it, she says, the 'something that would tell how it had been . . . how she had lived'. It is a sticking-point. Yet she has the idea that in some way 'she'll be purged' and the play ends with her still trying: 'keep on . . . hit on it in the end . . . then back . . .'.

HEAVEN

At its shadowy borders Beckett's earth that is purgatory looks on to heaven as well as hell. Here the Void reappears showing its more benign though still ambiguous, potentially terrifying, aspect. The vision of nothingness pursued by Victor in *Eleutheria* is one such. It can't be explained in words, as the play makes aggressively clear. 'Explain yourself', demands the Glazier, 'It is time that you defined yourself a little [. . .] you are quite simply nothing.' Victor's reply, 'It is perhaps time that somebody was quite simply nothing', leaves his interlocutor in the dark as it presumably would a real-life audience unless they'd had the sort of help supplied by Dougald McMillan and Martha Fehsenfeld in their trenchant account of the play and the ideas behind it: Democritus' theory of the whirling atoms and the void; Geulincx on 'nothing'.[12]

It is true that we get a hint at the nature of the vision from the austerely bare room Victor chooses in place of oppressive comforts (including a fiancée). But essentially we are made to feel that we are dealing with a mystery, one that can be experienced, not taught. Victor comes down twice to the footlights as if to explain himself, getting no further on the first occasion than telling the audience: 'I must say . . . I am not.' At the final curtain, having pulled his bed downstage and taken a long look at the audience from close quarters, he turns his back on them, lying on the bed, in his own space. We are left to feel either frustrated like those on stage or brooding on the one credo he has offered: 'I don't know.'

The 'no thing' behind everything might be benign. In *That Time* Voice B ponders on the fictions he has made 'to keep the void out just another of those old tales to keep the void from pouring in on top of you the shroud'. Yet when it descends, 'billowing' around him like a live thing, he finds himself 'little or nothing the worse'. In *Words and Music* the Void is positively sought—and attained, in a strange, lyric consummation made up of negatives.

All dark no begging
No giving no words
No sense no need
Through the scum
Down a little way
To whence one glimpse
Of that wellhead.

Reader and Listener in *Ohio Impromptu* descend still further into 'profounds of mind. Of mindlessness. Whither no light can reach. No sound.' Yet the effect is not of despair but achievement: 'The sad tale a last time told.' In *A Piece of Monologue*, where nothingness comes very close, Speaker transforms it by the addition of a single adverb: 'Nothing stirring. Nothing faintly stirring.'

Other visions or dreams of a heavenly dimension are more open to view, more common. Dan Rooney can be understood, even though he doesn't understand his own feeling of being not quite at home in the world: 'I dream of other roads, in other lands. Of another home, another—(*He hesitates.*)—another home. (*Pause.*) What was I trying to say?' Clov's dream involves dense mysteries, yet there is a human feeling all can recognize in his poignant 'I open the door of the cell and go.' A homely vision of paradisal contentment was originally held out in *En attendant Godot* (1953); they would sleep *chez* Godot, said Vladimir, 'au chaud, au sec, le ventre plein, sur la paille'. And in an early draft of *Fin de partie* (1957) the boy glimpsed by Clov outside the shelter was 'looking at his navel' like a youthful Buddha, bearer of enlightenment. (Neither of these visions made their way into the English versions, though Beckett included the first when he directed *Godot* for the Schiller-Theater Werkstatt in 1975.)

Traditional religious imagery occurs and God's name is invoked in many tones, including gratitude for hoped-for blessings: 'When first this change I actually thanked God.' May's lament for the crucified Christ—'His poor arm'—is the mystical centre of her long reverie; the opening of *Godot*—'Nothing to be done'—is followed by the meditation on salvation—'one of the thieves was saved'—which haunts the play. Angel-like messengers appear, offering tantalizing half-evidence, for the existence of a 'beyond'. In *Ohio Impromptu* the 'sad tale' turns on such a visitation: 'I have been sent by—and here he named the dear name—to comfort you.' In *Come and Go* God is invoked each time the trouble threatening the woman who moves into the shadow is whispered about by the other two and followed up with the question, 'Does she know?'

God grant not
God forbid
Please God not.

Is this just conventional usage, meaning nothing very much? Audiences sometimes smile at the repeated pieties as if they took them so. But of this we can't be sure. In the later years of our knowing each other Beckett often used to say 'God bless' on parting, a habit others have noted. It was *only* a habit, John Beckett assured me: his cousin had no religious belief and simply used the expression conventionally as Irish people did in the Dublin of his youth.[13] This couldn't be argued with, yet I retained the feeling that the expression hadn't been used quite conventionally at my last meeting with Beckett, a few weeks before his death; it seemed like a farewell with a true blessing in it. Some such impression is given, I believe, by the serene final tableau in *Come and Go* when the women, back together again in the circle of light, sit holding hands 'in the old way' (an intricate linking) and show their ringless hands as Flo speaks the enigmatic closing line: 'I can feel the rings.' The calm of this strange ending has completely held the audience whenever I've seen the play performed, maybe because it suggests something we might all hope for; a communion surviving the spoiling hand of whatever time has in store for us.

Heaven is imagined at the start of the theatrical *œuvre* by the most unlikely character. In his stuttering 'think' Lucky sees into the flames where the exceptions to God's love are 'plunged in torment', then tells how these flames will 'fire the firmament that is to say blast hell to heaven'. Hell becomes its opposite, a place of stillness and serenity: 'so blue still and calm so calm with a calm which even though intermittent is better than nothing'. That comically unexpected 'better than nothing' puts us in touch with a Lucky who was not always out of his wits, lets us wonder if he might, despite all, be a true seer.

A halcyon calm gathers around recollected love in *That Time* and is felt when Krapp records the sad idyll with the girl in the punt, drawing from it a transcendent ecstasy: 'We lay there without moving. But under us all moved, and moved us, gently, up and down, and from side to side.' A hush always falls on an audience at this moment.

Gleams of heavenly stillness (not the 'static lifelessness' envisaged in that youthful essay) visit even those still 'plunged in torment'. M 'brings up' for the spotlight not only his guilt but his vision of a harmony sadly not achieved: 'Never woke together, on a May morning, the first to wake to wake the other two.' Mouth in her frenzied circlings returns not only to old wounds but to the fresh beauty of the April morning when everything 'went out' for her while she was gathering flowers to make a cowslip ball. The oblique allusion to an innocent childhood joy carries a faint echo, I imagine, from that trapped spirit, Ariel, whose longed-for heaven of freedom could only be glimpsed through nature: 'Where the bee sucks there suck I | In a cowslip's bell I lie'. A 'distant bell' is heard by Mouth as she wanders in the cowslip field: she is back there at the end of the play, telling herself to 'pick it up'.

Endings are alien to Beckett's theatre. Even the characters who long for an end can't quite manage to believe in it. When Clov quotes the magisterial saying, 'It is finished', he has to blur it: 'Finished, it's finished, nearly finished, it must be nearly finished.' It is not enough to have lived: talking about it can't be imagined coming to an end. James Acheson suggests that Bam in *What Where*, though (in Beckett's words) 'something from beyond the grave', is still pursuing the riddle of the world through questions of a 'simple perceptual' kind, having given up the unanswerable ones.[14] The characters are haunted, as many are in life, by imaginings of life without end, that dream which could be a nightmare. Like most of us, they want more life, not less of it, for all they often say to the contrary. Krapp grumbles understandably about the 'sour cud and the iron stool' of old age but can't lose his longing to wander in the kind dark and 'be again':

> Be again, be again. (*Pause.*) All that old misery. (*Pause.*) Once wasn't enough for you.

Vistas open up of the many ways that have been imagined for reliving a life—or many lives, as in Hindu theories of reincarnation. One of Beckett's favourite actors, David Warrilow, believed in that possibility. In 1989, when he played Krapp at Leicester, he told me how he had talked of it to Beckett, getting the reaction—not too surprising—'I hope you're wrong.' Yet it was Beckett who created Krapp with his poignant longing to 'be again' and who used the word 'reawakening' like a life-wand. Opener in *Cascando* broods, 'You know, the reawakening', and Reader in *Ohio Impromptu*: 'Or was it that buried in who knows what thoughts they paid no heed? To light of day. To sound of reawakening.'

Agonizing contradictions recede in the late dramaticules; the view into eternity becomes calm, even confident. In the great closing apotheosis of *That Time*, time itself—the time through which lives come and go with painful swiftness—is transcended. By the rhythm of the words and the intonation they impose on the actor, a vision of infinity is achieved, of 'no time': 'come and gone come and gone no one come and gone in no time gone in no time'.

For the woman in the rocking chair of *Rockaby* (1981) death means going 'down the steep stair [. . .] right down | into the old rocker'; and then, 'those arms at last'. We may catch a biblical echo here: 'and underneath are the everlasting arms'. But even without it, there comes through an overwhelming sense of death as leading into some kind of continuation for the 'living soul', the Woman's own way of seeing herself.

Above all, heaven makes itself felt in Beckett's theatre, as in life, through the workings of the sympathetic imagination. It is the domain where Vladimir reflects, as Estragon sleeps, 'Was I sleeping while the others suffered? Am I sleeping now?' and imagines an infinite extension of sympathy: 'At me too someone is looking, of me too someone is saying, He is sleeping, he knows nothing, let him sleep on.' Actors often look out to the audience at this point, as if to encourage us to ask the question of ourselves: this would not be out of tune with the feeling in the play. Krapp takes us into the same domain when he recalls his mother's death in terms of the little things of life that gathered round it: the blind going down, signal of the end; the 'small, old, black, hard, solid rubber ball' he'd been throwing to a dog; the dog's 'yelping and pawing': 'Her moments, my moments. (*Pause.*) The dog's moments.' The episode touches off for me thoughts of E. M. Forster's Hindu mystic, Professor Godbole, who succeeds, after long meditation, in bringing into the zone of contemplation two once living creatures, now dead: an old Englishwoman and a wasp. 'It does not seem much', he says, 'still it is more than I am myself.'

In this power of becoming 'more than I am myself' Beckett's characters find their austere heaven. The Woman in *Rockaby* brings alive—for us as for herself—the dead mother who sat in the rocking-chair before her, dressed in the same touchingly incongruous 'best black', its jet sequins glittering. The 'prematurely aged' daughter enters into the experience of the old mother before and after her death, an experience the stage image helps us to visualize with uncanny vividness.

Music often sets the tone for this heaven. Music leads Words to the mystical consummation of *Words and Music*. Faint strains of the slow movement from Beethoven's 'Ghost Trio' (Op. 70, No. 1) issue from the tape recorder clutched by the mute figure in *Ghost Trio*. It brings into the bare, silent room the sense of some ethereal, tensely awaited visitation. Schubert's music opens up a visionary dimension in the early *All That Fall* and in the almost-last play, *Nacht und Träume* brings solace from the same distant space. Here it is the human voice, humming the last seven bars of 'Lied, Nacht und Träume' that prepares the way. There is a going out from the self into a 'kinder light' where hands appear, gently touching the head of the man in the dream, conveying a cup to his lips, wiping his brow with a cloth. The tantalizing 'above' of *Act Without Words 1* that withdraws solaces, has been replaced by a benign presence—even if it is only in a dream.

Beckett said his was an art of 'excavation', his concern was with 'impotence, ignorance'. In these regions we are all ignorant and in need of someone brave enough to excavate the dread spaces of the hidden psyche and the enveloping void. This he does for us.

3

Lifelines: Humour and Homely Sayings

PEOPLE have got used by now to the idea of Beckett's being funny as well as formidable. Donald Davie's idea might once have been right: 'So black is this comedy that most English readers and theatre-goers cannot see it as comic at all' (*Independent*, 27 December 1989). But it has been many times contradicted, as it was by the theatre-goers who flocked to Peter Hall's new production of *Godot* in 1997. At the performances I saw there was a palpable sense of general enjoyment as well as a *frisson* among aficionados looking forward to comic highlights like the battle of insults.

With *Endgame* too there's often the same sense of anticipation as set-piece drollery approaches. Like opera audiences savouring a favourite aria, people can be felt getting in tune for Nagg's story about the tailor who took three months to complete a pair of trousers. Nagg has only to put on the 'raconteur's' voice called for by Beckett to have us with him, relishing each stage of the joke and waiting for the witty pay-off line when he reaches the customer's exasperated comparison between the tardy tailor and God who needed only six days to make the world: 'But my dear Sir, my dear Sir, look—(*disdainful gesture, disgustedly*)—at the world—(*Pause.*)—and look—(*loving gesture, proudly*)—at my TROUSERS.' 'I never told it worse', he says wryly, confident in the knowledge that it will go down well in the auditorium, if not with his stage audience (Nell remains '*impassive*'). It usually does so, even when rather muffled as in Katie Mitchell's production in 1996: the unusual placing of the dustbins back instead of front stage may have had something to do with this.

Times have changed since the first audiences of *Godot* and *Endgame* were provoked by laments in the plays over the boredom of it all: 'nobody comes, nobody goes, it's awful!', or 'This is not much fun'. The first English Pozzo, Peter Bull, told how people in 1955 often reacted with irritated shouts of agreement and protest.[1] Beckett seemed to see beyond all this to a time when audiences would feel linked with the actors in companionable conspiracy to play around with the illusion. He did so even before having had experience of writing for the professional theatre. 'Nothing bores like boredom', quips the Glazier in *Eleutheria*, and the Audience Member amusingly climbs out of a stage box to demand on our behalf more action and at least *some* meaning.

The relatively large casts of the early plays (eleven in *Eleutheria*) gave Beckett chances he seized on with relish to introduce a rich variety of eccentric characters. Comic-label names encourage a humorous view. We expect comedy from somebody called Mr Slocum and get it in riotously farcical form when he offers Maddy Rooney a lift—and a dubious helping hand into his car 'from the rear' ('There! . . . Now! . . . Get your shoulder under it . . . Oh! . . . (*Giggles*) . . . Oh glory!'). Another character in *All That Fall*, Miss Fitt, expresses her sense of being 'not there' in grotesquely comic terms (disconcertingly, for anyone who knows *Footfalls* where that feeling is ghostly, tragic). The 'dark Miss Fitt' has her pathetic side, but we're bound to laugh when she assures Maddy that in church she is always alone with her Maker and often feels 'not there, Mrs Rooney, just not really there at all': 'Ah yes, I am distray, very distray; even on week-days. Ask Mother, if you do not believe me. Hetty, she says, when I start eating my doily instead of the thin bread and butter, Hetty, how can you be so distray?' Her 'distray' is the sort of pronunciation joke dear to bilingual Beckett. He shares it more than once with less than bilingual English audiences: it turns up in *Godot* as a dubious compliment on Pozzo's party piece: 'Oh, tray bong, tray tray tray bong.' Real strangeness connects with ordinary absurdity and oddity in the passing show. This is the 'earlier, funnier Beckett', to borrow a title used by a lecturer once at Sligo.

Companionship is a keynote. We're invited behind the illusion into fellowship with the actors and the writer himself. Awareness of us, the audience, is strong in Hamm and Clov and Didi and Gogo (to give the latter pair the sportive nicknames appropriate to this topic—and the ones they use themselves). We're all in it together is how the feeling goes when Gogo comes front stage, to survey us and say 'Inspiring prospects' or, more warily, when Clov turns his telescope on us, reporting to Hamm 'I see . . . a multitude . . . in transports . . . of joy. (*Pause.*) That's what I call a magnifier.' Dangerous jokes, all: the sort that make us take up a position, get involved (but Beckett later lost his taste for them; see *TN* ii. [56]).

We're drawn in too by the actors' shared jokes about their craft; Hamm announcing 'I'm warming up for my last soliloquy'; Clov asking 'What is there to keep me here?', being told 'The dialogue'. 'Don't we laugh?', he asks Hamm after the bit of fun with the telescope and later describes the world beyond the windows as 'corpsed', actors' slang for being made to laugh in the wrong place. Companionable links, these, between players and audience.

It's hardly surprising that stand-up comics have seemed natural casting for parts calling for this quick-fire repartee and adroit game-playing. Another layer of the familiar and companionable was added with such casting as Lucien Raimbourg, a cabaret performer, in the first production of *Godot*, and Bert Lahr in the first American one (to judge from a recording made by CBS in 1973, Lahr brought to the play the rapid, dry, deadpan style known to the whole world from early Hollywood film comedy). In London at the Queen's Theatre (20 September 1991) a popular British duo, Rik Mayall and Adrian Edmondson, took the roles in a more easy-going, out-to-the-audience style that obviously won the sympathy of the many young people present and, with reservations, of seasoned Beckett viewers such as Hersh Zeifman and myself.

When the music-hall veteran Max Wall played Didi at the Royal Exchange Theatre, Manchester (13 November 1980) he brought to the play amusing specialities like rolling the hats down his arm in the 'three hats for two heads' routine of Act 2, along with a zest for comic sounds[2] and formidable powers of working the audience. One of his music-hall routines involved picking on a latecomer and continuing the joke he built around him/her with any subsequent unfortunates, to ever-increased mirth from an audience safe in their seats. Or were we safe? There was just a touch of that apprehension, I thought, at the in-the-round performance in Manchester where Wall's Didi was close enough to pick us out for improvised sallies, had he wanted to. The sense of this potential threat curiously added to enjoyment of the warmth that flowed from the actor's protective relationship with his fellow, played with endearing bluntness by Trevor Peacock. Wall also brought to the role, so he believed, a maturity or wisdom born of hard experience in a long life; he felt he shared much with Beckett, whom he met about this time.

Enjoyment of easy repartee would be one thing they *would* share. Beckett and his wife, according to his first biographer, Deirdre Bair, were thought of by friends (not named) as 'being like two Irish "butties", trading vaudeville one-liners in the best music-hall tradition'. Elsewhere she cites Roger Blin and Jean Martin (first director of *Fin de partie* and first Lucky) as evidence for a remark made by Beckett at rehearsals in Paris, to the effect that Hamm and Clov were Suzanne and himself.[3] There may be doubts about the backing for these views but it's not hard to believe that some real-life habit of intimate, quick-fire argument, dry joke, and low-toned riposte lay behind Beckett's love of such interchanges in his plays. It is a form of companionship delectably open to audiences as well as to those engaged in the sport.

Existential anxieties, if not exactly exorcized, are kept in place by comic business and repartee. The dread of life that broods over *Endgame* loses its solemnity when Clov squirts flea powder into his pants, remarking that the flea may be 'laying doggo' to which Hamm returns, 'If he was laying we'd be bitched'. Similarly the oppressive weight of time in *Godot* is eased by the jokes the pair draw out of it:

VLADIMIR. That passed the time.
ESTRAGON. It would have passed in any case.
VLADIMIR. Yes, but not so rapidly.

'We always find something, eh, Didi', says Gogo, 'to give us the impression that we exist?' Dry turns of phrase like these keep at a distance the shapeless threat they struggle against with their 'elevations' and 'relaxations':

VLADIMIR. What about a little deep breathing?
ESTRAGON. I'm tired breathing.

In similar vein Maddy Rooney's inward, anxious sense of unreality takes a jocose turn when she slips into an unconvincing literary style—'I am agog, tell me all'—and is rebuked by Dan: 'sometimes one would think you were struggling with a dead language'. It is a terrible feeling, she agrees, and he—aiming mischievously at the listeners—admits to having it too at times when he overhears himself. She takes the chance to talk them into the public world again with a provocative Irish joke: 'Well, you know, it will be dead in time, just like our own poor dear Gaelic, there is that to be said.'

The comic duo in *Happy Days* is a marital team too. Willie isn't the best of company but he contributes to the comedy in his clippy way, as in answering Winnie's query whether hair should be referred to as 'it' or 'them' (a joke probably funnier in French) or giving her chances for 'innocent' laughs in the comic business with his dirty postcard. She gives the audience the same chance as she studies it with horrified relish, putting on her spectacles and using her magnifying glass to see it better: 'Heavens what are they up to! [. . .] What does that creature in the background think he's doing? (*Looks closer.*) Oh no, really!' When she spots an emmet (ant) on the mound and asks her mentor the meaning of its carrying 'like a little white ball' his laconic pun 'Formication' cheers her up in the end though her first reaction is an appalled 'God'. Horror at the idea of life being so irrepressible weighs on her, it seems, as on Hamm and Clov. But she does laugh.

The failure of jokes to register is a comic motif on which Beckett plays many variations. 'Laugh, Henry', says Ada when she gets no response to her little sally about backing horses that don't run: 'it's not every day I crack a joke.' Poor Henry; he's in danger of being swamped by his obsessions, though he can turn a joke himself when in the mood.

The audience in the auditorium is tested too for its sensitivities. 'Nothing is funnier than unhappiness, I grant you that.' Nell says this, after rebuking Nagg for reacting unfeelingly to Hamm's anguished 'A heart, a heart in my head'. Does our laughter tend to be unfeeling? Do we, for instance, laugh at the miserable figure who produces a dance and a 'think' to order as his share in our entertainment? Perhaps not when Lucky was played by Greg Hicks in Peter Hall's 1997 production with almost non-stop shivering and salivation. Yet the episode is an interlude with a zany comic aspect and people do laugh at it (rather nervously, it's to be hoped). The stage audience don't laugh, we might notice. Beckett charts their reactions very exactly in the text: they vary from anguish (Pozzo) to the other pair's alternations of intentness and protest.

Some clowning exists in the earlier plays even when there is no live company to provide companionable give and take. Krapp joins in laughter with the earlier self on tape who laughs at the still younger recorded self, the 'young whelp' with his voice ('Jesus!') and his aspirations and resolutions. Flesh-and-blood Krapp continues to laugh, without his previous self, at the resolution to 'drink less'. Some take this as a grim, others as a refreshingly philosophic, recognition of things as they are. The heads of *Play* are more isolated from each other than Krapp from the tape recorder which he handles so lovingly. Yet they too create a lively sense of company. In their unregenerate Narrative the two women are bitchy about each other with a verve which always amuses the unregenerate audience: 'Pudding face, puffy, spots, blubber mouth, jowls, no neck, dugs you could—'. M invites laughter by speaking out as if to an all-male audience whose macho solidarity he can take for granted: 'God what vermin women'; 'Adulterers, take warning, never admit'. On the second round the fun is dampened down but its aura can't quite be extinguished. *Play* might from this angle almost have deserved the title Beckett at one time designed for *Happy Days*, 'A Low Comedy'.

Beckett touches a great common chord in giving his characters so many clownish aspects. He toned down the clown look assigned to some in the early days: Krapp's purple nose, the red faces of Hamm and Clov. But much of the style remained, to touch off memories of the 'little man' of music hall and silent film who can't cope with all the awkwardness of life—but somehow does. Echoes, visual and verbal, go back and forth. Many a routine silent film comedy lies behind Clov's battles with objects and laborious stage business like the ladder-climbing with its built-in repetitions and frustrations ('I'm back again, with the glass'). In the way of clowns and stand-up comics everywhere, Hamm and Clov are aware of their own oddity—'No one that ever lived ever thought so crooked as we'.

Moments of dream-like *déjà vu* occur. When Lucky takes off his hat on command, letting loose his disconcerting cascade of long white hair, we might see, as in a mirror behind him, that other famous mute, Harpo Marx, enigmatic, slightly sinister with his wild hair and staring eyes, capable, like Lucky, of manic eruptions (and of getting fun from an incongruous telescope). Affectionate allusions these, often very bold as in the take-over in *Godot* of the hats routine from *Duck Soup*. Krapp starting on his second banana has a touch of Harpo in *Room Service* going straight to bananas from a speedily eaten meal, a hint at other kinds of insatiability. Actors playing Krapp usually point up the implication, making the banana an unmistakably phallic object (the trick can be overdone, though audiences revel in it, as in the well-loved tripping on the banana skin). Another family likeness suggests itself between *Below Zero* of Laurel and Hardy and *Rough for Theatre 1* where a lame man in a wheelchair contemplates partnership with a blind street musician. Laurel and Hardy, street musicians playing for money in the snow, are bumped into by a blind man who adroitly makes off with the coins spilt as a result. The 'blind' one adjusts his dark glasses as he goes; a saturnine touch of comedy well in tune with Beckett's *Rough*.

To revisit these old films is to receive many little pleasurable shocks of this kind, including a verbal one in *Room Service* when Chico hits on a device for warding off ejection from their hotel room—'How about one of us being sick?'—and Groucho approves: 'That's the idea. They can't put a sick man out.' We may get an advance echo of Didi taking up the way out of an impasse inadvertently offered by Gogo: 'That's the idea, let's abuse each other'. The ability to improvise—or seem to—is a part of the comic's repertoire Beckett actors need to have. It's ironic—and a real test—given that never in any play will they be more firmly tied to the minutiae of the text.

Beckett touches a rather mysterious common chord in making the use he does of physical opposites. In his own production of *Godot* with the Schiller-Theater Wertkstatt in 1975 his Didi and Gogo perfectly struck the visual note of contrast—tall, thin person, short stout one—epitomized in the Laurel and Hardy combine, or that of Morecambe and Wise and endless other duos. Pozzo and Lucky were envisaged in an early draft of the French text of *Godot* simply as 'le grand' and 'le petit'. People tend to find this combination funny in real life even when not as neat and complete as the stage can make it. Perhaps the universal affection for these duos springs from the resolution they offer, in comic lightness, of unacknowledged anxieties about the splits and divisions we all have within the self.

Charlie Chaplin, bowler hat on head, twirling his stick as he goes into the distance with splayed walk down an empty country road, is the great icon in the background of all, shedding an extra glow of poignancy on the wanderers of *Godot*. Beckett praised one performance of the play as 'very chaplinesque' and would have liked Chaplin for the role in *Film*. Instead he had Buster Keaton, another icon of the 'little man' with his own trademarks; the expressionless face, the hat (a flattened-down stetson) which he received Beckett's permission to wear in his role as the protagonist in *Film*.

A few words on hats. They are deeply congenial to Beckett as playwright, especially when they have an archaic period look, like Winnie's, described by Beckett in his French text as 'Une toque très bibi'.[4] The pale grey toque worn by Natasha Parry in *Oh les beaux jours*, with its discreet hint of diamanté and sad, once elegant feather, perfectly captured the mixture of the comical, bright, and poignant which characterizes Winnie herself. Beckett evidently loved that 'Gay, frivolous, fragile, drooping, pathetic, mangy feather' (as he described it in his Schiller Notebook[5]). Willie also has his hat, or rather two: the yellowing straw with a striped band—tapped jauntily as he put it on, in Peter Brook's production, as in Beckett's—and the wedding topper of his final manifestation. It was one of those shocks in which Beckett delights—part comic, part upsetting—when he took it off to lay quite bare a totally bald head.

There is a great deal of real life in these hats. As in real life, they often contribute to the sense of companionability. It can go wrong: the bowler hat is an inflammatory emblem of solidarity in Northern Ireland where Beckett went to school and taught for a while. And the British building society which bought Stan Laurel's legendary bowler, to match their well-known logo, found soon after that hats can change meaning: though still reassuring, the bowler had become 'too old-fashioned, sexist and stuffy to survive into the Millennium' (*Sunday Telegraph*, 3 May 1998). Hats can hint at the fragility of human identity. It's a mix capable of amusing and troubling in one, as when Stan Laurel tries on hats, reacting with growing uneasiness as he disappears into one too big or is made ridiculous by one too small.

Beckett's intuitive contact with the communal imagination is nicely shown by his appropriation of the comic's hat. He has made the Chaplinesque bowler hat so much his own that it's likely nowadays to be as much associated with *Godot* as with silent film. It would have been a surprise to many, as it was to me, when Peter Hall's 1997 production opened with Ben Kingsley's Gogo not in the classic battered bowler but a black beret-style cap, its brim worn to the back. It seemed wrong at first but immediately became right as an expression of a personality that was consistently there: shrewd, earthy, warily sceptical, just the man who would wear that cap (it reverted to shapeless bowler when Alan Dobie took over the role in March 1998).

Paris has its place in the dream kingdom of hats. The 'old world Latin Quarter hat' on the table between Reader and Listener in *Ohio Impromptu* will conjure up for many thoughts of a bohemian world devoted to art, perhaps romantically distant—*La Bohème, Trilby*—or taking more modern form as the literary ferment around the composing of *Finnegans Wake*, or tales of Beckett's walks with Joyce on the Ile des Cygnes.

As with everything in Beckett's theatre, the light and the dark coexist in the jokes and games: the running joke on 'No more of anything' in *Endgame* leads inexorably from 'No more sugar-plums' to 'No more pain-killer', drawing from Hamm a scream real enough to make us shudder: 'What'll I do?' So too with the hat. It takes a turn into black symbolism when Didi follows Pozzo's instruction to end Lucky's 'think' by snatching off his hat, drawing from Pozzo, as he tramples on it, terrifying words of approval: 'There's an end to his thinking.' Lucky is never heard to speak again. On a different note, I thought Ilan Reichel captured something both droll and mysterious with the hats of *Come and Go* when he presented the play in a programme of Beckett 'shorts' by his In Motion Theatre Company at the Etcetera Theatre (1 February 1996). At the end of the evening, with the stage bare, the light fell on the three hats alone, frail reminder of the comedy and pathos in the lives we had glimpsed.

I turn now to the question: what happens in the later plays, especially those from *Not I* onwards when company has left the stage and characters are isolated in ethereal solitude? They may still hear the sound of their own voices but scarcely engage with them: they often seem close to death and content to be so: Listener's smile at the end of *That Time* might suggest this. The smile is '*toothless for preference*', a textual direction that shows Beckett still thinking humorously. The speakers of the lonely monologues also manage as a rule to hold on to the humorous perspective with little reminders to themselves of the oddity of things. Intent listening, as to music, is required of an audience to catch this quiet humour, showing itself in a wry turn of phrase, an impishly unexpected switch of mood.

A disconcerting switch of that kind occurs in *Footfalls* when the dimly lit figure who has just conjured up a still more shadowy 'semblance' changes key and speaks out to the audience, addressing them as if they were Victorian novel-readers: 'Old Mrs Winter, whom the reader will remember'. People are sometimes too mesmerized by what has gone before to react to the little joke. This seemed to me the case with Katie Mitchell's production at Stratford-upon-Avon in 1997: the audience were deep in the spell Juliet Stevenson had cast, though perhaps they smiled to themselves. The programme as a whole tended to draw from reviewers headlines like 'Life in the Bleak Lane': for some it was evidently an entirely humourless, if affecting, experience. Yet humour was wonderfully there, all the same.

It is there at the start of the 'dramaticule' mode (Beckett's word). The fragile *Come and Go* can't afford too much change of mood in its three minutes' playing-time if it's to hold on to its deep inward intensity. Yet it opens with a line which usually draws a quiet, probably rather surprised chuckle from an audience, with its playful suggestion of the witches in *Macbeth*: 'When did we three last meet?' The actors I worked with in the Drama Workshop at Sligo in 1988 found that reaction from a dauntingly large audience in Sligo Town Hall immensely companionable, as too the murmurs of amusement as each of the three women in turn enquired whether the one out of earshot 'knows' what has just been whispered about her. Within the other-worldly space created by stylized movement, rhythmic patterns of sound, and the women's half-hidden faces, a whole ordinary world of people gossiping about each others' troubles had been recognized.

Again at Sligo, this time on the stage of the Hawk's Well Theatre, Robert Gordon, playing *A Piece of Monologue*, told me how grateful he felt to Beckett for opening the taxing, brooding play with the nicely rueful joke, 'Birth was the death of him.' The appearance of Speaker itself refuses total solemnity. We see in the dim light an apparition with white hair, white nightgown, and—comical anticlimax—white bedsocks. We wanted the light to be not so dim as to obscure the effect of these homely bedsocks. To smile at them is to be in tune with a play which often calls for quiet smiles, as when Speaker tells how he can light a match by striking it on his buttock 'the way his father taught him'. This wryly humorous mind succeeds in keeping its balance even while preparing to go to bed for good.

Opportunities for comical Krapp-like interchanges with a recorded voice shrink in the later plays, but the voices listened to in silence can strike their own note of humour. The voice in *Eh Joe* gets saturnine fun by quoting at Joe his own well-turned phrases—'voice like flint glass', 'mental thuggee'. People usually smile at these jibes though perhaps not at the dark joke the voice makes when she tells of the abandoned girl's repeated attempts to kill herself, first by lying face down in the sea, then with a razor: 'Cut a long story short doesn't work [. . .] Cut another long story short doesn't work either.' It's a horribly apt joke, bringing out the awful reality of the struggle with the razor: 'You know how she always dreaded pain.' Yet it allows too a moment of slight relief before the tension mounts, uninterrupted, to the bitterly affecting climax. The conscious wit of the voice taunting Joe is a deliberate turning of the knife in the wound. There is also in the late plays the more playful humour that springs from characters just being themselves. An endearing moment of that kind breaks the somnambulist rhythms of *Ohio Impromptu* when the Reader interrupts himself and a different persona appears for a split second: a pedant who checks his manuscript and likes to have his references clear, even in the midst of a profoundly poetic passage:

In this extremity his old terror of night laid hold on him again. After so long a lapse that as if never been. (*Pause. Looks closer.*) Yes, after so long a lapse that as if never been. Now with redoubled force the fearful symptoms described at length page forty paragraph four.

When he starts to turn back the pages, in search of page forty presumably, he is prevented by the Listener's sharp knock. It's a joke open to all, though with special charm for authors with a pedantic streak, among whom Beckett would no doubt, so the play suggests, have included himself.

We wouldn't expect mildly comic self-mockery of that kind from Mouth, so far gone into a humourless hell of 'raging'. Billie Whitelaw felt she was producing an 'animal' sound: it certainly came near to seeming inhuman at times. But Mouth is human and humour, of a saturnine variety, is not absent from her monologue. Her 'spared that' when she speaks of God and love tells us that. The sarcasm is part of what is wrong with her but also of what might go right. If she could make that effort she finds so terrible and accept herself, the same words could be said quite differently, still with irony perhaps, but the more good-humoured kind that helps to keep us going rather than pulling us down.

Even in the bleak *What Where* notes of the humorous absurd are struck in the jingle of names and clock-like repetitions as Bim succeeds Bom, and Bem, Bim. We are surely invited to smile at the oracular saying which closes the play: 'Make sense who may. | I switch off.' *Quad* often draws similar murmurs of amusement for its mechanical variations on the one theme as yet another solitary mime emerges on screen, distinguished from the last only by the colour of the masking robe and hood.

These 'moments of reprieve', if I may call them that (with deep respect to Primo Levi's book of that name) slide unobtrusively in and out of the late plays, usually with perfect naturalness, though on occasion with a little shock which is a joke against us and our expectations. We hardly expect the 'Fuck life' that emerges from the 'prematurely old' woman in the rocking-chair at the very close of her mesmeric reverie. I have heard faint, uneasy half-laughter in response; a tribute to the fact that life never ceases to spring amusing surprises, even at the point where it is turning into death.

This refusal of humour to be quenched tells us that deep in the grain of Beckett's plays runs the vital force described by Wordsworth: 'the grand elementary principle of pleasure'.

HOMELY SAYINGS

Warmth and companionability spring too from the frequent intertwining of Beckett's fantastic scenes with the well-used sayings of every day: tags, proverbs, clichés, and the like. We could all produce a list 'off the top of our heads' (a start in itself). Homely sayings like 'two-faced' or 'up against it' or 'blowing the mind' have fantastic images in them waiting to be let out. Beckett does this, amazing us while allowing us still to feel in an odd way at home. His fictional character, Belacqua, speaks for him when he stresses the value to the writer of 'humble tags and commonplaces'. They are he says; the 'flints and pebbles' necessary to show up the 'margarita' or pearl; 'the sparkle, the precious margaret'.[6]

There are many of these common bits of earth in the plays. Take 'beside herself'. We all know what it means, but only Beckett could have converted it into the awful vision of Mouth, placed 'beside' the mute figure, the 'other' she needs but can't connect with. Or consider the simple words 'that time': we all use them as Listener repeatedly does in *That Time*, trying to chart a memory—was it 'that time' when we went to this or that place, saw this or that? Eloquently Listener feels for those footholds in a personal past: 'was that an earlier time a later time before she came after she went or both'. But 'that time', so intimate and personal, takes on another sense as he broods on it—'was there ever any other time but that time'—till finally it is projected, along with all the other times, into the immensity of 'no time'.

Even through the dreamy, hypnotic murmurings of *Rockaby* faint echoes of homely sayings reverberate; voices are heard whispering about the old lady 'gone off her head | but harmless'. A more vulgar version, 'off her rocker' might come to mind. If so, it would tie the gossiping talk to the rhythms of the rocking-chair and be absorbed, like everything said in the play, into that rhythm, go with the 'living soul' down to 'the old rocker | mother rocker'.

Happy Days marries the fantastic and the homely on epic scale. Its humble tags and commonplaces could be thought of as the 'flints and pebbles' that have built up Winnie's mound; an accumulation of the common sayings that have dropped from her over the years. Often she leaves them for us to finish, as when she muses 'can't be cured' while looking for signs of decay in her teeth. She might reasonably expect us to provide the saying's other half—'must be endured'—and notice as we do so how supremely appropriate it is to her situation and how she probably knows it.

That she does know it very well is confirmed in the rest of the tooth-brushing episode. She hisses out 'Good Lord! . . . good God!' as she pulls her mouth about to get a better view. It's amusing but only those who have never had tooth trouble will fail to appreciate in addition the philosophic calm she manages in the face of what the exhaustive scrutiny tells her: 'no better, no worse'. There is 'no pain', she claims, then adds with her usual honesty 'hardly any'.

A common saying dear to Beckett lies behind the fantastic central image of the woman stuck in earth up to her waist, then neck. He plays many variations in his correspondence on the odd little metaphor, 'up to her/his neck in it'. 'Up to my navel in sudden work', he will write, or 'Up to my eyes and in rather a panic'.[7] From here it is only a step to Winnie; yet who but Beckett could have taken it? We might remember though that even in his uniqueness he contributes to a long-standing comic tradition, one which takes in the Marx Brothers acting out 'burning the candle at both ends' and, still further back, music-hall performers like the British Harry Clifton who enjoys a curious connection with Beckett through his song, 'The Weepin Willer'. It tells how a miller's daughter had second thoughts about hanging herself from a willow tree: 'I'm not very bold and I may take cold | I'll wait till the weather is hotter.' 'Oh Vladimir and Estragon!', as Peter Davison, collector of the song, aptly comments.[8]

Finally, the saying that provides Beckett with his title *Happy Days*. We probably know it as a euphoric song, 'Happy days are here again', and a toast (an important sense for Winnie, so taken up with wedding memories). The cheerful implications can soon be swept away by a different intonation. 'Happy days!' said with a sigh by someone looking back on youth, is heavy with nostalgia. Beckett plays with these contrasting implications through Winnie's facial expressions and her speech habits. Her 'happy expression' comes and goes with speed, drawing attention to the difficulty of maintaining it. And her 'happy day' is placed at an ironic distance by her careful use of the future or future perfect tense. 'Oh this is going to be another happy day!', she exclaims, when Willie follows her directions about applying suntan oil. His laconic reply to her query about how hair should be referred to draws the same burst of euphoric anticipation. Is there ever going to be a present tense, we wonder, or is happiness always to be located in the nebulous future typified by wedding toasts? Only once does she break the pattern. Willie's response to her query 'What is a hog?' brings out the 'happy expression' and a confident 'Oh this *is* a happy day.' But she slips straight back into the strange hypothetical past represented by the future perfect:

This will have been another happy day! (*Pause.*) After all. (*Pause.*) So far. (*Pause. Happy expression off.*)

We could hardly be sure what her reaction will be when Willie makes his astonishing entrance in Act 2, in morning dress, living embodiment of 'that day' which she has been recalling: 'The pink fizz. (*Pause.*) The flute glasses. (*Pause.*) [. . .] The look. (*Long pause.*)'. As always, she records exactly, registering the shakiness of the memory—'What day? (*Long pause.*) What look? (*Long pause.*)'—and the awful incongruity of the aged Willie's appearance: 'What a get-up, you do look a sight!' Yet she holds on to 'happy days' moving from the present into that almost indestructible future perfect. Is this stupidity or wilful self-delusion, as some have thought? Rather, it is need. She works on the facts of life; not to evade them (no chance of that) but to surmount them, as she surely does despite the sinister uncertainty of Willie's 'look' when she makes her last defiant assertion that it will have been another happy day: 'After all. (*Pause.*) So far.'

It is then—at last—that she gives us the song we have been waiting right through the play to hear. It is the pearl, the 'precious margaret': always, in Beckett's theatre, to be sought among the 'flints and pebbles'.

4

Taking the Life Journey and Telling It

IN the earlier plays the journey through the mysterious space we all inhabit is still felt in part as physical and actual, taken in present time. Later, as the travellers' movements are frozen it becomes more obviously a journey of the mind. Old tracks are gone over again; there is a pressure, sometimes resisted, to 'see' it truly ('As you could not at the time', says the voice in *Company*). Whole lifetimes are revealed, in forms increasingly elliptical and compressed; only sixteen minutes of stage time is needed for *Not I*, three or four for *Come and Go*.

We are in the middle of the road in *Waiting for Godot*, feeling its ordinary, daily rigours down to the last blister on the hard-worked feet—and its consolations and hopes, which are both immense and vague. The immersion in the present is complete; perhaps one of the reasons why many have found it such a liberating play.

The pressures of the physical journey are to the fore: the heavy bags Lucky can't put down, Vladimir's prostate trouble, Pozzo's neurotic tics, Estragon's ill-fitting boots. Friendly echoes sound from Chaplin and silent film—and Beckett's own troubles with tight-fitting shoes, much mentioned by commentators. The audience laughed with obvious fellow feeling as Ben Kingsley's Estragon struggled to put the boots on and off with resigned matter-of-factness and were still sympathetically with him—to judge from their intent listening—when he took off from these irksome necessities into a domain we might not have realized he thought about at all:

VLADIMIR. Your boots. What are you doing with your boots?
ESTRAGON. (*Turning to look at his boots.*) I'm leaving them there. (*Pause.*) Another will come, just as . . . as . . . as me, but with smaller feet, and they'll make him happy.
VLADIMIR. But you can't go barefoot!
ESTRAGON. Christ did.
VLADIMIR. Christ! What's Christ got to do with it? You're not going to compare yourself to Christ.
ESTRAGON. All my life I've compared myself to him.

On a later occasion he soon earths himself—'That's enough about these boots'—but in the 'barefoot' passage the journey takes on the look of a pilgrimage, one not unrelated, though so different, to that most famous one, *The Pilgrim's Progress*. Compared with Christian, armed with his 'book' and sure of his destination Beckett's travellers are laughably ill equipped and uncertain. 'I must have made a note of it', Vladimir says, searching his pocket for the detail of the appointment with Godot. We don't expect him to find it, any more than we expect Godot to turn up. Is it the right tree, the right day, the right place in the void? They can't be sure. Bunyan found room for doubt but nothing quite so disorientating as this. His Christian carries a heavy burden but it rolls off, as Lucky's never will.

For all the distance between Beckett's travellers and Bunyan's, they are equally on a 'quest', the term used by Julie Campbell in her comparison of *The Pilgrim's Progress* with the early novel, *Mercier and Camier* (written in 1946).[1] The wavering, erratic, blatantly unexplained journey of the louche pair in the novel is an ironic reflection on Bunyan's pilgrimage but also, she persuasively argues, a quest in its own right: 'a journey through the maze of conflicting pressures, apathies, escape routes, and blind alleys of contemporary thought'.[2]

There is a relevance to *Godot* in this but something has changed between the novel and the play. Vladimir and Estragon are much closer to Bunyan's Christian in having a purpose, one they intend to hold to:

VLADIMIR. He didn't say for sure he'd come.
ESTRAGON. And if he doesn't come?
VLADIMIR. We'll come back tomorrow.
ESTRAGON. And then the day after tomorrow.
VLADIMIR. Possibly.
ESTRAGON. And so on.

In Peter Hall's production Ben Kingsley produced a wonderfully varied range of intonations—surprised, resigned, weary, irritated—for the 'Ah yes' he returned to Alan Howard's patient reminders of the reason for being there. There was pleased laughter in Act 2 when Pozzo asks Vladimir what Estragon is doing and the latter makes the unexpected, pat response, 'I'm waiting for Godot', identifying himself with the waiting for the first time and in the first person.

The Pozzo/Lucky journey also has an end in view: to sell Lucky at the fair. Shades of *The Pilgrim's Progress* thicken here. Pozzo is easily seen as an inhabitant of Vanity Fair, primed with picnic basket and pipe ready for a luxurious smoke. Ignorance, Vain-glorious, and the rest of Bunyan's unsaved are not far off. Although the tree is on Pozzo's land it seems to have no special meaning for him, no more than the road has. 'The road is free to all', he tells the other pair indifferently, 'It's a disgrace. But there you are.' His stop at the tree is for company; he likes an audience—when they know their place (a trait Dennis Quilley's jovial, brigadier-like Pozzo in Peter Hall's production made alarmingly ordinary and familiar). Yet the tree pulls him back. He returns in Act 2 (Lucky unsold) from the wings into which he disappeared in Act. 1. It's as if they have fetched a circle, yet it's not a closed one. Their journey has moved into another spiral where a dumb man leads a blind one by a rope, now clearly a lifeline for both.

By the end there is a sense of mysterious purpose in both journeys, with Pozzo claiming a place for himself as a blind seer: 'They give birth astride of a grave, the light gleams an instant, then it's night once more.' This image is picked up in *Breath* (1969) where a faint light comes and goes and we hear cries and the inhalation and exhalation of breath; all in a playing time of thirty-five seconds.

Pozzo's pronouncement feeds into the sense that, as Vladimir says of himself and Estragon, the travellers are 'all mankind'. Some have seen the separate individuals as making up a composite being, along the lines of the 'trine' personality which the self-analysing Belacqua attributes to himself in *Dream of Fair to Middling Women*.

Similar speculations might be sparked off by the complementary pair of *Endgame*. Blind master and lame servant make up an effective whole like the pairs in Yeats's *The Cat and the Moon* who go in search of a saint and a cure, with the lame man riding on the blind man's back. But the overwhelming first impression in *Endgame* is of constriction and stasis. With three of the four characters immured in dustbins and a wheelchair, and the fourth lame, it seems that here journeys in present time must come to a stop.

They do not. On the contrary, in such a context Clov's slow, hobbling travel across the stage takes on the quality of epic, an only part-comic one: Don Quixote and Sancho Panza in one. Hamm too still manages to travel in present time; pushed around his room by Clov in his makeshift vehicle, the chair on castors. Katie Mitchell's production brought out the lively comedy in this laborious trip, with Hamm fussing about being returned 'right in the centre' and Clov humouring him, poker-faced, pushing the chair 'slightly' at each command.

Hamm isn't allowed too much sympathy. But there was no doubt of the intent, sympathetic feeling in the audience when the blind man reached out to the wall as he passed, hugging it as if drinking in life, a traveller still.

Offstage space has shrunk to almost nothing in this play, compared with *Godot* where it is felt as vast and all-embracing, a place each character goes in and out of, where Estragon has bad dreams and the Boy makes the almost unimaginable journeys back to Godot. Clov's kitchen is that space in *Endgame*: it becomes equally potent and mysterious for an audience. Only he has access to it; his one great advantage over Hamm. When we have listened for some time to the short, sharp blasts on the whistle by which Hamm summons him we are made to feel on our pulses what Beckett said of the tension built into Clov's struggle to get back to the kitchen and Hamm's to call him out of it.

We know we will never see into that mysterious space where Clov looks at the wall and sees 'my light dying'. It sounds grim yet might suggest the possibility of change; the dying of the light as prelude to a new day. Some have thought of another tyrannized spirit, Ariel: this one is more divided, more content with his kitchen ('Nice dimensions. Nice proportions') even if it is also the 'cell' from which he hopes to move on.

Can this happen? We're invited to dwell on the possibility by Clov's final appearance in outdoor clothes, astonishing sight in this room-bound play. The long-held final tableau, with Clov standing mute throughout Hamm's soliloquy, gives us plenty of time to take in the incongruous panama hat with the tweed coat and the anticipations of real 'weather' in the raincoat over the arm, the umbrella. Hamm undermines the idea of an 'outside' by returning to his opening posture, preparing for the next move in the game: 'Since that's the way we're playing it . . . (*he unfolds handkerchief*) . . . let's play it that way.' Yet Clov in outdoor clothing is a strong visual statement, not easy to resist. Perhaps the door of the 'cell' has opened and his journey will take another direction; we can't rule it out.

A curiously veiled attempt is made to tell of the journeys that lie behind what the play shows us when Hamm tells his story, the one, says Clov, 'you've been telling yourself all your . . . days'. It's hard to know how to take it, told as it is in Hamm's most actorish tones. When he relapses into 'normal tone' it's only to congratulate himself on his literary powers: 'Nicely put, that.' Though it's a tale about himself, and has the feel of real life in it at moments, he keeps it histrionic, half a fable, presenting himself as a kind of god from whom a nameless character, a 'pale man', begs bread to keep his young son from starving to death, then when Hamm offers him a place in his service, asks him to take the child also.

The story breaks off here, with Hamm apparently working up to a caustic refusal. Hints are dropped of connections between the story and the story-teller. Clov reminds Hamm how he rejected Mother Pegg's plea for oil for her lamp ('I hadn't any', he says, weakly). And Hamm asks Clov if he remembers coming to the shelter, reminds him that he, Hamm, has been a father to him. Clov's reaction is inscrutable. 'Yes', he says, 'You were that to me'. A thin line of consanguinity emerges, threading together the one undoubted father, Nagg, who left Hamm to cry in the dark when he was a child, Hamm who prophesies that Clov will end up blind and paralysed like himself, and Clov who is acknowledged as a kind of son: he came to the 'shelter' as the child in the story might have come. Outside, never to be seen, a small boy, a dream child, approaches, troubling Clov but leaving Hamm unperturbed.

Probably the clearest impression we are left with is of someone driven to tell of the bitter journey of the man and child in need but unable or unwilling to 'say' it fully, reach out for the truth of it. Hamm keeps his tracks covered. Only when without an audience does he let out more of himself: Clov is offstage when he says 'I'll have called my father and I'll have called . . . my . . . (*he hesitates*) . . . my son.' 'Calling' involves pain. Yet, though evasive, the story contributes to the impression that there is purpose here; 'Something is taking its course'. Clov jeers at Hamm's question 'We're not beginning to . . . mean something?', but I don't think the audience does. In one of those more natural, unaffected exchanges the pair have in the midst of the acrimony and jesting Clov asks, about the story, 'Will it not soon be the end?' and Hamm replies 'I'm afraid it will', drawing a kind of reassurance: 'Pah! You'll make up another.' In its way, so very different from that of *Godot*, this play is also a quest, a heroic effort to keep journey and story going. Hamm says the No against the nothingness, Beckett told Ernst Schröder, playing Hamm, when he asked about the 'No' inserted into his final monologue during rehearsals at the Schiller-Theater Werkstatt in 1967 (MF 224).

With *Krapp's Last Tape* comes a shift to out-and-out telling. Krapp at 69 still makes ordinary journeys in present time. 'Crawled out once or twice, before the summer was cold', he records. But the journey he makes in front of our eyes is the one he is dedicated to; the going back and forth between the cubby hole where ordinary life continues—'Ah finish your booze now and get to your bed'—and the table where he makes his annual audits, 'separating the grain from the husks'. The task is a deep pleasure mixed with irritation and anguish. Once he seems to rebel against the discipline he has set himself, following up the accidental fall of a box of tapes by 'violently' sweeping boxes and ledger to the floor. Rick Cluchey gave this moment an unsettling degree of force, approved by Beckett, so I gathered (in a conversation we had in 1986).

Picking his way to the cubby hole through the spilt tapes, Krapp was 'treading on his life', Beckett said, and this he makes us feel. Krapp has something in common with Hamm in his attitude to endings. He may be 'drowned in dreams and burning to be gone', but far stronger is the wish to relive some of the journeys of the past: 'Be again in the dingle on a Christmas Eve, gathering holly, the red-berried. (*Pause.*) Be again on Croghan on a Sunday morning, in the haze, with the bitch, stop and listen to the bells.' The loneliness in which he is left at curtain fall, still listening to an old idyll, dims but can't extinguish the sense of creative joy involved in retrieving the journey, with its high moments of feeling. The tone tended to the feminine, Beckett interestingly said of this play (*TN* iii. [23]).

The radio plays of this period, in the 1950s and early 1960s, follow a similar pattern. The journey is taken in present time in *All That Fall*, moves back and forward in time and in and out of fiction in *Embers*, and becomes a tale trying to be told in *Words and Music* and *Cascando*.

The sound of journeying feet and labouring bodies runs through them all. *All That Fall* opens with dragging footsteps, *Embers* with the noise of Henry's boots on shingle—and his voice calling 'On!'. Croak in *Words and Music* is heard first and last as shuffling carpet slippers; not an easy sound to project, David Clark and I found when working on a production of the play in 1973, but it had to be done.[3] Beckett set store by these slippers, presumably to establish Croak as old and failing (an idea feelingly conveyed by Words' lyric on old age: 'if you're a man . . . were a man'). *Cascando* is dominated by a gasping, rushing voice conjuring up the equally rushing sound of Woburn on his endless journey, in his 'same old coat', going down slopes ('boreen . . . giant aspens . . . wind in the boughs . . . faint sea'), falling in the sand, 'ton weight', picking himself up, stumbling over dunes, getting into a boat, heading for the island, then the open sea, missing the 'lights' in the sky ('he need only . . . turn over . . . he'd see them . . . shine on him . . . but no').

There's no time for dwelling on the purpose of the journey in *All That Fall*. We get little glimpses into the Rooneys' home life as when Dan looks forward to Maddy reading a novel to him ('I think Effie is going to commit adultery with the Major') or grumbles about the noises of domesticity, the '. . . washing, mangling, drying, mowing, clipping, raking . . .'. But the focus is on the journey to the end of the long day and the effort required to circumvent its hazards. Maddy labours against her 'Two hundred pounds of unhealthy fat!', the blind man's stick spells out the peril for him of steps: 'I have been up and down these steps five thousand times and still I do not know how many there are.' Maddy refuses to count them yet again. 'Not count!', he exclaims, 'One of the few satisfactions in life!' A nice reminder that there are pleasures as well as miseries on this path. It is a Bunyanesque way of many encounters, many methods of dealing with life's vicissitudes.

Embers begins a shift away from the act of travel to the act of narration. Henry's is still a journey through present time but he spends much of it in monologue, struggling to get at the meaning of his life (and that of the father thought to have drowned himself). He calls up ghosts to help him, composes a piece of fiction which obliquely reflects his own 'deep trouble' over his father, tries desperately to shut out the sound of the sea heard monotonously in every gap in the talk. In our production of the play in 1976 David Clark and I opted for a naturalistic sea sound with crashing waves rather than the surreal electronics of the original BBC production. This admittedly undermined Henry's 'the sound is so strange, so unlike the sound of the sea', but Beckett had left the choice open and the real sea noise seemed to accord with the solid real-life journey that can be picked out from the world of dream and story Henry builds around it.

Bits of that life emerge from tart, intimate conversations with Ada and amusing snatches of piano- and riding-lessons endured by their child, Addie, heard at one point crying when scolded by Henry for not enjoying herself (that well-known syndrome). A flashback, unusual with Beckett, recreates a former 'present time' when Ada murmured 'Don't' before their first love-making, a sardonic contrast with her bossy 'Don't' to Henry in the 'now' of the play.

Henry blurs the links between life and story with a Hamm-like emphasis on artifice and melodrama in the tale of the two old men, Bolton and Holloway, the former pleading with his friend, a doctor complete with black bag, for an injection: 'Please, Holloway!' It's a shock for the listener when Ada innocently makes the connection with the story-teller's life, advising Henry to see a doctor about his compulsive talking: 'you ought to see Holloway, he's alive still, isn't he?' She is a catalyst, needed by Henry for his arduous reconstructions. Elvi Hale (in our production) seemed to me to catch the right mix of matter-of-factness and oddity in her reminiscing: Beckett approved her vocal tone.[4] Yet she told quite simply the story of the last time Ada saw her father, on a day of uproar in the family home: Henry's bed not slept in, everyone shouting, his sister threatening to throw herself off the cliff, his father going out, slamming the door:

> I left soon afterwards and passed him on the road. He did not see me. He was sitting on a rock looking out to sea. I never forgot his posture. And yet it was a common one. You used to have it sometimes. Perhaps just the stillness, as if he had been turned to stone. I could never make it out.

Broken and incomplete as the process of retrieval is (Henry thinks it a failure), it does give us for a fleeting instant the sense that there is a meaning, if our minds could reach out to it, in the father's posture, looking out to sea. It begins to connect with the poetic feeling captured towards the end of the story: 'that's it, that was always it, night, and the embers cold, and the glim shaking in your old fist, saying, 'Please! Please!' But all is still veiled, as in the story-telling of *Endgame*. Henry is left alone on the beach, finding in his diary only one entry, for the plumber ('Ah yes, the waste'), otherwise 'nothing'. It isn't quite like that for the listeners; we have seen—through the veils—into a tormented mind, endlessly turning over the story of his father, trying, if failing, to bring out of it a work of truth.

When music enters the scene in *Words and Music* and *Cascando*, the focus is on efforts to bring alive a particular stretch of journey, an erotic one for slippered Croak in the former play. He enters the soundscape muttering of a 'face' seen on the stair, in the tower: echoes here of W. B. Yeats's love poems in *The Winding Stair* and *The Tower*. But the romantic Yeatsian vision can only be achieved when Words and Music, the 'servants', drop the platitudes they first offer on the theme, 'Love', and go roundabout, by the rough way of 'Age' ('old age, I mean . . . if that is what my Lord means'). An image is made between them; an old man huddled in the ingle, waiting for comforts, a warming-pan, arrowroot, a 'toddy' to be brought by a 'hag', close kin perhaps to Fanny, the 'bony old ghost of a whore' who solaces Krapp. Harsh allusions both, but touching on a supernatural world of ghost and legendary 'hags': the 'blue-eyed hag' of *The Tempest*, Milton's 'Blue meagre Hag, and stubborn unlaid ghost', or, most pertinent, the hag of medieval romances who would reward a knight for keeping faith with her by transforming herself into her opposite: the beautiful young girl of his desire.

Words and music work this kind of magic for Croak. In the ashes of the old man's fire they find 'the face', then take him—and us—into a mystically all-white, cold vision of a young beauty lying in the moonlight, as if dead but with life slowly creeping back. Croak groans and suffers as her 'matchless' features are enumerated by Words in a pompous rhapsody: his cry, 'Lily!' is 'anguished'. He can take no more: we don't know what he makes of the more intensely lyrical vision of the 'wellhead' to which his 'servants' advance. He is heard shuffling away, letting fall the club whose thumps directed them, drawing from Words a shocked 'My Lord!' He may have been given a revelation he can't use or interpret, like the incomplete one Ada relays to Henry: 'I could never make it out.'

In *Cascando* the directing character, Opener, makes a great point of having no personal involvement in the story Voice and Music tell: his role, he claims, is simply mechanical, to 'open' and 'close'. Whenever he opens, Voice and Music are there, waiting to come on-stream (an idea that fascinated Beckett: he tried it out in *Rough for Radio 1*). People say 'it's in his head', but, says Opener, 'There is nothing in my head.'

The story of Woburn which Voice and Music project is simply one long journey. When David Clark and I worked on the play in 1984 with David Warrilow as Voice (he later played Words in *Words and Music* for Everett Frost[5]) I thought his distinctive gravelly tones exactly conveyed the roughness in the ups and downs of the journey and the persistence required, both of Woburn and of Voice and Music who have to 'change' him from one bar to the next, keep him moving, grasp him, get him 'right'. Then it will be 'sleep . . . no more stories . . . no more words'. The story acquires tremendous momentum: enough to force Opener away from his aloof stand, and admit that he is also a traveller taking 'outings':

Two outings, then at last the return, to the village, to the inn, by the only road that leads there.

These 'outings' are his life: 'I have lived on it . . . till I'm old.' It's a burden—we're made to feel that—but there is excitement and satisfaction too as Woburn is impelled toward some undefined goal. The listener is drawn into the work of creation, feels its exhilaration as well as its frustrations, guesses there can be no end to it till Opener's life journey ends. Typically the play closes with shouts of 'come on . . . come on—' from both Voice and Opener (Humphrey Searle's music in our recording added a suggestion of exuberant arrival[6]).

The word 'outings' is connected with holiday, freshness, birth. We are told at the start that the month is May: 'You know, the reawakening.' Reawakening in spring to set out on a journey of imagination chimes with a great tradition of odysseys and pilgrimages such as those taken by Chaucer's pilgrims 'Whan that Aprill with his shoures soote | The droghte of March hath perced to the roote.' Or by Langland's Piers Plowman who went wide in the world 'wondres to here' and on a May morning in the Malvern Hills had a mighty dream of a wilderness, a 'felde ful of folke' and a tower of truth. There are hints at an Irish ambience in Woburn's journey—'boreen' rather than 'lane' for instance—but it is essentially an open landscape into which we can fit our own well-loved places. To 'go on' is the imperative: 'to go out . . . go on . . . elsewhere . . . sleep elsewhere . . . it's slow'. Warrilow's 'it's slow', in his ruminative tone, struck me as linking Voice, Opener, and playwright in one rich sound. Finally we may share in the sense precious to Opener of an 'outing' from the self, an exhilarating journey into an imagined world.

Just such 'outings' keep life fresh and interesting in *Happy Days*, first performed in 1961, the year before *Cascando* was written (in French). Winnie is a kind of Opener, keeping torpid Willie moving, guiding him on his trips to and from his hole in Act 1 and—spectacularly—calling him back after his absence from the whole of Act 2 (who else but she could have done it?) for his out-of-the-blue crawl across the stage to her mound at the end. This astonishing crawl was important to Beckett. Billie Whitelaw and Leonard Fenton have told how he did it himself during rehearsal break,[7] measuring and timing no doubt, but one might imagine also enjoying the chance to enact on stage the journey that figures so often in his fictional world (there is a fine crawl in *Company*).

Winnie takes little journeys in present time so far as she can, putting things in and out of her precious bag, dealing with toothbrush, parasol, revolver—all the items carefully listed in Beckett's Production Notebook.[8] She throws herself into Willie's little trips in Act 1, crawls with him, so to speak. All the time she is going over old tracks, not just in Act 2, though there it's inevitable: Willie is gone as also (almost) her power of movement. She brings the places and phases of her life into the here and now triumphantly: the toolshed, site of her first kiss, the wedding breakfast, the memory of a coarse fellow commenting on her rudely and his wife castigating him for 'dragging me up and down this fornicating wilderness'.

Is it a wilderness, is Winnie asking questions of that kind, revaluing her life as Krapp does and Henry tries to do? Beckett is quoted as saying that she was 'unaware', an 'interrupted' being.[9] We see of course that she does interrupt herself continually, goes off at a tangent. But she wrestles with hard thoughts too and in Act 2 seems to attempt an obscure self-revelation with her story about a little girl, Mildred, her doll, and a mouse: it is usually taken to reflect a sexual trauma. Her scream as the mouse begins its run up Milly's thigh was an alarmingly real-life sound when Billie Whitelaw played Winnie under Beckett's direction in 1979. He made a connection in his Production Notebook between Winnie's clothes and the doll's.[10] But the story breaks off and remains obscure, perhaps too painful to face more directly.

In the end, however, Winnie is shown to be fully aware. When Willie comes crawling to her ('*dressed to kill*') she sees him with awful clarity; a grotesque mixture of the romantic wedding-day image she has been holding on to and the old man with a disfiguring anthrax, bald head, and disconcertingly unreadable 'look': 'Don't look at me like that!' It's her reward that, having seen, she is allowed to hear from him the sound of her name, gasped out with true feeling: 'Win'. It is then that she is able to produce her own pure sound: the waltz duet that closes the play on the words 'It's true, it's true | You love me so!' In performance the song never fails to achieve the heart-rending poignancy told of by friends who visited Beckett just before his death when he sang it for them himself.

A new phase begins in 1964 with *Play*. Characters in this and many of the plays that follow feel themselves under a stern demand (usually resisted for a time) to rerun their life journeys in order to see and 'say' them in the light of the truth. Two journeys are taken in *Play*.

The first, poured out in fragments in the Narrative, is full of the bustle and agitated movement of people involved in 'ordinary' affairs. Energetic verbs abound. A sexual challenger strolls, bursts, or comes crashing into a room where her rival sits stitching by an open window or doing her nails; the husband slinks in, the butler goes to and fro, 'letting people in, showing people out'. There is no time for long thoughts.

On the second journey the heads in urns follow the movement of the spotlight, perceived as poking and pecking at them, liable to 'blaze me clean out of my wits'. Their journey is all mental now, going back over past incidents, searching for a way to 'placate' the tormenting light: 'Is it that I do not tell the truth, is that it . . .?' In new form there return little ordinary noises of the day-to-day life they have left behind. The commonplace hand-mower heard in the background of the Narrative when M admitted to his mistress that he had confessed all to his wife, returns in the Meditation as a great mental weight, to be shifted before the journey can continue: 'Like dragging a great roller, on a scorching day. The strain . . . to get it moving, momentum coming.'

Throughout the seeming stasis and fixity of *Play* activity never ceases: the audience are kept continually on the move, following the rapid switches of the spotlight, listening from one voice to another, coping with the zigzags and interruptions in the journey's purposeful course. We share in the strain and the achievement of 'momentum coming'.

Characters in the plays of this time may try to disconnect themselves from their life journeys, by refusing the first person, as Mouth does, or by obliterating stretches of it. Destroying the family photographs is a potent image of this compulsion, twice used. In *Film* the camera dwells on Buster Keaton checking through photographs which lay out his life in the traditional seven stages, then on his methodical tearing and scattering of them. There is a shock here for those who recognize the child praying at his mother's knee as a photo of Beckett himself with his own mother; it isn't quite what it seems, however. The photo has an unmistakably stagey look and was in fact set up for a friend of May Beckett's at her request.[11] This tunes in with the sense of the artificial half-real running through the film, the exaggerated horror of the passer-by who catches sight of O's face, for instance. Irony rules, until O's efforts to separate himself from the self reflected in the family photos are annihilated by the powerful image of the actor's face, black patch over one eye, staring at the twin face that stares back from the tattered wall.

Family pictures are torn up again in *A Piece of Monologue*, more passionately, although this is a play of a later, calmer phase. Speaker makes intermittent attempts to disconnect himself from his life journey, stopping himself from acknowledging direct emotional involvement—'he all but said the loved ones'—and distancing himself from funerals. These he reruns at ever-faster speed, presenting them in a frame, like shots in a film: 'Coffin out of frame. Whose? Fade. Gone . . .'. It is a shocking moment (given a strong actor) when the dim, white-haired figure in the lamplight abruptly switches from the ritual check of his properties—'Socks. Nightgown. Window. Lamp'—to bring before our mind's eye a rather terrible act: the family pictures 'Ripped from the wall and torn to shreds one by one'.

They can't so easily be obliterated: the wall remains for a time 'pockmarked' with memories: 'There was father. That grey void. There mother. That other.' Later, Speaker tells himself they have really gone: 'Swept out of the way under the bed and left. Thousand shreds under the bed with the dust and spiders.' Then the ghosts come, and the funerals, over and over: 'Again and again gone'. Like him, we the audience will remember those pictures all the more for the violence of the attempt to blot them out; a reminder here, if needed, that to hear a thing told can be more thrilling than to see it done, as it was in *Film*.

A Piece of Monologue is moving into calmer mode all the same, like most of the plays after *Not I*. That terrifying monologue can be thought of as a crescendo of protest against being tied to a life that seems to have no value and being compelled to value it: 'something she had to—'. The first person is not often used by the speakers of these late plays; avoidance of it is for Mouth an obsession expressed in awful screams: 'what? . . who? . . no! . . she!' These screams make it hard to interpret in Buddhist terms of detachment, as some do, her refusal to say 'I'.

We may feel instead that by the violence of her passion she identifies herself with the journey, even in the act of repudiating it. She knows it so well in all its harsh, often shaming detail: the woman standing mute in the supermarket, 'mouth half open as usual'; having a periodic burst of dyslexic speech in the public lavatory; in court facing an unfeeling judge who shouts 'speak up woman'. A miserably believable life journey unrolls before us, or, rather, draws us into its heart. It was a very odd experience, in January 1973, to arrive at the Royal Court for the British première—punctually—to find the performance seemingly already started, with a voice behind the curtain muttering words hard to hear. As always with Beckett, it is some such physical stress or strain laid upon us that compels us to go into the thick of the journey. This one covers the whole of a life, from the careless moment of procreation to the careworn telling over, after 'all went out'. We have to race and concentrate to keep up.

Walking continues in some of the late plays as a painful necessity, a going over some stretch of ground in order to see it more clearly, perhaps to lay a ghost. It's an inward walking now: the voice of the unseen mother in *Footfalls* assures us that May has not been 'out' since girlhood. Her ritual pacing—nine footfalls (originally seven) ending in a 'wheel'—must be repeated until the light dims and renews itself for the last time, showing only the place where she was: she will walk no more. Even here, in this most ghostly play, convincing detail of a real-life journey pushes through: we are present at a mother's sickbed, glimpse a stunted girlhood, take part in a revelatory church service. But Beckett said that the 'life-long stretches of walking' were 'the centre of the play, everything else is secondary'.[12]

In the latest phase of the *œuvre* a new relationship is achieved between the traveller and the journey that must be told, a different kind of distance set between the speakers and their stories. They listen unresisting to their own voices telling how it has been. In *That Time* Listener is simply that: the one who has taken the journey and now receives it back from some space beyond himself. Rounded, rhythmic, it is a work of art though still full of human feelings, including doubt about there being any point in journeying: 'not a thought in your head only get back on board and away to hell out of it'. The seven stages of life represented by photographs in *Film* are here compressed to three: A focuses on childhood, B on young love, C on old age but they cross over into each other's field of vision, driven by the same need to see the journey as whole. Linking images recur. The child sits with imaginary playmates 'ten or eleven on a stone among the giant nettles'; the lovers sit together at the far ends of 'a long low stone like millstone'; the old man in the portrait gallery sits on a marble slab gazing up at the picture of 'some young prince or princess of the blood black with age'.

There is no first person, only an ever-changing second person, asking and answering questions about the endless journey:

that time you went back that last time to look was the ruin still there where you hid as a child when was that

The intimate 'you' keeps Listener—and us—close to the journey while the fact that it is related by his own voices from a distance seems to declare that an independent truth has been arrived at. Similarly in *Rockaby* the separation of the Woman from her recorded voice suggests something completed and authentic in the account of her life. Unlike Listener, who seems content to have reached the end, W is divided, joining in the intermittent call from the recorded voice, 'Time she stopped', then cancelling consent in her living voice. In Alan Schneider's production which came to the National Theatre, London (9 December 1981) the high, weak sound of Billie Whitelaw's 'More' in contrast to the steady, hypnotic flow on tape was deeply affecting. The 'prematurely old' woman in the rocking-chair is rocked, never rocks herself. I recall Martin Esslin being upset by a performance set up for a Beckett conference in Austin, Texas in 1984, where the actress was visibly helping the chair to move, implying a command over her life journey not permitted by Beckett's note that the chair is mechanically controlled 'without assistance from W'. The simple act of rocking in a chair had probably become in all our minds a statement about the nature of the strange journey we undertake by being born.

Always there is a parallel pattern of movement and cessation of movement in the story told by the recorded voice. The woman in the story goes to and fro, searching for 'another | another like herself | a little like'. Then movement fades away and she sits instead by her window, looking out to other windows, all their blinds down; an image of stasis and frustration we might think.

But it is not so. It is when this point is reached that she begins the movement 'down the steep stair' into 'mother rocker', that force which moves her as it moved her mother before her. Mother and daughter coalesce and go beyond themselves: the figure we see in the 'best black' seems in the end to be rocked for all living souls. Two journeys merge, then the rocking stops for good, the head falls forward; it is over. Yet perhaps we still hear those words that spoke not of stopping but going on, or rather down into awaiting arms: an image of human reunion, invested with transcendent force.

In the late screenplays this characteristic flavour of a distance which does not divide is achieved by the use of a persona, sent out by some controlling force to walk over old ground, retracing it sometimes, as Enoch Brater has brought out,[13] in close-up repeats, making it familiar to the viewer too. In . . . *but the clouds* . . . a walk is taken many times under the eye of M who crouches on one side of the screen, quiet, absorbed, while 'M in set' walks for him. In *Ghost Trio* an unseen female, V, presides over the walks round the familiar room taken by the male figure, F. Her surprised 'Ah!' when he stops by the mirror suggests that the journey is not just a retrospect but could still develop. Ronald Pickup's look into the mirror, unsurprised, added a different note; a sense of something understood, accepted.

Among these ghost plays (to which I return briefly in the next chapter) . . . *but the clouds* . . . draws Beckett's walking rituals into a single austere and serene image: the walker's calm movements across a bare screen are a world away from the neurotic anxiety of earlier travellers like O in *Film*. The figure dressed in walking-clothes who brings the roads and night 'home' might be thought of as the quintessential persona of Beckett's theatre, even, indeed, of his entire *œuvre*. It was through the images of walks together that Beckett movingly expressed his grief at his loved father's death: 'I can only walk the fields and climb the ditches after him.'[14]

In another late play, *Ohio Impromptu*, the journey seems completed. 'Nothing is left to tell', says Reader to Listener: the posture of the two at the close, sitting looking at each other, '*Expressionless*', enacts the concept: 'So sat on as though turned to stone.' As always we have glimpses of journeys past; walks by the Isle of Swans and the confluence with its 'two arms', the traumatic move to an unfamiliar place in hope of relief after bereavement: 'Out to where nothing ever shared. Back to where nothing ever shared.' That 'back' hints at a whole life stretching before some 'dear face' came and after it went. It is all here now, in the book; a sad tranquillity can descend.

The journeys become more overtly mystical in this phase yet even here real place-names are heard and whiffs of real-life journeying occur. The Isle of Swans, where Beckett in youthful days walked with James Joyce, erupts with the solidity of Paris in the 1930s into the timeless dimension of *Ohio Impromptu* (it has encouraged some, plausibly, to identify Joyce as the much-missed 'dear face'). *Godot* keeps contact with the world beyond the theatre with jokes about the Eiffel Tower, Estragon's longing to 'wander in the Pyrenees', and thinly veiled references to Beckett's wartime years at Roussillon: 'But you were there yourself, in the Macon country [. . .]'; 'But down there everything is red!' Like the reminiscing of Nagg and Nell about Lake

Como these allusions bring an extra personal warmth into the fable without diminishing the sense of the fabulous. W1 in *Play* drives back from her rival's deserted house 'by Ash and Snodland' (real places, unlikely as it may seem).[15] Krapp recalls a real place dear to Beckett ('Croghan on a Sunday morning') and *All That Fall* and *That Time* evoke images of Leopardstown racecourse, 'Foley's Folly' (where Beckett played as a child), Dublin's 'Doric terminus of the Great Southern and Eastern'. The terminus is 'all closed down' says the voice of A: like the rest of these real places it has been transfigured into a landscape supernaturally remote, still, and permanent.

The allusions are actual and personal but carefully left open too. 'Foley was it Foley's Folly', A muses, then offers a description which we could easily fill in from our own memories: 'bit of a tower still standing all the rest rubble and nettles'. Generic terms are used: Post Office, Public Library. The Portrait Gallery where C slips in out of the rain could be in Dublin or London; he gazes hard at a portrait of some famous person but doesn't know who it is: again, we may view it as a frame, open to our own images.

These journeys surely come to seem heroic, all the more for containing so much that is fiercely or comically unheroic. Humdrum or oppressive bodily processes loom large, especially in the earlier plays. Audiences tend to enjoy this, taking for comedy—as no doubt intended—Estragon's cry during the 'fall', 'Who belched?', which later became 'farted' (*TN* i. [74]), or Vladimir's troubles with urinating (actors often accentuate the comic effect, as when Alan Howard's Vladimir clutched himself while saying 'Never neglect the little things of life'). We're invited to see ourselves as all in the same boat by light-hearted jokes about finding the Gents ('At the end of the corridor, on the left. | Keep my seat') and rather more sour ones on the theme of 'crap', the name (in different spellings) bestowed on a character in one play and a whole family in another.

Friendship and interest in the lives of others are great energizing forces for the travellers. Interviewed just before they opened in *Godot*, Alan Howard and Ben Kingsley dwelt on the special closeness between the two they played. 'If you took one away the other would evaporate', said Howard. He had just had the curious experience of spotting in public a 'female Vladimir and Estragon', recognizing them 'by the way they walked, talked. Their dependency.' Ben Kingsley thought any attempt to distinguish between the two would be 'like asking, which part of the circus donkey are you? . . .

It doesn't really matter. You are the donkey' (*Guardian*, 18 June 1997).

The travellers on these journeys have to uphold each other, often literally, as when Didi walks Gogo about the stage or Clov pushes Hamm around. Bickering, even revulsion from each other doesn't destroy the deep dependencies. Didi and Gogo come together again with relief after the different relief of being apart, and Clov can't do without Hamm, though he means it at the time when he says 'If I could kill him I'd die happy'. Beckett noted that Pozzo and Lucky should exchange a 'hypno look' over the picnic paraphernalia; Winnie has Willie, Henry, Ada; even Mouth has her Auditor, though she doesn't know it. When no living soul strays into the field of vision, the lonely tale-spinners of the later plays evoke them as voices, creating twin souls, one that talks, one that listens.

The purpose of any life journey, so those in Beckett's theatre suggest, is to take the way we discover to be ours and open it to others by 'seeing' and 'saying' it in the light of the truth. From the start his travellers intuit this purpose and struggle to follow it. They pause, doubt, resist, are impelled forward, fall, pick themselves up, 'fail better', and go on, telling themselves, 'this time it's the right one'; 'I see it all now'; 'something I had to tell . . . how it was'.

It's an irresistible drive, one that could be seen as central to an age of individualism like ours, with its emphasis on finding and being 'oneself', its passion for memoirs in any form, from book-length biographies to television and drama-documentaries aiming to identify the dominant thrust of a famous life. Out of the limelight, individuals still feel, as probably they always have done, the need to reflect on the nature of their life journey as it approaches its end. The 'obligation to express' which drove Beckett is not confined to writers, though he does so much with it on our behalf. He encourages us—despite the fearfulness of the project—to try for a true 'audit', presenting our reckoning. Or, as Yeats put it, in a poem so loved by Beckett that he wove it into the substance of a play (*. . . but the clouds . . .*) written when he was 70: 'Now shall I make my soul'.

5

Be Again, Memory!

FORGETTING

FORGETTING is a fact of life that Beckett turns into a treasure hoard, connecting it by fine threads to acts of remembering; those that come of their own accord, swimming up as if from nowhere, and those methodically sought, collected, sorted, as Krapp collects and sorts his 'retrospects'. Writing as a young man on Proust,[1] Beckett followed him in being caustic about the latter kind, the inferior 'voluntary' memory which Proust had categorized as 'turning the leaves of an album of photographs'. Beckett's own image was even more caustic: the person who claims 'I remember as well as I remember yesterday' cannot *remember* yesterday, he said; he only contemplates it, 'hung out to dry with the wettest August bank holiday on record a little further down the clothes-line'. 'Involuntary' memory was the only true 'instrument of evocation' and evocation was the purpose of the artist. Beckett jibbed a little at Proust's habit of reiterating the idea 'ad nauseam', but like him he pursued it in wonderfully free and varied form—not omitting the washing on the clothes-line.

Forgetting and 'extreme inattention' were, he surmised in the Proust study, crucial to the writer's attempt to tap the deep springs of the self, to release the 'pearl', the secret stores, the 'fine essence of a smothered divinity'.[2] The first of his 'memory' plays, *Krapp's Last Tape* (1958) might seem to diverge from that view. Krapp has all his past collected in boxes of tapes, catalogued, ready to be played over and contemplated, not too unlike the yesterdays on the washing-line. But for all his precautions, forgetfulness keeps breaking in. The tape he made at the age of 39 assures us he will never forget the feel of the 'small, old, black, hard, solid rubber ball' he was holding in his hand at the moment his mother died. Now, aged 69, he is baffled by the memory marker in his ledger, 'The black ball'; he repeats the words, 'puzzled'. Long echoes run back and forth, linking Beckett with Proust, Freud, and those playwrights—Shakespeare supremely, and, among moderns, Pinter—who have made subtle connections between forgetting and remembering. The black rubber ball temporarily forgotten by Krapp is of the same order as the *madeleine* dipped in tea or the stumble on the uneven flagstones that restored to Proust's Marcel—as his efforts at recalling it could not do—a full sense of the past. So too the flight of steps in Beckett's pre-Krapp short story, 'The Expelled' (1955 in French; 1963 in English) where the narrator begins by failing to remember the exact number of some often-climbed steps, then from his forgetfulness draws the 'important thing', that 'there were not many, and that I have remembered'. Conversely, he suggests that if you want to forget 'killing' memories the best way is to remember them regularly, 'every day several times a day'. 'That's an order', he wryly tells himself.

Barbara Hardy has pointed out that Shakespeare 'suggests something of the gains of forgetfulness' in Sonnet 77, when he advises writing down 'what thy memory cannot contain' so as to retrieve it like a 'new acquaintance'. 'Lost it can be found', she aptly comments.[3] Krapp has followed the Shakespearian line, using a tape recorder instead of a blank notebook. It is the lapse of memory, we might deduce, that has kept the 'black ball' memory fresh and potent: it comes to us infused with the poignancy of the forgetting and the restoration.

Not all Krapp's cherished moments retain their force in this way. The vision on the pier which so excited him thirty years before he now sweeps away impatiently. There was such a revelation, we know, in Beckett's own life, though not on a jetty with the great waves crashing but, so he told James Knowlson, 'in my mother's room'.[4] A phrase of real remembering, this, alive with the rhythm of *Molloy* (published in 1951) which opens so arrestingly: 'I am in my mother's room. It's I who live there now. I don't know how I got there.' The rhythm of the 'vision' memory in the play, though it has gleams of revelation in it, becomes increasingly strained and unconvincing as Krapp emphasizes its landmark status: 'unshatterable association until my dissolution of storm and night with the light of the understanding and the fire—'. At this point he curses loudly and switches off, understandably. The 'vision' has shrunk to washing on the line while the other memory of the 'black ball' has been transformed into an evocation that will live on, certainly for us. So too with the memory of the girl in the punt: Krapp thought when recording his last meeting with her that it was all done with. But the haunting rhythm he achieved keeps it blowing in the wind, not hanging dank and static, waiting to be counted.

Winnie is on the face of it the antithesis of Krapp, utterly disorganized, unable to finish a quotation or a story, not in command of her memories. But they are two sides of the same coin, one we all use: being Krapp at times, methodically storing; at other times (maybe more often) Winnie, flitting from memory to memory, forgetting as much as she remembers. She doesn't assess her life as Krapp does; sifting the grain from the husks. It's all grain to her, we might say, everything is alive for her and she brings it alive for us—through the broken rhythms of her forgetfulness. They keep us on the *qui vive*: in filling in and completing for her we recognize how she continually reaches out for poetic enlargement of her life. Her interrupted memories join a mass of half-lines and unfinished phrases which lead in the end to something complete, the song that can't be sung to order. When she sings it at last it comes over as the pure 'involuntary' release of her 'essence', the 'smothered divinity' which Beckett imagined when writing on Proust. She achieves what Clov reaches for in his pathetic, never-to-be-realized 'I want to sing' (the song he had in the French original was cut in the English version) (*TN* ii. [65–6]).

At the other end of the *œuvre* in *That Time*, Listener is a master of memories, even better organized than Krapp in that he has grouped them in three distinct stages of life, while keeping them unified by a regular, ever-flowing melody which he as Listener never interrupts or questions. This might bring him perilously close to the 'clothes-line' effect were it not for the evocative force in the vocal music, and the thread of questioning and wonderment that runs through it: 'was that another time all that another time was there ever any other time but that time'. We receive a sense of something very familiar, the forgetfulness that comes with age, and something that may not seem so common but surely is: the effort to grasp the 'self' revealed in the remembering—and the forgetting: 'making yourself all up again for the millionth time forgetting it all where you were and what for'.

Through the brooding and questioning the thing he is trying to recover will often float up, half-unsought, from a tangle of overlapping memories. A creative unruliness and diversity breaks through the well-ordered patterns. Typically, a thought of the girl on the stone 'at the edge of the little wood and as far as eye could see the wheat turning yellow' pushes its way in to disperse C's doleful vision of old age, or, contrariwise, the idyll will be darkened, as if by infiltration from another voice, by the vision of a dead rat floating in the water. These comings and goings help to give the images an astonishing immediacy. We are there with the child on the stone 'talking to himself being together that way where none ever came', then suddenly with the old man struggling through the rain or sheltering in the public library with a 'bevy of old ones'. Beckett's manuscript (in the Reading Archive) shows the pains he took to find the right alternations for the voices of A, B, and C.

The forgetfulness and the questions asked without expectation of an answer are true instruments of evocation, summoning up the 'real', the mystical state Beckett takes for truth in his Proust study. But human feeling is always there. It is sometimes desperate, as when C feels his identity slip, wonders 'whose skull you were clapped up in whose moan had you the way you were'. B tries for detachment, perhaps aware that he is, as Beckett said, 'the most emotional voice'. He constructs round the remembered girl slightly surreal pictures, framing her, keeping her fixed, unmoving, sitting 'on your right hand always the right hand on the fringe of the field'. But deeper feeling creeps in: there comes 'a whisper so faint she loved you hard to believe you even you made up that bit till the time came in the end'. Is it a memory, dream, imagined thing? There is no longer a way of knowing. It is real in its own right; the 'one thing could ever bring tears till they dried up altogether that thought when it came up among the others floated up that scene'. These high moments create a sense of going beyond the analytic probing that runs through the reverie, and beyond the personal memory into a universal space of 'unknowing' where nothing is forgotten.

Forgetting is universal in *Godot*. In Beckett's Schiller Notebook half the notes he made under the heading 'Remembering' are to do with forgetting. Pozzo admits in Act 1 to a defective memory, proving it in Act 2 by totally forgetting the meeting in Act 1. Estragon forgets that too. It is how he is: 'Either I forget immediately or I never forget.' Lucky's memory has disintegrated but throws up fragments of thought which accuse God, among other things, of 'divine aphasia'. The despairing thought is never far off: 'God has forgotten us', a cry often heard from humanity. And the Boy seems to have no memory. It is one of the most disconcerting moments in the play when he denies having spoken with Vladimir in Act 1 though we know he did (or think so, anyway).

Vladimir is the only one with a memory, but it's a strange one. He puzzles us after the exit of Pozzo and Lucky in Act 1 by his comment, 'How they've changed', though on their entrance he had, like Estragon, reacted as to strangers. We can only share his friend's incomprehension:

VLADIMIR. . . . Didn't you see them?
ESTRAGON. I suppose I did. But I don't know them.
VLADIMIR. Yes you do know them.
ESTRAGON. No I don't know them.
VLADIMIR. We know them, I tell you. You forget everything.

How does Vladimir know them? Was there another act before this one, not shown to us? Is he having a prevision of the act to come when the Pozzo–Lucky combine is indeed 'changed'? A disorientating idea develops: time may be going round in circles like Vladimir's dismal 'dog' song of Act 2 that could go on for ever.

Then comes a second thought: 'Unless they're not the same'. Alan Howard's Vladimir made this compelling. He turned away, seemed to be looking in on himself, ransacking his mind: he repeated the delphic words like a mantra, as if locating Pozzo and Lucky in some mental realm where enigmatic shades appear and reappear in changed form. Vladimir lives a good deal in such a space.

Estragon seems not to, but one of the most arresting instances of forgetfulness in the play connects him too with this other world beyond the visible and actual. On the Boy's first appearance Estragon is unsurprised. 'Off we go again', he says, as if knowing, after all, that this has happened before. It might be enough to account for his violent loss of temper with the Boy. Knowing what he is going to say—Godot won't be coming this evening—he takes out his frustration on the timid, bewildered messenger, accusing him of telling a pack of lies in saying he belongs to these parts, shaking him, demanding 'Tell us the truth'. Twice Vladimir asks him what's the matter with him. It's simple: 'I'm unhappy.'

VLADIMIR. Not really! Since when?
ESTRAGON. I'd forgotten.
VLADIMIR. Extraordinary the tricks that memory plays!

What has Estragon forgotten? The question is left open for each to answer in their own way, but one thing can't be left out of account: the youth of the messenger. Without effort, in his innocent simplicity (which so affects Estragon) he is close to Godot, at home in that country the older pair can't reach; something deeply instinctive has been lost. Wordsworth in his 'Immortality' Ode imagined such a loss:

> Our birth is but a sleep and a forgetting:
> The Soul that rises with us, our life's Star,
> Hath had elsewhere its setting,
> And cometh from afar:

The Boy in the poem still lives in the light shed from this mystical source, as to a lesser degree does the Youth 'who daily farther from the east | Must travel':

> At length the Man perceives it die away,
> And fade into the light of common day.

Beckett taps a similar vein of uncomprehended nostalgia behind Estragon's unhappiness, so it seems to me. A cloud of forgetting hovers, such perhaps as that imagined by mystics like the author of *The Cloud of Unknowing*. The figure of the Boy in his theatre always brings with it a powerful sense of some dimension closed—or half-closed—to the older characters. It is felt for a split second when a small boy is perceived by Clov outside the shelter of *Endgame* or the Boy in wet oilskins appears at the door of the 'familiar chamber' in *Ghost Trio*. It is disconcerting, even alarming, yet a faint promise stirs: perhaps something lost is to be recalled, relived.

REMEMBERING

Tenacious ghosts stand at the door of this divine forgetfulness, refusing entry, demanding a listener. They are there at the start in *Godot*, rustling in the gentle sounds of nature:

> All the dead voices.
> They make a noise like wings.
> Like leaves.
> Like sand.
> Like leaves.

And they are there at the end, more insistent, taking visible shape at times, determined to tell their story. They may bring pain or comfort, usually mixed, as in *Ohio Impromptu* where the Reader tells how a man sunk in the grief of bereavement tried to assuage his pain by moving to a place with no shared memories, though in a dream he had 'Seen the dear face and heard the unspoken words, Stay where we were so long alone together, my shade will comfort you.'

The potent word 'shade' has a throng of ghosts behind it, rooted in intuition and memory. In his Proust study Beckett categorized Memory, along with Habit, as the 'cancers of Time'. The shades that haunt his stage have cut free from this malign Time: they open up another way into the space beyond, the Great Memory, in Yeatsian phrase, or, in Beckett's, the 'smothered divinity' waiting to be released by the magical touch of involuntary memory. We feel the breath of it in that moment of stillness in *Godot* when Vladimir and Estragon make space for the dead voices that haven't yet done with life:

VLADIMIR. To have lived is not enough for them.
ESTRAGON. They have to talk about it.
VLADIMIR. To be dead is not enough for them.
ESTRAGON. It is not sufficient.

The supernatural intensity here is unlike anything else in the play, but along with it goes a sense that these 'voices' are known, familiar, like the sound of leaves and sand through which they are heard. Beckett finds many ways of conveying this distinctive mix of the familiar and strange in his ghosts. In the early plays especially he makes witty use of ghost lore and fiction. Nagg and Nell in their white nightcaps, heads sticking out of dustbins, are ghosts of a kind, in the vein of Dickensian grotesque. When Nell dies it is the death of a ghost, to be lived through over and over, like everything else in *Endgame*. It also opens up a new, distant dimension: the pure grief of Nagg, crying for her. Ada in *Embers* may not seem very ghostly: called up by Henry to assist his narrative, she comes over as entirely lifelike: shrewd, tartly humorous, impatient of dreamers. But Beckett lays down the clues. In the way of ghosts her voice is low and remote, there is no 'sound as she sits' (on the abrasive shingle), and she has been there 'for some little time', so she says, before Henry is aware of her.

Another ghostly female voice, in *Eh Joe*, also enjoys jokes, sour ones. Her task is to induce memories that are 'involuntary' in a special sense: Martin Dodsworth has called it a 'horrifying parody' of the Proustian kind.[5] She moves him inexorably, with each camera move, further into himself till he is deep in a 'beyond' where another ghost waits, to be recovered and 'realized', with pain. At first the accent is on what can be assimilated without too much agony; the Voice tells of how her failed affair with him left her bitter but able to get over it: 'I did all right'. Then she moves into the story of the other who did not recover from betrayal: 'The green one . . . The narrow one . . . [. . .] Spirit made light'. Joe has access to these stories through memory of scenes already in his mind, like the last meeting with the green-eyed girl. The Voice reminds him how he assured her 'The best's to come', while preparing to ditch her: 'Ticket in your pocket for the first morning flight.' The 'you' here comes close to the 'you' of *That Time*, the form of address used to Listener by his own voices.

Then Joe is taken a further step, beyond what he can know from personal memory, into the story of how the girl died. 'Will I tell you?' the Voice says, severely: 'Not interested . . .? Well I will just the same . . . I think you should know'. He resists, as we most of us tend to resist, the full imagining of another's pain. He is made to see what he would rather not see: the distraught girl in her lavender slip ('You know the one') swallowing lethal tablets on her last journey to the seashore, lying, 'Clawing at the shingle', her face and breasts in the stones. 'Now *imagine*' says the Voice, 'Before she goes'. The repeated sound 'stones' batters at Joe's resistance.

In the rushing, agonizing lyricism of her story the Voice creates a space that allows no escape from the command, 'Imagine!' It extends far beyond the unwilling memory. A ghost—a mysterious psychic function—is needed to speak for the one who can't speak for herself. Harshness is needed too. 'You've had her, haven't you?', says the 'whisper' in Joe's head, 'You've laid her?' Then she changes to 'he', a suggestive distancing: 'Of course he has.' A savage pun and a warning: the betrayer laid the living girl but may not find it so easy to lay her ghost.

Whether he does so in the end we don't know. He has 'throttled' unwanted voices up to now and this one fades out too. Patrick Magee's Joe registered the increasing anguish that might be expected from someone sensitive enough to discern the spiritual beauty of the dead girl. 'Spirit made light' was his expression, the Voice reminds him. Magee's face at the close filled the screen like a tragic mask.[6] Jack MacGowran in the original production showed less emotion and—surprisingly to me—smiled at the end, as if to say, 'One more voice dealt with', or perhaps 'I have my story'. The smile was not called for in the text: Beckett remarked in a conversation I had with him on 11

January 1987 that it might have been a mistake. Perhaps the effect of the story on Joe must always be ambiguous, however.

There is less doubt about its effect on viewers. I have never known it fail to move and disturb (in many showings to students and other audiences). It acquires a mysterious autonomy and completeness; an evocation is achieved through an unwilling memory driven by a 'ghost', the voice in the head whose watchword is 'Imagine!'

The word 'ghost' comes to seem ever more inevitable in the last plays. 'Make it ghostly' Beckett urged Billie Whitelaw when directing her in *Footfalls*. The play's subtle mix of images suggests both the ghost of tradition and a more ambiguous modern vision. One kind of ghostliness comes through stage effects: the eerie sound of the chime echoing in the darkness; the dim light on the woman in the worn grey wrap; her obsessive pacing on a narrow strip of light, always wheeling on the ninth step. What ritual is this? The 'nine' steps invite the kind of metaphysical discussion they have received from critics (somewhat lamed by the fact that Beckett changed to nine from his original seven, for practical reasons).

We are bound to pursue such questions. But above all we need to feel the tenuous nature of the ghost, combined so strongly with its tenacity. I recall a rehearsal at the Royal Court (in May 1976) when Beckett directed Billie Whitelaw as May and Rose Hill as the offstage voice of the mother (a particularly fine vocal combination). He very much wanted the feet not to be seen at all, an effect, could it have been achieved, which would have added to the impression of a ghost gliding—and the terrifying sense of being 'not there' which May, speaking for 'Amy', confides to the surrogate mother at the end of the play.

Why does she walk? A reason suggests itself briefly at the start in the play's only dialogue between two separate voices: those of May and the invisible mother. As in *Eh Joe*, a ghost calls up a ghost. May speaks into the void—'Were you asleep?'—and receives from the void an answer: 'Deep asleep. (*Pause.*) I heard you in my deep sleep. (*Pause.*) There is no sleep so deep I would not hear you there.' There comes through overwhelmingly a sense of the bond between mother and daughter, the pain of it—and the fidelity. An evocation is achieved, rooted in homely if harrowing detail of human life; the routines of the sickbed: sponging, changing the drawsheet, passing the bedpan. The mother seems both infinitely far away and disconcertingly near; a patient, being asked if she would like an injection again, murmuring 'Yes, but it is too soon.' The daughter pities her—'Moisten your poor lips?'—and she pities the daughter for her compulsion to revolve it all 'In your poor mind'.

Darkness blots out the pacing figure, the footsteps cease, the chime becomes a little fainter. Preludes in traditional style to the manifestation of a ghost and followed by words in the same tradition: 'I walk here now', spoken by the unseen mother. She is for the moment the ghost walking—and, as a ghost must, she speaks of the past, of the daughter who walked obsessively even when a child, who has not 'been out since girlhood' from the home where 'It all began'. It is a voice of sorrow and understanding, bringing us a little further into the strange heart of the play, May's overpowering need to 'hear the feet, however faint they fall' and tell 'how it was'; the last a little like the ghosts of the Noh theatre whose remote kinship with Beckett's has been traced by Yasunari Takahashi.[7] Mother and daughter merge in this walking; by the end the image seems to reverberate with all the footfalls ever heard on the human way.

The mother falls silent on the refrain, 'It all' and is not heard again except through her daughter's voice, in the mysterious 'sequel': 'A little later, when she was quite forgotten, she began to—(*Pause.*) A little later when, as though she had never been, it never been, she began to walk.' The correction from 'quite forgotten' is telling. Nothing has been forgotten, as we are reminded in every recurring echo from chime and light. They grow fainter but can't go out till some release is achieved. Words like 'exorcism' come to mind in a context which increasingly draws on Christian imagery, centring very precisely on the little church where, so May tells us, a 'semblance' appears—at Vespers 'Necessarily' (a cryptic comment, inviting speculation). In that church, we may guess, hangs the crucifix which inspires her recurring sigh, 'His poor arm'.

What is this ghostly 'semblance'? May urges us to 'Watch it pass', then corrects to 'watch her pass': the semblance is never to be thought of as less than human. The solitary figure on stage appears to have seen as if in a psychic mirror the twilight self which can only be perceived 'in a certain light. (*Pause.*) Given the right light.' The light in the theatre has been carefully made 'right', so that we can see what she sees: a twilight shape in a trailing grey gown: 'Grey rather than white, a pale shade of grey. (*Pause.*) Tattered. (*Pause.*) A tangle of tatters.' The figure on stage walking 'up and down, up and down' before our eyes seems to contain in herself both the semblance and the whole story of mother and daughter.

It is a mischievous change of mood when Beckett dissolves the mesmeric reverie and transforms May into a narrator, addressing us as readers who need reminders and clues: 'Old Mrs Winter, whom the reader will remember' (very teasing, since we have heard nothing at all of Mrs Winter. Addicts at this point enjoy thoughts of Beckett's favourite word play with Ms and Ws). Only Beckett could risk such a break with the fragile, precarious illusion.

May has to produce new voices now, for Mrs Winter and her daughter, Amy, and set their scene: domestic interior, the couple just back from a church service; the mother troubled by something strange about this Evensong, Amy saying she noticed nothing, couldn't do so as she was 'not there'.

I thought of this sequence in *Footfalls* when directing a workshop group at Sligo in 1990 in Yeats's *The Words upon the Window-pane*.[8] In this play a professional medium, operating in a shabby Dublin house of the 1930s, once a Georgian mansion visited by Jonathan Swift, produces from her throat the voice of Swift and induces her clients (and us) to 'see' him in painful episodes with women and in his terrible old age. The medium explains the abrupt changes in the voices that come and go: 'Now they are old, now they are young. They change all in a moment as their thought changes.' A grim prospect of eternity; glossed, however, by one seance member as simply part of life, a kind of mental replay and suffering we all of us must endure at some time, to be dissolved only when 'God gives peace'.

Such a release finally comes about in *Footfalls*, so it seemed to me, at least, when Billie Whitelaw in the first production 'did' the mother's voice insisting that May must have been at Evensong because she joined in the 'Amen' following the benediction. Then, still in the mother's voice, she spoke with great simplicity and gravity the majestic words of the Authorized Version:

> The love of God, and the fellowship of the Holy Ghost, be with us all, now, and for evermore.

For that moment the theatre felt like a church, the audience, hushed and awed, a congregation, taken out of themselves into a spiritual dimension beyond our normal reach. The question is still asked of May, by herself now, 'Will you never have done . . . revolving it all?', but a blessing had been given; it seemed natural and right when the lights went out and then slowly faded up on the strip, to find '*No trace of May*'. Echoes from the chime might still linger but the weary pacing was over, there was a sense of release, of a story having been fully told or taken as far as the narrator can reach, in the broken rhythms of a modern self-consciousness.

The two television plays written (1975–6) about the same time as *Footfalls* focus on the long, hard creative process involved in calling up a shade ('Shades' was the joint title under which they appeared when first shown by the BBC on 17 April 1977). Everything in *Ghost Trio* prepares us for a mysterious collaboration between the silent figure (F) and the invisible speaker (V) who instructs us to see the room as abstracted from nature, all grey geometry (Beckett wanted it to have 'no shadows', a well-known attribute of ghosts). The haunting music from the slow movement of Beethoven's 'Ghost Trio' issuing at certain points from F's cassette, intensifies the sense of psychic expectation. Commentators have pointed out that the music is not under F's control; nor, say Beryl and John Fletcher, is there any indication that he hears it: it 'has an existence which is outside of time, place and the human perspective'.[9]

V tells us we are concerned with 'shades' a direction which brought Yeats again to my mind; it was a word he often used. In his poem 'All Souls' Night' the Yeats persona sits in an Oxford room by a table set out with 'two long glasses brimmed with muscatel'. He is alone, waiting: 'A ghost may come'. Then he raises his ghosts himself, in a roll-call of dear friends, now dead. They are guests who will drink from the wine breath, their element too fine for 'the whole wine'. F in *Ghost Trio* waits for such a guest. She does not come, though we are made to feel her near when V says 'He will now think he hears her.' Psychic changes occur in the room: the door and window open of their own accord, with a 'crescendo creak' (followed by a decrescendo: Beckett's humour never goes). Then there is a silence, in which a ghost appears, the Boy, in his oilskins wet with rain. He shakes his head, an ambiguous negative that we are left to interpret for ourselves. What we might all agree on is the expansion the room undergoes through this visitation. The so-unexpected young creature, with his fresh, benign air, brings with him another world: his shake of the head might indicate postponement, not refusal. He could seem to be keeping open the way to a dimension that was shut off by the obsessive 'remembering'.

In . . . *but the clouds* . . . the longed-for being does appear; in the form of a woman's face in close-up. Again, the act of evocation requires a complex collaboration, in this case among three elements of a psyche: M, in his light grey robe and skullcap, sitting bowed over an invisible table; M1, who walks for him (M in set), and V, his voice. Like Mrs Henderson in Yeats's play, M1 goes through careful routines and rituals to prepare himself. Yeats's medium takes a rest before a seance, has a hymn sung, and so on. M1 changes into his magician's garb, or, as V puts it, 'assumed robe and skull'. The sardonic play on 'skullcap' keeps us in touch with humour and common life, as does the phrase V uses about the place of evocation: 'my little sanctum'. It's an expression, I was told by Augustine Martin, that used to be a familiar Dublin turn of phrase for any old comfortable retreat. I have wondered if Beckett was having a friendly dig here at Yeats's penchant for ceremonies like those solemnly practised by the spiritualist Order of the Golden Dawn, of which he was a very active member. The other side of that, of course, is the good use Yeats made of such theatricalizing in *The Words upon the Window-pane*. Brilliantly, he plants equivocal connections between the spiritualist's dubious art and that of the dramatic artist, actor or playwright: the seance when taken over by the spirit of Swift is seen by one disgruntled participant as 'some kind of horrible play'.

Yeats's medium fails to produce what her clients want—including contact with their own dead—but with the aid of her ghostly child 'control', Lulu, achieves an uncanny materialization: voices that are not hers issue from her throat. By his splitting up of narrative voice, figures on the screen and the woman's face mouthing words, Beckett achieves just such an effect. M1 may be controlled by the M who crouches in a corner of the screen, or perhaps it's the other way round; we can't know. What we do come to know is the labour and weariness involved in the process of materializing an unseen reality. Four stages are spelt out by V and illustrated on the screen. The woman's face appears but only for two seconds, then lingers a little, then is seen mouthing words 'inaudibly'. The fourth stage, the commonest, is for nothing to happen, 'when I begged in vain', says V, and 'busied myself with something else, more . . . rewarding, such as . . . such as . . . cube roots, for example'. Another of those humorous notes which keep things in proportion. Effort is continuous: there has to be a rerun—'Let us now run through it again'—in which we, the viewers, must share before the full materialization can be achieved.

When the face returns in the final sequence, still mouthing inaudible words, the sense of human yearning is strong. It's one of the most moving moments in Beckett's theatre when V drops the past tense used up to then and moves into the present, directly addressing the face with the 'unseeing eyes' which 'I so begged when alive to look at me'.

Look at me.
Speak to me.

No response; the eyes remain 'unseeing' and the words inaudible; it is seemingly an image of frustration. Yet there is a sense of approaching revelation. The face so longed for has acquired a mythic quality, it hovers there like the spirit of Memory itself (supposed mother of the Muses). So at least we might imagine when we are at last allowed to hear, from the voice of M, what the lips have been suggesting: the four lines of exquisite poetry which end the play. The full impact of the effect depends on our not hearing the words till then (ideally, not even knowing what to expect, an experience we can only have once). When heard, they will conjure up, for those who love Yeats's poetry as Beckett did, another shade, author of 'The Tower', that self-searching poem which declares itself in its last stanza with majestic serenity: 'Now shall I make my soul'. In the course of the 'making' the poet gives proper weight to those pains of life that might pull the spirit down in old age: 'wreck of body', 'testy delirium', 'death of friends'. Then he makes them recede into an infinite calm and—

Seem but the clouds of the sky
When the horizon fades;
Or a bird's sleepy cry
Among the deepening shades.

No one need feel cut off from this magical calm by not knowing Yeats's poem: Beckett knew what he was doing in trusting his ending to its delicate rhythm and evocative, simple words. Of course we gain more if we sense too the presence of Yeats. 'Presence' was one of his words; he throngs his stage with figures involved in creative acts of 'dreaming back'. We join a charmed circle of friendship when Beckett brings him so potently on to his own stage. But even without this, there is a sense of hands joined across an infinite distance, bringing release into a beyond where shades no longer fret. And crucially, for those who know nothing of Yeats, the lines gain power from the patient efforts and poignant frustration that preceded them.

In my last illustration, *A Piece of Monologue*, Beckett shows the world of nature and human complexity in the act of fading into a world of ghosts. Standing 'Stock still head haught' in his all-white nightwear Speaker himself is half a ghost. He has moved away from those emblems of mortality that troubled him, the funerals with their 'Streaming canopies. Bubbling black mud. Coffin on its way. Loved one . . . he all but said loved one on his way. Her way.' That has receded into an unknowable distance, as a ghost does: 'Ghost light. Ghost nights. Ghost rooms. Ghost graves. Ghost . . . he all but said ghost loved ones.' The light is going, the ghosts must go with it: this was written as a play about death. But something remains; a story has been told before the departing, an 'unaccountable' light perceived, and a space 'Beyond that black beyond' has been made mysteriously real. Memory has transfigured itself.

6

Shared Words: The Camaraderie of Quotation

FAMILIAR sayings, literary and theatrical allusions, lines of verse, proverbs, and the like are one of the pleasantly open ways into Beckett's imaginative domain. It is true that his erudition and wide range make it hard if not impossible to keep up with him entirely, in the spontaneous, 'at first hearing' way I have especially in mind. But there is the pleasure of discovery too: what we have to look up at the start in an annotated edition may end up among our own favourites. It happened to me when a friend, Leonee Ormond, who knew of this gap in my reading presented me with a copy of *Effi Briest*, a novel I knew about but didn't know as Krapp does, from within ('Scalded the eyes out of me reading *Effie* again, a page a day, with tears again. Effie . . .'). It became for me too a haunting book, with its equivocal ghost and dream-laden dunes.

It will be clear, I hope, that I am not attempting to trace sources or chart quotations comprehensively: that herculean task is already well advanced by Beckett scholars, his editors in particular. My wish is to illustrate Beckett's subtle and varied uses in his plays of the common stock, and the pains he takes to make it accessible as well as to tease us (one aspect of camaraderie).

The pleasures of quotation are more obviously open to the solitary reader than to an audience intent on keeping up with the action on stage, unable to turn back a page. Beckett clearly keeps the latter's need in mind, offering in his plays more help than in his fiction with quotations, and minimizing arcane allusions. A glance at his production notebooks or scripts where he gives detail of passages quoted from (full reference provided with scholarly exactness) will show how mainstream most of the sources are. He could reasonably hope for the fragments he uses to be recognized or just 'sensed' as familiar, in the way we recognize a tune we couldn't name.

Winnie is the prime exponent of this faculty, one we all have, though not too many have her literary range. It sometimes tests us severely, as when she makes covert allusions to Browning's *Paracelsus*, first by calling that ominous prop, the revolver, 'Brownie', then alluding to the poet and in one breath the poem: 'Ever uppermost, like Browning' ('I say confusedly what comes uppermost': *Paracelsus*, III. 372–5). Beckett refers to this in his notebook as 'hint of Browning'.[1] Though there may be few in any audience who would unaided find their way spontaneously from Winnie's scraps to *Paracelsus*, the clue has been well laid for us to follow up at leisure. And in any case something has been said about Winnie, her attachment to the revolver and its ambiguous connection with the poet often parodied as the great exponent of Victorian optimism.

A little trick of Beckett's for highlighting a quotation is to have a character hesitate and feel for a word, as Krapp does before hitting on 'chrysolite' as the right adjective for the fine eyes of the nursemaid he has been watching, pushing the 'big black hooded perambulator'. It is a clue to the colour of her eyes (green), but beyond that points to Othello, who uses the word with anguish. In the copy of *Krapp's Last Tape* Beckett annotated for the 1973 production at the Royal Court Theatre, he carefully wrote out the three lines in question:

> If heaven wd [would] make me such another world,
> Of one entire and perfect chrysolite,
> I'd not have sold her for it.[2]

This is a poignant gloss on the reason for Krapp's remembering the word: the sadness he shares with Othello over a love lost.

The air Beckett's characters breathe is thick with quotation. Often there is a sense of life lived through literature, as with Krapp, a professional if not successful writer ('Seventeen copies sold [. . .] Getting known'). He draws continually on his reading to register high points in his life, using the title of a poem by Donne, 'Farewell to Love', for a momentous sequence on his spool, and slipping into the style of Herrick when recalling how his mother 'lay a-dying'. The oddity of 'lay a-dying' invites us to remember the original in the background; it is certainly part of the common stock:

> Gather ye Rose-buds while ye may,
> Old Time is still a-flying,
> And this same flower that smiles today
> Tomorrow will be dying.

The conflation of 'a-flying' with 'a-dying' makes a telling suggestion that his feelings about his mother and the women in his life are inextricably tangled—and that he dreads the end of life, though also longing for it.

The occasional appearance of a line unlikely to be known to the general reader—Winnie's 'I call to the eye of the mind', for instance—shows up by contrast how heterogeneous and popular the mass of quotations are. Famous lines of Shakespeare and Milton rub shoulders with the Bible and there is a plenitude of sayings which everyone quotes but few, probably, could ascribe to their source. 'Cheerfulness was always breaking in' is one of these, wittily amended by Winnie to 'sorrow keeps breaking in'.[3]

Fragments of quotation are artfully placed to make an impact, whether or not likely to be recognized. Estragon's reply to Vladimir's query about the state of his leg—'Swelling visibly'—is funny even if we don't catch the Dickensian echo (though funnier if we do). And Dan Rooney's morose fantasy of nipping some young doom in the bud is explicable without reference to Gray's 'Ode on a Distant Prospect of Eton College' though if we do catch the allusion, the word 'doom' opens up on a complex vista of thought, including a vision of lost childhood paradise as well as the inevitable suffering in store for the little victims who play 'regardless of their doom'. Each time Gray's poem surfaces in Beckett's plays (it is a favourite) the echoes acquire appropriateness through his artful placing of them. We can appreciate the relevance to her situation of Winnie's garbled 'something something laughing wild amid severest woe' even if we don't recognize the source in Gray's Ode, with its grand universalizing drive. And Hamm's 'Every man his speciality' is a nicely black joke without benefit of the original on which it is a variation: 'To each his suff'rings: all are men, | Condemned alike to groan'.[4] Something of Gray's original is likely to be lingering in many minds in the audience, however. In this instance, as so often, Beckett is drawing on a poem which has entered the common stock and acquired proverbial status. Its closing couplet, 'No more; where ignorance is bliss, | 'Tis folly to be wise', might tell us something about Winnie's attitude to life.

We have to work at the quotations, and in doing this—filling out an unfinished phrase, identifying a variation—we gain fascinating glimpses into the creative process from which the variations sprang. Often a tiny scrap will be enough to conjure up famous lines; most will identify the best-known stanza of *Omar Khayyám* for instance, from Winnie's minimalist 'paradise enow':

> A Book of Verses underneath the Bough,
> A Jug of Wine, a Loaf of Bread—and Thou
> Beside me singing in the Wilderness—
> Oh, Wilderness were Paradise enow.

In completing the scrap we taste to the full the ironic contrast between FitzGerald's lover, content in the wilderness, and poor Winnie, for whom Willie is the inadequate 'thou' and who has to do the singing herself (with one notable exception when Willie produces his 'hoarse' burst of song to her tune). Winnie points up the incongruity of the quotation with a comical hesitation—'. . . er . . .'—as if she knew well that her romantic dreams don't ring quite true (like the word 'enow'). Yet they bring a paradisal gleam into the wilderness for her. Beckett doesn't demean the quotations he uses, even those that might seem obvious candidates for derision. He may draw satirical effects from them as in Mouth's bitter recall in *Not I* of statements like 'God is love'. But even when seeming to undermine or annihilate familiar sayings he is often preparing to restore or recharge the feeling that first established them in the common stock.

This is a most touching achievement. It sometimes looks like a testing of lines in romantic or sublime mode which haunt Beckett as well as his characters, an attempt to find if they could ring true in a more sceptical, in some ways anti-romantic, framework. Krapp's hesitation over 'chrysolite', for instance, seems like part of the test he is conducting on the false rhetorical notes in his view of himself. Throughout the *œuvre* familiar sayings are planted in a tough modern soil which both threatens and, through Beckett's alchemy, renews their life. Quotations from some lofty source may be first pulled down into a low context, then given their wings again. Milton's 'sublime' is earthed (it seems the right word for *Happy Days*) when Winnie strikes the Miltonic note while applying lipstick: 'Oh fleeting joys—(*lips*)—oh something lasting woe'. The lipstick pause and her favourite fill-in word, 'something' are amusingly reductive, though it can be noted that they also serve to preserve the scansion of the original and 'something' of its power: 'Oh fleeting joyes | Of paradise, deare bought with lasting woes!' (*Paradise Lost*, x. 741).

More corrosively reductive is her vision of the vulgar pair coming by 'hand in hand', caricature version of Adam and Eve leaving

1–2. 'just a few regulars, nursemaids, infants . . .', 'hats with enough brim to shade faces.' Postcards from Beckett. See pp. 16–17.

3–4. Original set design by Peter Snow for Peter Hall's production of *Waiting for Godot*, 1955, and 'road in room' variation (gouache). See pp. 26–8.

5. Set design by Louis le Brocquy for Walter Asmus' production of *Waiting for Godot*, Gate Theatre, Dublin, 1991. With Barry McGovern and Johnny Murphy. Photograph by Tom Lawlor. See pp. 28–9.

6. 'From the Wings'. Pencil and wash drawing by Brian Bourke of Barry McGovern as Vladimir and Johnny Murphy as Estragon at Dublin in 1991. See p. 29.

7. *Godot*-like image in a painting by Bo Jeffares: *Winter, Four Seasons I* (oil on canvas).

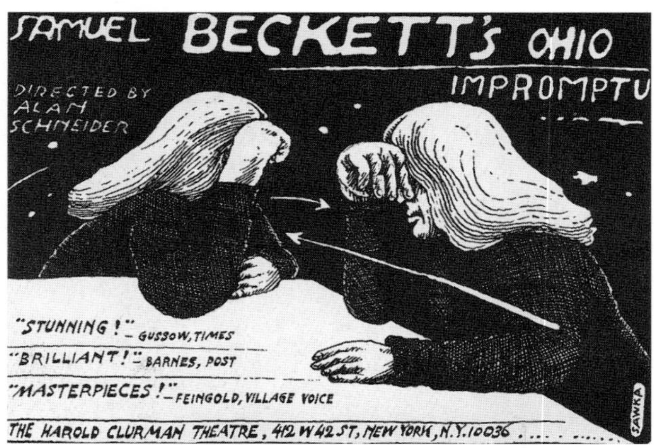

8. Witty publicity postcard for Alan Schneider's production of *Ohio Impromptu*, Harold Clurman Theatre, New York, 1983. See pp. 38–9.

9. Julian Curry in *Company* with 'shadow' in background. Donmar Warehouse Theatre, London, 1988. See p. 170.

10. 'Ah earth you old extinguisher'. Natasha Parry with parasol on fire in Peter Brook's production of *Oh les beaux jours*, Riverside Studios, London, 1997. Photograph by Laurence Burns. See p. 155.

11. The pacing feet of Fiona Shaw in Deborah Warner's production of *Footfalls*, Garrick Theatre, London, 1994. Photograph by Neil Libbert. See pp. 158–9.

12. Juliet Stevenson in the dark of *Footfalls*; production by Katie Mitchell, The Other Place, Stratford-upon-Avon, 1997. Photograph by James F. Hunkin. See pp. 161–2.

13. David Warrilow as Protagonist in Antoni Libera's production of *Catastrophe*, Haymarket Theatre, Leicester, 1989. With Tom Knight as The Director, Christina Paul as Assistant. Photograph by Nobby Clarke.
See p. 56.

14. Closing image of hats from *Come and Go* in Ilan Reichel's production of Beckett 'shorts', Etcetera Theatre, London, 1996. Photograph by Nat Rea.
See p. 74.

15. Ben Kingsley and Alan Howard in Peter Hall's production of *Waiting for Godot*, Old Vic Theatre, London, 1997. Photograph by David Harrison. See pp. 96–7.

Paradise. The man asks crude questions about what Winnie 'means' and the woman taunts him for thinking he has meaning just because 'you're still on your two flat feet, with your old ditty full of tinned muck and changes of underwear, dragging me up and down this fornicating wilderness'. At this point Winnie interjects 'coarse creature', immediately adding 'fit mate': another Miltonic echo degraded (*Paradise Lost*, X. 899). So are we to take satirically her declamation at the start of Act 2, 'Hail, holy light'? In its original context (*Paradise Lost*, III. 1) the words lead into Milton's infinitely moving reflection on his blindness and his heroic resolve to 'see' into 'things invisible to mortal sight'. Winnie seems placed at a far distance from that grandeur. Yet even if we smile a little at the incongruity, we must surely feel it is moving and heroic when the Miltonic invocation issues from the depleted head which is all that is left of her. Having first been brought down to earth, the lofty words are shown to be the right ones for her.

A similar earthing occurs in *Godot* when Estragon amuses himself by misquoting the opening lines of Shelley's 'To the moon', changing 'Art thou pale for weariness | Of climbing heaven and gazing on the earth', to 'climbing heaven and gazing on the likes of us'. It is a deflation, but the kind that in making us smile draws us closer to the speaker and the poem he has misquoted. The vision in the poem must have sad meaning for him. Shelley's moon is pale for weariness of solitude, of 'Wandering companionless | Among the stars that have a different birth'. A key note of the play is struck: the sense of human beings troubled by deep loneliness, feeling themselves adrift in a universe which is in some ways mysteriously alien.

It is never a simple matter of ironic contrast between high and low art. On the contrary Beckett achieves some of his most subtle and moving effects by way of 'low' elements which make for comedy but also feed into the poetry and tragedy intertwined with it. Winnie's singing of the *Merry Widow* waltz at the end of *Happy Days* is an affecting example of this 'treasure of the humble' (to use the Maeterlinckian phrase which often seems appropriate to Beckett's use of 'little' words and phrases).

Total recall is not a prerequisite in this sharing. On the contrary, it would probably be a disadvantage never to have to fumble for a line; it would for one thing cut us off from Winnie, whose hit-and-miss way with quotations reflects common experience, even if taken by some critics as a particular failure in her. Haven't we all at some time or other felt for words through the beat of a line, as she amusingly does: 'Go forget me why should something o'er that something shadow fling'?[5] Most of us will laugh with fellow feeling at her frustrated cry 'What is that unforgettable line?' She is at an age when the tricksiness of memory begins to show, around 50 (Beckett's age when he wrote the play). Yet memory is her guiding star. Only what has been stored in her mind since her younger days is any use to her now; no books to hand, in Act 2 no hands to turn the pages if there were any. She forgets much but remembers more. It is no idle boast when she says 'a part remains, of one's classics, to help one through the day'. Quotation refreshes her, even when carrying with it bitter contrasts. Her brief recall of Keats in 'beechen green', for instance, evokes a romantic image that might seem a cruel mockery, the 'beechen green, and shadows numberless' of 'Ode to a Nightingale'. Yet while she holds it in mind it affords a fleeting moment of relief from the hard, unsparing light trained on her.

We too must enter into the struggle for recall, try (for the time of performance) to accept our own gaps in knowledge and failures of memory. We are rewarded by having words that may have faded or receded restored to us in pristine freshness, as Yeats's exquisite reverie from 'The Tower' is restored in . . . *but the clouds* . . . Outside the theatre there are other pleasures to be had with quotation: sharing with friends in the search for some elusive allusion; sharpening our knowledge with the aid of a helpful footnote. But first we need to go along with the dramatic process, let ourselves be plunged in the universal sea of 'not knowing'.

Often it's hard to know which of several possibilities a speaker on Beckett's stage might have in mind and equivocal echoes abound. The 'little cloud' in *Godot* could point both to the Bible and James Joyce ('A Little Cloud' in *Dubliners*); the wind in the reeds to the Bible and Yeats. Winnie might have a predecessor in Dickens's Flora as well as Joyce's Molly Bloom, whose kinship with her has been convincingly traced by Antonia Rodríguez-Gago. She suggests that when Beckett started writing the monologue called 'X female solo' he couldn't resist drawing on 'perhaps the most famous female monologue of this century'.[6] When the voice in *Eh Joe* mutters 'silence of the grave' it is in tune with her many allusions to biblical warnings about death and judgement, but might also call to mind Sir Walter Ralegh's moving poem (re-written on the eve of his execution) about the Time that takes away our joys:

Who in the dark and silent grave,
When we have wander'd all our ways,
Shuts up the story of our days.

Favourites of our own will insinuate themselves; it's a part of the pleasure and the fellowship. I wondered, for instance, whether there was an echo from Henry James when I first heard Voice C in *That Time* describing his experience in the Portrait Gallery, peering at the 'vast oil black with age and dirt' and trying to make out what lay behind the glass: perhaps a 'child such as a young prince or princess some young prince or princess of the blood'. Just so the governess in *The Turn of the Screw* reacts to the children in her care when she first encounters them, before the ghosts make their way in: 'a pair of little grandees, of princes of the blood'. A ghostly manifestation of a kind occurs in *That Time* too: a 'face' appears as C peers at the glass: 'had you swivel on the slab to see who it was there at your elbow'. We are left to imagine for ourselves what the experience means: there has been no shortage of suggestions, any more than for James's ghosts.

That echo chamber, *Ohio Impromptu*, similarly sets the mind going in various directions. 'Profounds of mind', says Reader as the story draws to its close: 'Buried in who knows what profounds of mind. Of mindlessness.' For a lover of Yeats there can't but spring to mind his expression for those distant, mysterious spaces: the 'deep of the mind'. Though Wilde spoke of the depths with different emphasis, his *De Profundis* may also contribute to the complex harmonies we construct from our own reading and the words of Beckett's Reader. In that work Wilde quotes Goethe on the value of suffering as, more cryptically, does the voice in *Eh Joe*: 'Ah she knew you, heavenly powers!'

It is true, as Barbara Hardy once reminded me, that camaraderie involves exclusion as well as fellowship. Not everyone will recognize or even notice the less obvious half-concealed quotations. Most are from a culture (Anglo-Irish, Protestant, old-style European) that is slipping rapidly into the past. Will audiences of the future, including all those who never learnt verse by heart as children, be able to enjoy the pleasure offered by quotation on Beckett's stage? I believe they will, each in their own way, as with everything in life. His plays have the power to stimulate us into seeking out those things that fascinate his characters. It is a process of recall or discovery such as many have had through Shakespeare: enjoyment of his plays on stage or screen has enabled them to tap into the wealth of a far more distant culture.

The common stock is a great survivor. Shakespeare and the Bible are a part of it much used by Beckett, a topic I glance at now. (I should say that I don't discuss quotations in the French texts; that rich subject requires a study to itself. It has been interestingly opened up by James Knowlson, Colin Duckworth, and Harry Cockerham among others.)[7]

To begin with the Bible. It is one of the most quoted texts in Beckett's *œuvre* and overwhelmingly the dominant shadowing text in *Godot*, as Ruby Cohn has commented. This is not the Bible as sacred text nor even as literature but as folk property, issuing in popular forms such as proverbs and hymns as well as direct quotations. Emphasis falls on well-known narratives (the Creation, Noah's Ark, the Crucifixion) that have often provided subjects for performance art, as in the medieval miracle plays, Handel's *Messiah*, and Britten's *Noye's Fludde*. Beckett's emphasis is on what 'everyone' knows—including what they know wrong. Vladimir worries about this, brooding on a crucial discrepancy in the Gospel accounts of the fate awaiting the two thieves crucified with Christ: 'But one of the four says that one of the two was saved.' Why believe this one rather than the others?

ESTRAGON. Who believes him?
VLADIMIR. Everybody. It's the only version they know.
ESTRAGON. People are bloody ignorant apes.

As Yeats put it, speaking of myth and legend, 'everybody and nobody built up the dream bit by bit'.[8] Vladimir's deep anxiety about salvation is fuelled partly by what 'people' have chosen to believe about the fate of two thieves: a brilliant rooting of the story in the folk imagination.

Only when the context of ordinary suffering—with corns, bunions, and the like—has been established does the first direct biblical quotation in the play occur. Vladimir reminds Estragon that he suffers too, with his prostate trouble: 'I'd like to hear what you'd say if you had what I have.' 'It hurts?' asks Estragon sardonically, and then: 'What do you expect, you always wait till the last moment.' It's a flashpoint:

VLADIMIR (*Musingly.*) The last moment . . . (*He meditates.*) Hope deferred maketh the something sick, who said that?

'Who said that?' is a question we probably couldn't answer, any more than Estragon can. But we could no doubt supply the missing word, the 'something' he knows is needed to keep the scansion. 'Hope deferred maketh the heart sick' is one of those sayings dear to Beckett which seem to have an inspired anonymity: in fact it originated in the Bible (Proverbs 13: 12). We don't need to know that to be affected as Beckett intends. It is enough to balance, along with Estragon, between knowing and not knowing; just the equilibrium the pair maintain throughout their waiting for Godot. The missing word in the quotation, 'heart', gains extra emphasis from Vladimir's seeming loss of memory. He is heartsick for something undefined which is endlessly deferred. The keynote of *Waiting for Godot* is characteristically announced in a drolly unfinished quotation.

Those with further-reaching memories of the Bible (or maybe childhood books like Arthur Mee's *Children's Encyclopedia* with its pages of proverbs and biblical sayings) may also recall the half of the proverb Vladimir does not quote:

> Hope deferred maketh the heart sick; but when the desire cometh it is a tree of life.

The method is pursued throughout, by way of truncated quotations or fleeting allusions, verbal and visual. Vladimir tries out the names, 'Cain' and 'Abel' on the fallen Pozzo and Lucky in Act 2 and at different times he and Estragon take up a crucified posture, arms outstretched. Many sly, parodic allusions occur, as in Vladimir's tart 'I've had about my bellyfull of your lamentations'. The incongruously sonorous 'lamentations' points us towards the Old Testament prophet declaiming 'Behold, and see if there be any sorrow like unto my sorrow, which is done unto me' (Lamentations 1: 12). For those who catch the allusion, a mythic grandeur touches the everyday comedy of the friends' competition in suffering. Parody has a cutting edge in the question-and-answer sessions with the Boy, from which a God of tradition emerges: one who divides up the sheep and the goats and conforms to popular Christian iconography by having a white beard. The depressing thought of an Ancient of Days having seemingly learnt nothing from his aeons of experience (Beckett's tentative gloss) draws from Didi the cry, 'Christ have mercy on us!' Mockery yields to mournful longing, a recurring undertone in these veiled biblical quotations.

Another such is Lucky's dance. Powerful, distorted echoes sound from the prophetic books of the Old Testament when the run-down prophet, white hair streaming from under his 'thinking' hat, performs his shambling, inscrutable dance. Pozzo informs his stage audience that the dancer calls it 'The Net'. In his 1975 production with the Schiller-Theater Werkstatt Beckett thought of having faint shadows of bars cast on the stage floor to suggest that Vladimir and Estragon too were trapped: '2 caged dynamics'.[9] The Bible is full of nets spread for the unwary soul; it is apparently one of the commonest images in the Old Testament. The narrator in Lamentations complains, 'He hath spread a net for my feet' (1: 13), and the most cruelly and unjustly tormented of God's servants, Job (often in Beckett's mind)[10] used the same image: 'Know now that God hath overthrown me, and hath compassed me with his net' (Job 19: 6). He also says, 'and mine hope hath he removed like a tree' (19: 10), another echo with relevance for *Godot*.

For those with some memory, however faint or garbled, of these ancient sayings, there must also be ominous recollections of God's unpredictable tendency to turn into his opposite. 'The Lord was as an enemy', complains the speaker of Lamentations (2: 5). Yet 'The Lord is my portion, saith my soul; therefore will I hope in him' (3: 24). For Vladimir and Estragon hope has to coexist with black scepticism—and the horrific thought (surfacing each time Pozzo appears) that the monster who keeps Lucky as a slave might really be Godot. Repetition of the word 'Lord', reflecting an ambiguous relationship with some dubious God, echoes through Beckett's theatre, as in *Eh Joe* when the voice taunts Joe: 'How's your Lord these days? . . . Still worth having? . . . Still lapping it up? . . . The passion of our Joe. . . . Wait till He starts talking to you [. . .] When He starts in on you.'

The prophets loom over the horizon again in *Godot*—in the cryptic form appropriate to them—when in Act 2 Didi calls on Gogo to look at the 'little cloud'. In Walter Asmus's production at the Gate Theatre, Dublin, in 1991 there was at this point a moment of weighted stillness which the word 'silence' always indicates in Beckett's stage directions. Gogo can't see the cloud and we are not told why Didi finds it so significant. It is another of those gaps which draws attention to unheard words. As ever, without necessarily being able to place it, some may hear—or half-hear, like Winnie—the biblical words which told Elijah a deadly drought was broken: a little cloud had appeared on the horizon, no bigger than a man's hand. Seven times he had asked his servant to look into the sky (they were up on Mount Carmel from where both sea and earth could be viewed) and seven times the servant had seen nothing. Then came the awaited sign, the 'little cloud', which was also the harbinger of a great personal change. God tells the prophet to prepare for his death, a state of rest from wandering for which he yearns, in common with all the driven servants of the Old Testament God (1 Kings 18: 44).

The vision of the prophet ordering his servant to scan the skies on his behalf becomes a central image in *Endgame*. The play rings with biblical echoes but they evoke a universal myth: the Flood. Beckett enjoys himself with the Noah's Ark flavour of Hamm (a resonant 'Ark' name) and the 'creatures' marooned with him in nothingness. It's common stock again; myth fusing with child's play, making it seem fitting that the apocalyptic vision towards the end should be embodied in a small boy.

Clov carries biblical echoes of his own: he is the look-out, climbing the ladder and reporting back to Hamm, as if to Noah or Elijah, what he sees through windows giving on to earth and sea. Both are visible, as from Mount Carmel, but not in one view; the ladder has to be laboriously moved for that. Prophecy has become more difficult. Mostly the biblical echoes are ambivalent. 'It is finished' loses its finality as Clov moves it towards the doubtful 'must be nearly finished', though lurking in the quotation, even in its modified form, remains an elusive possibility of an ending which is not random but meaningful, even perhaps the beginning of a new world. Characteristically, Beckett weaves specific biblical quotations into a universal web, where many beliefs and visions touch. In an early French draft of *Endgame* he had Clov report that the small boy approaching the shelter was looking downwards 'in the direction of the navel': Buddha joining hands with Noah and Elijah.

In the first of the radio plays, *All That Fall* (1957) biblical quotation is 'naturalized' by the Rooneys being church-goers, well able to fill out the tantalizing half-sentence that is the play's title. Less well versed listeners coming new to the play have to wait till near the end to feel the impact of the completed line, when Maddy answers Dan's query about the lesson for the coming Sunday: 'The Lord upholdeth all that fall and raiseth up all those that be bowed down' (Psalm 145: 14). Their shrieks of hysterical laughter at the idea are disturbing, though the play doesn't end on that note but with another kind of quotation, music from Schubert's 'Death and the Maiden'; a remote, heavenly sound.

A deep religious anxiety asserts itself in *Eh Joe*. The scraps of unfinished, often threatening biblical quotation are presented in quotation marks, as if requiring the voice to suggest authority as well as a sarcastic view of 'the passion of our Joe': '. . . Till one night. . . . "Thou fool thy soul. . . ." '. That can be felt as a voice of judgement even if we don't know the source, a parable in Luke's Gospel about the man who thinks his life belongs only to him but is warned that some night he will hear a knock at his door and a voice saying: 'Thou fool, this night thy soul shall be required of thee' (Luke 12: 20).

Another fragment carefully printed in quotation marks in Beckett's text will have a familiar ring to anyone who has attended a funeral service. A sardonic shorthand, 'Mud thou art', it darkly conflates the rain and mud conventionally associated with funerals with the sombre reminder of life's fragility which regularly punctuates Bible narratives: 'for dust thou art, and unto dust shalt thou return' (Genesis 3: 19); 'All flesh shall perish together, and man shall turn again unto dust' (Job 34: 15); 'they die, and return to their dust' (Psalm 104: 29).

It is mud rather than dust in *Eh Joe*, horridly appropriate to what is happening to him as he is forced down into the muddy depths of his mind. Dust is the image that takes over in the great final vision of *That Time* when the ordinary dust of the public library is transfigured:

> C. not a sound only the old breath and the leaves turning and then suddenly this dust whole place suddenly full of dust when you opened your eyes from floor to ceiling nothing only dust and not a sound only what was it it said [. . .] come and gone no one come and gone in no time gone in no time.

The poetic force behind Beckett's words tells us this is the dust that has haunted human minds since antiquity; many echoes could make their way in from visionary works of the world, the Bible being one: 'Then shall the dust return to the earth as it was; and the spirit shall return unto God who gave it' (Ecclesiastes 12: 7).

Not all the biblical quotations are doom-laden. The threatening voice in *Eh Joe* summons up images of faithful as well as faithless love. 'Great love', she says, apropos the dead girl: we may hear in the background a familiar saying, 'Greater love hath no man than this, that a man lay down his life for his friends' (John 15: 13). Close listening is demanded to catch these oblique allusions and the comparison into which they lead between human sexual love and the self-sacrificing love of the 'Lord' (disrespectfully referred to earlier as 'His Nibs'): '*There's love for you*. . . . Isn't it, Joe? . . . Wasn't it, Joe? . . . *Eh Joe*? . . . Wouldn't you say? . . . Compared to us. . . . Compared to

Him. . . . *Eh Joe*?' The text provides us with clues like the capitalized 'Him' which an actor will aim to convey by vocal emphasis. But the biblical quotations are on the edge of the action here. In *Not I* they are very much at the centre of Mouth's agony. Like those church-goers, the Rooneys, she knows her Bible; well enough to mock it with precision: ' . . . brought up as she had been to believe . . . with the other waifs . . . in a merciful . . . (*Brief laugh*.) . . . God . . . (*Good laugh*.)' Little fragments of benign teaching such as 'God is love' float through her mind; she derides but can't lose them: '. . . can't go on . . . God is love . . . she'll be purged . . . back in the field . . . morning sun . . . April . . .'. Once she has allowed her thoughts to flow this way, she hears whispers of mercy: '. . . then forgiven . . . God is love . . . tender mercies . . .'. Perhaps we too hear at these points, if only distantly, from childhood memories, the hymns and psalms that hold out these promises of mercy: 'Withhold not thou thy tender mercies from me, O Lord, let thy loving-kindness and thy truth continually preserve me' (Psalm 40: 11).

Her quotations are likely to bring with them, for some, familiar hymn tunes, deep-rooted in the common stock even if no longer regularly sung. An animated correspondence on this subject took place in *The Times* (September 1993) when readers were invited to choose the 'top ten' hymns: lists of favourites were sent in and feelings ran high. Beckett would have understood this well: the plays are full of hymnal sounds. In an early draft of *Happy Days* he gave Winnie a hymn to sing, though in the text as it stands she only repeats, soulfully, a fragment, 'Great mercies' (Beckett once thought of using it as the play's title). Krapp for many years quavered out 'Now the day is over': Beckett gave a variety of reasons for cutting it, including the nice idea that Krapp was by then probably too tired to sing. The hymn in *Not I* is represented like everything in the play by a fragment —'new every morning'—but how easy for anyone brought up as Mouth was (or Beckett) to complete it by hearing in their heads its confident tune:

> New every morning is the love
> Our wakening and uprising prove;
>
> . . . . .
>
> New mercies, each returning day,
> Hover around us while we pray.

Mouth takes a derisive line as most members of contemporary audiences (and probably congregations) would do at the point where the hymn continues along an excessively pious line, advising us, for instance, to be content with 'the trivial round, the common task'. This is not quoted by Mouth, however, nor is the hymnwriter's appeal for divine help to 'live more nearly as we pray' (*English Hymnal* (1951 edn.), 378).

What she does quote, repeatedly, is the hymn's opening line, 'New every morning', along with the snatch from the psalm, 'tender mercies'. Her frenetic, violent delivery makes it hard to distinguish changes of mood, but we can tell that there are struggles going on within, and might wonder about the words she leaves out of her quotations. Some she should heed perhaps, as when the psalmist appeals to the Lord 'Withhold not thy tender mercies', claiming, in support, 'I have not concealed thy loving kindness and thy truth' (Psalm 40: 10). The broken quotations come together at the end, a grace-note, we might say:

God is love . . . tender mercies . . . new every morning . . . back in the field . . . April morning . . . face in the grass . . . nothing but the larks . . . pick it up—

After *Not I* comes a remarkable change. The carapace of mockery is cut away or so thinned down that biblical words emerge with calm authority, as does the Evensong benediction in *Footfalls*. Ordinary little words of every day are moved towards biblical grandeur. It happens in *Rockaby* with 'living soul', an ordinary enough way of referring to loneliness: 'I didn't see a living soul all day'. The Woman in *Rockaby*, sitting at her window with its blind up, always looking for 'another like herself', is lonely in that common way, we may assume. The blinds of the others are always down. But a long echo from Genesis endows her longing for 'another living soul', with a greater loneliness, akin to that of Adam, the first-made 'living soul' (Genesis 2:7); alone in the universe until God created the 'other', Eve. Human and divine touch in oblique quotation throughout the Woman's dream-laden reverie. The human longing in her cry, 'those arms at last' reaches out also to the mystical consummation in the biblical vision she alludes to so elliptically (it has been incorporated into the language of her life): 'The Eternal God is thy refuge, and underneath are the everlasting arms' (Deuteronomy 33: 27).

A similar shift of mood can be traced in the patterns of quotation from the other most-tapped source, Shakespeare. Black irony broods over the near-quotation from *The Tempest* that emerges from wild, garbled fragments when Lucky imagines the sufferings of those in hell: 'and suffers like the divine Miranda with those who for reasons unknown but time will tell are plunged in torment.' In those few words (Lucky's 'think' is a masterpiece of compression) he evokes the shipwreck magicked up by Prospero and the anguish of Miranda's response to it: 'O, I have suffer'd | With those that I saw suffer!' Lucky's epithet, 'divine' plays with Shakespeare's word 'admired' ('Admir'd Miranda! | Indeed the top of admiration!'), taking even further the Latinate sense the word had then: 'to be wondered at'. Miranda's capacity to feel so keenly the suffering of strangers, seems to place her in another dimension than that inhabited by the unpitied carrier.

In other early plays ebullient variations are played on famous lines, first startling us with comic incongruity, then opening up deeper connections between the quoters and the quoted. The line that opens *Come and Go*—'When did we three last meet?'—amuses with its echo from *Macbeth* ('When shall we three meet again?'), but by the end of the play the allusion falls like a sombre shadow over Ru's commonplace question. We see that for the three refined women in their decorous long dresses and shady hats a sombre destiny lies in wait as for Macbeth; it can't be averted, only responded to, with feelings good or bad.

Hamm, openly histrionic, declaims or parodies Shakespearian lines with mocking relish: 'Our revels now are ended'; 'My kingdom for a nightman'. We can't help but laugh: Prospero's word, 'revels', seems the last word for the dour routines of *Endgame*; Richard III's swashbuckling 'My kingdom for a horse' comically inappropriate to the homely needs that bother Hamm ('What about that pee? I'm having it').

Or, conversely, the echoes elevate Hamm and his creatures, give them heroic status, as they struggle with the need for pain-killers, a rest in the kitchen, clean sand in the dustbins. The 'revels' too are real in their way. The quotation certainly prompts us to see Hamm as a magician. Chair-bound, earth-bound, he yet creates a world in which Clov, Nagg, and Nell gain a strange extension of life, though always on a knife edge. When Nell ceases to speak ('Is she dead?') she vanishes as instantly as the spirits performing the betrothal masque for Prospero. He has only to turn his mind from them, and—'These our actors, | As I foretold you, were all spirits, and | Are melted into air, into thin air'.

So it is with Hamm, with the difference that his Ariel, if such Clov is, can't quite be imagined vanishing. Much 'quotation comedy' of this equivocal kind occurs in *Happy Days*. It can cause slight shocks, as when Winnie uses a resonant line from *Cymbeline*—'Fear no more the heat o' the sun'—as a hearing test for Willie: can he hear it from his hole? 'Is this literary vandalism?' might be our question. The line comes from the touching dirge spoken by her brother over the seemingly dead body of Imogen, unrecognized by him in her boy's disguise. Should something so delicate and moving be reduced, made to amuse us, as it certainly does when Winnie shouts it at an increasingly irritated Willie?

But it is not to be reduced. If we know *Cymbeline* and its emotional complexities, the quotation, though so brief, will cast a piquant light on Winnie. It might give a different slant, for one thing, on her devoted subservience to Willie, rather provoking to feminist critics, as when she thanks him profusely for kindly answering her: 'I know what an effort it costs you.' Imogen's husband received similarly inappropriate gratitude. Yet there is an eventual triumph of love in Shakespeare's play which audiences tend to take as touching and right: perhaps some of that feeling will flow over to Winnie, who reminds us of it. Even if we don't pick up the context, however, the line itself speaks to us; calmly it holds out the prospect of release from the 'heat o' the sun', for Winnie an only too real and terrible condition. It is a wonderful moment, growing easily out of the absurdity of the hearing test, when Willie, tired of assuring her that he can hear, shouts back 'violently' the first half of the line only: 'Fear no more'. Consolation can come through unlikely channels.

Winnie's hyper-consciousness of time's depredations on her body finds expression in scraps of Shakespearian verse so truncated ('no damask', 'ensign crimson', 'pale flag') they can only be thought of as said to herself, not us, even if a quick ear will catch them. With the first she reminds herself of beauty's decline and its connection with frustrated love in Viola's tale of the 'sister', unable to reveal her love, who 'let concealment, like a worm i' th'bud, | Feed on her damask cheek'. Poor Winnie, long frustrated in love, has lost the damask from her cheek, but can't conceal that, or anything else, any more.

Her other fragments, 'ensign crimson' and 'pale flag', also refer to feminine beauty, this time strangely enduring. Romeo is conjured up, gazing painfully at Juliet in her tomb, wondering at the crimson ('beauty's ensign') on her lips and cheeks: 'And death's pale flag is not advanced there'. It is a dream that Winnie can't part with, of a beauty never to be lost: 'brief dream' is a recurring instruction in Beckett's production notebook. Yet she, who quotes from the dirge in *Cymbeline*, can't but have in mind its grave reminder: 'Golden lads and girls all must, | As chimney-sweepers, come to dust.' The word 'golden' trembles on her tongue and she almost breaks down when she remembers how Willie once used it of her hair.

Minute fragments such as these last depend for their recognition to some extent on support from a context brimming with quotations, artfully placed and projected as quotation, like 'Fear no more the heat o' the sun'. A sea-change occurs in the plays of the final phase. Now the words of Shakespeare flow in a continuum with the narrators' own; they have become part of their account of themselves, are felt to have been always that, always deep in their minds. Speaker in *A Piece of Monologue* says that the 'he' in his story has no identity of his own, is only 'The words falling from his mouth'. Among these words, in the first account of the recurring funeral, a Shakespearian echo sounds; faint, incomplete, yet unmistakable for those who know the play it comes from:

> Umbrellas round a grave. Seen from above. Streaming black canopies. Black ditch beneath. Rain bubbling in the black mud. Empty for the moment. That place beneath.

In such a context 'That place beneath' must in the first place suggest the grave in the black mud ('seen from above', that obsessively recurring stage direction). A sombre vision, it is modified by an echo from *The Merchant of Venice*; Portia's lofty appeal for mercy which rises above the earth, to invoke heaven:

> The quality of mercy is not strain'd,—
> It droppeth as the gentle rain from heaven
> Upon the place beneath.

The grim finality of the grave in the 'bubbling black mud' is lightened and softened by that humane echo.

In *Ohio Impromptu* Beckett joins hands with Shakespeare as if the two writers were themselves the twin souls we see on the stage before us, weaving their story out of their sorrow and finding consolation there. In a persuasive argument for seeing the play as tragi-comedy, Verna Foster has traced the connections between *Ohio Impromptu* and *The Winter's Tale*, a play tied by Beckett to his own with the finest threads.

'So the sad tale a last time told', says Reader at the end, bringing before the mind's eye Shakespeare's Mamillius, responding to his mother's request for a story ('As merry as you will') with an ominous choice: 'A sad tale's best for winter'. It's the prelude to the 'real-life' sad tale of a young boy who dies and is mourned over, as the 'dear face' in Beckett's play is mourned. Shakespeare allows a spring awakening after the years of sorrow: Hermione's statue comes to life on a magical command. There is no such 'reawakening' (Reader's word) in Beckett's story. 'So sat on as though turned to stone' sounds like a reversal of 'Be stone no more'.

But it is not quite so bleak. Something has been achieved. 'As lived experience' suggests Verna Foster, 'the events narrated by Reader are painful but as story they comfort'.[11] The audience does receive this comfort, I believe, and so, we may imagine, do Reader and Listener. They may sit 'as though turned to stone', but Reader strikes the note of achievement in his last words: 'So the sad tale a last time told. (*Pause*.) Nothing is left to tell.' It is then that for the first time Reader and Listener raise their heads and look at each other. Their look was to be unblinking, expressionless, Beckett said. Yet it suggests that in their 'profounds of mind' they are at one: a calm consummation has been achieved, in which *The Winter's Tale* has played its kindly part.

In moments such as these the camaraderie we enjoy through quotation in Beckett's theatre becomes a communion of living souls: we share in words that bring long echoes with them and create echoes likely to be as long.

7
Rhythms

AT my first meeting with Beckett on 30 April 1976, sitting in the bar of the Royal Court Hotel, we almost at once went into a Yeatsian rhythm. I was telling him of the video recordings I had arranged to have made of two productions of Yeats's plays—*The Cat and the Moon* and *At the Hawk's Well*—when at the mention of the latter he instantly broke into its great opening line, 'I call to the eye of the mind'. It seemed natural to join in and we continued the extempore reading to the end of the first stanza, on the line 'The salt sea wind has swept bare'. It was an exhilarating, three-party conversation.[1]

Yeats's rhythm was compelling, but of course on that occasion it was Beckett's that had me gripped. It was almost a shock to find this genius so unaffected, so completely himself, speaking with the Irish intonations of his youth, ready to be interested, quizzical, sparing of words but generous with them too. He spoke of what he was engaged in at the time, the rehearsals for *Footfalls*, inviting me to attend if I cared to: they were happening just across the road, at the Royal Court Theatre. He was interested in the productions of his plays he had given me permission to make (we had already had correspondence on this). And he was interested in the life going on around: he told me how the hotel worker who greeted him as we left had confided in him a complicated story of his troubles: he had promised him a ticket for *Footfalls* but doubted if he would use it.

It was the sympathetic personality already known from the work, familiar in the way his appearance was, from so many photographs: tall, spare, erect, with the blue eyes that looked very straight at you. There was a feeling that anything specious or false would wither under his look, not that there was the least touch of the censorious in it.

In conversations over the years that followed, in Paris and London, rhythms of other writers found their way in, especially of those dear to Beckett from his youth on. He knew I had written on Yeats and his contemporaries and was engaged in trying for live performances and recordings such as those just mentioned, so Irish writers were a natural topic of talk. He had a strong feeling for Goldsmith, who 'wrote so well'. His tendency to say silly things, Beckett thought, was probably because of the pressure on him from Dr Johnson's circle. Lady Gregory came up in conversation as late as 1987 (11 January): he was inclined to blame her for the 'shocking' rejection of *The Silver Tassie*: 'She had the say in all to do with the Abbey. It couldn't have been rejected without her.' The rejection was still alive for him, as were plays by O'Casey he had seen at the Abbey: he glowed when recalling Barry Fitzgerald and F. J. McCormick in the famous parts.

Sometimes there were surprises as when, on 14 November 1986, he told me he had been rereading the whole of Synge and found some of it less to his taste than it had been. The plays suffered most in this revaluation. His own plays of course often contain echoes of Synge, sometimes very close. Anyone familiar with *The Playboy of the Western World*, for instance, will easily hear behind Lucky's mournful refrain, 'the skull in Connemara', the voice of Synge's Jimmy, relishing 'the skulls they have in Dublin, ranged out like blue jugs in a cabin of Connaught'. In a more general way, there are affinities between the blind couple who make the world for themselves from words in *The Well of the Saints* and Beckett's lonely tale-spinners. But he wasn't as impressed by that play, he said, as he used to be: the 'phoney' aspects of the language (as people had said then) seemed more obvious now.

Synge's poems, however, had for the most part retained their power for him. He recited one of them with much feeling. His admiration for Synge had not gone, only changed in emphasis; an experience most readers have as life goes on.

He hadn't changed his mind about Shaw so far as I could gather, but maintained the relative indifference he had expressed in 1956 when asked to contribute a few words on him to a centenary programme in Dublin. He would 'give the whole unupsettable applecart', he had said, 'for a sup of the Hawk's Well, or the Saints', or a whiff of Juno, to go no further'.[2] Shaw was too voluble for him though sly allusions in his fiction—like the 'hushabied' in 'A Wet Night'[3]—suggest enjoyment of the Shavian humour when at its most freewheeling, balanced on the knife-edge of farce.

It was the faculty he admired so much in O'Casey, whom he had called the 'master of knockabout', able to explode 'even the most complacent solidities . . . from the furniture to the higher centres'.[4]

Eleutheria seems only a step away! As late as our meeting in November 1986 his enthusiasm hadn't waned: he recommended to me, having heard well of them, productions of *The Plough and the Stars* and *Purple Dust* currently on the Left Bank, which, alas, I didn't have time to track down. He would speak too of Eileen and Shivaun O'Casey, knowing I had met Shivaun years before. He was very sympathetic to her attempts to establish a theatre in Ireland partly devoted to her father's plays. I would have liked to tell him how she and I met again, in 1996, when we were both involved in a BBC radio programme on O'Casey and music, a subject that would surely have interested him.[5]

Yeats was always a presence in the background of these talks, as he is in the plays from the moment when Vladimir murmurs 'The wind in the reeds', a slanted echo from the title of an early collection, *The Wind Among the Reeds* (1899). Some allusions are near-parody, like Words' pompous 'Arise then and go now', with its hint at 'The Lake Isle of Innisfree'; some, like Winnie's 'I call to the eye of the mind', need to be taken as seriously as it was by Winnie's creator. He told me once that *At the Hawk's Well* was his favourite among Yeats's plays, adding immediately, 'and *Purgatory*'. The poems were much in his mind. When I gave him as a birthday gift in 1986 an edition of *The Wind Among the Reeds*, he seemed pleased, telling me that he only had the *Collected Poems*. Yeats's celebrated readings of his poems rather amused him, I think: 'booming' was his nice word for it. He was greatly entertained by the rumbustious doings of Yeats's father, John Butler Yeats, described in William Murphy's biography (*Prodigal Father*, 1978). He had not been rereading W.B., he told me, but enjoying the life of 'old John': 'What a man!' (letter, 20 April 1987).

I turn now to another kind of rhythm, that of actors and musicians, so crucial to the appreciation of plays which construct subtle music for the speaking voice (and often yearn towards pure musical form). I came into close contact with these rhythms when working on productions of *Eh Joe* (1972), *Words and Music* (1973), *Embers* (1976), and *Cascando* (1984). I have written elsewhere on this subject,[6] but should probably explain here that in the early 1970s little of Beckett's theatrical *œuvre* was to be seen in performance, and recordings were rare. When invited by an adventurous university administrator, Winifred Bamforth, in 1972, to organize a course of public lectures on Beckett in central London, I found, with chagrin, that illustrations were not to be had for my own lecture on 'Audio-visual Beckett' (the BBC had no loan system and the original productions hadn't been broadcast since their transmission a decade earlier). This led me to try for new recordings, an aim generously supported by Michael Clarke, Director of the University of London Audio-Visual Centre, even though he knew well that the material would be more expensive than that usually requested. Beckett kindly gave consent for new productions to be made. A talented senior producer at the centre, David Clark, was to be director, responsible for all the technical work; I had overall responsibility for the realization of Beckett's texts; we rehearsed the actors together.[7]

By great good fortune we had Patrick Magee to play for us in our first three productions. He loved the plays and liked the chance to explore the roles again—or for the first time (the part of Joe had gone to Jack MacGowran). We were fortunate also in having my friend Elvi Hale to play the voice in *Eh Joe* and also Ada (and the child, Addie) in *Embers*. She had played Nell in the 1964 production of *Endgame* in Paris, with Patrick Magee and Jack MacGowran. When at one point in rehearsals the actors had become depressed, she told me, Beckett, who took a hand in the directing, said in surprise 'It's meant to be hopeful'; a wonderful ray of light on the play. One of the revelations that came from working with actors of this calibre was the variation they made possible, not by evading textual instructions, but simply by the impact of their distinct personal rhythms. For Magee, mute in *Eh Joe*, the rhythm came through his facial structure, with its suggestion of flamboyant emotional energy, its mobile, slightly mephistophelean eyebrows (he was a thrilling Mephistopheles in a production in 1980 of Marlowe's *Doctor Faustus*). His 'plangent monotone' was alive with energy as Richard Cave put it, in a sensitive account of Magee's vocal tone and its effectiveness in Beckett's monologues.[8] Magee's Joe created a different dramatic rhythm from MacGowran's; eventually more tragic.

There was a correspondingly strong contrast with Elvi Hale. She was a little worried at having to rely only on voice, being more experienced on stage and in film than on radio. But she brought to the role a highly individual vocal tone and rhythm: on the dry side, with a sharp, humorous edge and a capacity for startling change when she moved into a deeper register, as in the threnody for the dead girl in *Eh Joe*. She found herself pushed towards a slight Irish accent by turns of phrase like—'Will I tell you now?', 'Will I play my piece now?'—but the effect was unstrained, not always the case when non-Irish actors use an Irish accent. Again in *Embers* a similarly wry, level tone served as ground base for the frequent variations of mood called for in that play.

Music introduced a new, unknown dimension when we made *Words and Music*. I had expected to use the original music by John Beckett, Beckett's cousin, but on asking his permission received a courteous refusal: he had withdrawn it. In 1996 he told me more of this when we met at a Beckett conference at Goldsmiths, University of London: he was convinced that his music wasn't up to the level of Beckett's genius. I respected his modesty and great love of his cousin's art but felt sad too, for him, that he couldn't have let his music stand: by that time I had heard, and liked, it.

This came about after Beckett had given me permission for new music; he added that if I had no composer in mind, he would suggest Humphrey Searle (letter, 12 July 1973). My first meeting with Humphrey, on 12 October 1973, was at Broadcasting House where he had arranged for us to hear the original recording of *Words and Music* (he had a long-standing connection with the BBC). It turned out to be a curiously 'Beckettian' occasion, to use for once that overused word.

We were shown up to a room on a high floor where the recording was to be played to us on our own; our guide would just look in after a while to check that all was well. She left us in a slightly awkward silence: Humphrey was a shy man: we really needed the recording to give us our subject-matter. But the silence continued so long that it got us talking: what was wrong, what should we do? Our guide reappeared, was astonished, went off to investigate and returned with piquant news: the recording was playing away on the floor above—to an empty room. Silence and emptiness: a proper start to our venture!

From there on we moved into a fruitful collaboration. Humphrey Searle's music expressed a personality in tune with the modernist strain in Beckett: he had previously set to music works by Edith Sitwell and Joyce (*Gold Coast Customs*, 1949; *The Riverrun*, 1951), and he struck me as relishing the spiky ironies, discordances, and exaggerated 'warm' sentiments of Words and Music at the start of the play. We had much discussion of the fluctuating moods and the startling change when affectations give way to genuine feeling. For this Humphrey would find a new rhythm that couldn't be defined in advance: 'Music has its own logic', he said.

When I heard him conducting his music for our recording in 1973 with the Sinfonia of London, a small group of strings, woodwind, and percussion, it seemed to me that he had tracked very exactly the movement Beckett called for, from shallowness and false starts to depth and calm. Playfulness was maintained in a satisfying way almost to the end, a mischievous note in an ever-deepening lyricism. The sonorous bassoon would play comically with homely detail like the 'hag' arriving to put the pan in the bed—'And bring the toddy'. Then it produced a resonant, long-drawn-out sound, the viola made a dark-toned response, and together they led into the lyric of the 'wellhead', a melody so haunting, it seemed to me only natural that Words would plead 'Again' at its conclusion. He is 'trying' to sing it, says the text; this was clearly the right word for Patrick's rendering: he was forced to raise his voice upward, on the 'wellhead', to a harmony rather beyond him. Music had its own struggles but the final impression was that the little poems on 'Age' and the 'Wellhead' couldn't be reached without his aid.

Beckett heard the recordings of *Words and Music* and *Embers*. He was in London at the time of the 'hearing' David and I had arranged in May 1976 for an invited audience at Royal Holloway College (where I was at the time Reader in English Literature).[9] He wouldn't come to that, but told me he would like to hear them if he could do so without others present. I took this perhaps too literally and came to regret that I hadn't stretched it a bit and invited David to be there too. He met Beckett later, however, when showing his new version of *Film*.

It was a strange experience to sit alone with Beckett on the morning of 15 May in the empty lecture theatre at Royal Holloway, listening to plays which, he said, he had written so long ago he could hear them now almost as if they weren't his at all. *Embers* he hadn't looked at 'for ages': he seemed to enjoy it, chuckling, for instance, at the conversation about Addie's age: 'It took us a long time to have her. (*Pause.*) Years we kept hammering away at it.' He approved Elvi Hale's level tone and thought she had an 'interesting voice'; perhaps a touch over-emphatic here and there but with the right strangeness. She amused him as Addie, wailing at Henry's exasperated 'Go on with you when you're told and look at the lambs!' The sea sound rushing in over Ada's 'Oh' in the flashback pleased him ('exactly right'): and Patrick's sigh at the end was 'good'.

Some things might have been differently or better done, of course, but he just touched on them: we should, for instance, have had a sharper 'drip' (one of the hard sounds Henry calls for, to counteract the sucking sound of the sea). He was entertained by Patrick's rolling flamboyance at certain points in both plays. I wondered what he would think of the attempts to sing, those moments when, suggested Clas Zilliacus, the play becomes 'the closest thing there is in the Beckett canon to an opera'.[10] Words is meant to be groping and hesitant, but someone who had heard our recording thought Patrick seemed not to know what he was doing. He himself had joked that the direction 'trying to sing' would be only too well realized by him. Beckett might have agreed, I don't know: he only speculated tolerantly that perhaps he'd had a few jars.

It couldn't have bothered him much for he also said that the 'two little poems' came up well. The music was the determinant here. He liked it and asked me to convey his congratulations to Humphrey Searle. 'Music always wins', he said, though on a more general note he agreed that humour was usually outside its range; he didn't find musical jokes very funny. Later he was to approve our commissioning music from Searle again, for *Cascando*. All this was a great pleasure to Humphrey; he had met Beckett, once, I believe, in Paris and deeply appreciated the opportunity to create music for the plays as Fiona Searle confirmed some years after his death when I was trying, with kindly support from Edward Beckett, to find a way of making Searle's score for *Words and Music* available to potential directors.[11]

The college audio-visual technician who played the tapes for us admitted rather nervously to not having read *Embers*: yes, that would make playing it more difficult Beckett agreed, putting him instantly at ease. I'd kept strictly to his wish for privacy but the Principal, Lionel Butler, wanted to offer a gesture of hospitality before our return journey to London. In the hope of this happening he had laid on some Guinness, not his own favourite drink, but known to be one of Beckett's. It led to a rather charming ice-breaking incident when the Principal poured drinks for us and his one other guest (Christopher Ricks, who had stayed overnight in the college after giving an evening lecture). Though a most accomplished host, the Principal was having trouble with the unfamiliar Guinness when Beckett good-humouredly took the bottle from his shaking hand and saw to it himself, remarking 'I'm a dab hand at pouring Guinness'. I was moved to discover, when I told him of Lionel Butler's sadly premature death in 1981, that Beckett still remembered the meeting and 'the Guinness episode' (letter, 12 December 1981).

The distinctive dual rhythm springing from the personalities of Patrick Magee and Humphrey Searle was one we were not to experience again. Patrick had agreed to play Voice for us in *Cascando*, a play I was particularly keen to have recorded, being tantalized by the dotted line which is Music's only identity in the text. The production was delayed, first by Patrick's other commitments, then by the illness which ended in the sad blow of his death: we were shattered by this. In 1978, however, with the future still uncertain, Humphrey Searle was given the commission for the music for *Cascando*. It was possible for him to work on it separately; there was no quasi-operatic relationship with Voice here, though timing had to be very exact, to keep the two synchronized. I recall intensely concentrated sessions with Humphrey, trying to pin down for him my impressions of Woburn's strange journey with the requisite precision: so many seconds or minutes of this type of music here; such and such a phrasing there. As before, he conducted the music himself with a similar combination of instruments (the London Sinfonietta) and it was recorded by David Clark and his team in the BBC stereo studio arranged for by Michael Clarke.

Sadly Humphrey Searle never heard his music in the final production. He died in 1982: another great loss and grief. We were determined not to waste the music, which to my mind was exceptionally sensitive to the text. Renewed stirrings of life came about when we were able to cast as Voice another great Beckett actor, David Warrilow. Though already engaged in a Beckett programme,[12] he managed to fit us into his schedule. 'Good news indeed', Beckett said, when learning of this (letter, 6 January 1985). That piece of good fortune was matched by our securing Sean Barrett for Opener: the impeccable timing he brought from his radio theatre experience was very helpful to his fellow actor, so David Warrilow told me. The latter was a little concerned at first that their voices might be rather too alike in tone, but they came through in fact as utterly distinctive: David's gritty, panting, rushing; Sean's more mellow, full, and calm. The two met for the first time in Bloomsbury at the University Audio-Visual Centre where David Clark (now Director) had arranged for a weekend of rehearsing and recording. In the event we needed only one day, so well did the rhythms of the two actors play into each other.

The two voices had to flow in a triple stream with the music recorded so long before. It was an affecting experience to hear coming from 'above' (the studio source) as if out of the air, the mercurial sounds Humphrey had created: the flute motif summoning up

'Woburn', the occasional discordances among strings and woodwinds reflecting the uneasy, unreal distance between Opener and Voice; the delicate harmonies telling of the elusive 'island'. Voice and Opener calling out 'Come on' at the end, pursuing Woburn still, might seem immersed in failure, their story unfinished. But the sensuous impact of voices and music finally surging together suggested much more strongly, I thought, a kind of elation; or at least a desire to continue indefinitely in this magical, triple confluence.

Another kind of music, that of Maeterlinck, was much in my mind at this time. I was gathering material in Brussels and elsewhere for a slide-set on his plays in performance to be published in a series edited by my friend and colleague, Richard Cave, who shared my wish to communicate the concrete experience of theatre, through words, productions, slides, tapes, film: whatever medium best suited.[13] It was natural for Maeterlinck to make his way from time to time into conversations with Beckett. Though such different writers (most obviously in the matter of humour) Maeterlinck's technique of broken, interrupted speech often gave his plays a look of kinship. To be working on a play like *Words and Music*, that 'text-music tandem' as Beckett had called it, seemed an activity in tune with the Maeterlinck of the 1890s whose scripts, ideally, would be read almost like scores. He orchestrates the ordinary rhythms of common speech to suggest profound inner rhythms and the notation often has a musical tilt, as when a direction for 'silence' is followed by 'nouveau silence'.

The workings of this technique in *Pelléas and Mélisande*, that most romantic of his plays, seemed to me to bring it surprisingly close at times to *Godot*. Both plays plunge us into a world of 'not knowing'. *Pelléas* opens in the middle of a vast, empty forest, with Golaud helpless before Mélisande's silences. He can find nothing to explain her, where she came from, why she is there. As in *Godot*, only the present counts. She fends off intimacy—'Don't touch me! Don't touch me!'—and refuses to speak of how she has been hurt in a mysterious 'elsewhere':

GOLAUD. Who was it that hurt you?
MÉLISANDE. All of them! All of them!
GOLAUD. How did they hurt you?
MÉLISANDE. I will not tell! I can't tell!

At that point I was prone to hear Estragon's voice, similarly refusing to speak of his off-stage nightmares:

VLADIMIR. Gogo. (*Pause, Vladimir observes him attentively.*) Did they beat you? (*Pause.*) Gogo! (*Estragon remains silent, head bowed.*) Where did you spend the night?

ESTRAGON. Don't touch me! Don't question me! Don't speak to me! Stay with me!

The sense of lostness pervaded both plays, I felt. It's the most important thing we know about Mélisande: 'I am lost! . . . lost! . . . O! lost here . . . I don't belong here . . . I wasn't born here.' The style is different but the effect not too unlike the unease of Vladimir and Estragon, wondering if they're in the right place, on the right day; or are they really alone in the 'void'?

Maeterlinck is often over-rhetorical to modern taste, but the hesitations and silences of his early style can still affect us. There may be nothing quite equal to the potent stillness of the tableaux by the tree that close each act of *Godot*. But *Pelléas* has great moments of this kind too, notably the extraordinary entry of the servants in the final act, into the room where Mélisande lies dying. They come uncalled, range themselves around the walls, and wait; all in perfect silence. No one knows why they have come—and yet we all know. It's one of those uncanny expressions of intuition which in this play (as elsewhere in Maeterlinck's early theatre) make their way in to surprise us with their confidence, their freedom from the need to explain themselves.

The opera Debussy made from the play (in 1902) projected these moments into a musical idiom that broke with choruses and arias, and wove dialogue into union with pure orchestral sound. I wasn't sure whether it was the play or the opera Beckett had in mind when he took up my remarks about *Pelléas*. He thought of it as something that had been totally new, and known in this way to everyone. On this same occasion (30 April 1976) he called it 'marvellous'. I had the temerity once in London to try and take the subject further by reading him a passage from Maeterlinck's essay, 'The Tragedy of Everyday Life', in the Edwardian translation (*The Treasure of the Humble*, 1897) which I had with me at the time. It wasn't really fair to Maeterlinck, I'm afraid: the early translations are ponderous. I was in fact engaged at the time in trying for new ones, though not inclined to follow Beckett's suggestion that I should translate *Pelléas* myself; the French was simple he said.[14] Possibly the old translation had a certain appropriateness to the surroundings, the lounge of the Hyde Park Hotel, liked by Beckett, so he had told me, for being stately and shabby. But it wasn't enough to commend the passage I read: he only commented that it seemed rather turgid.

I came to feel that *Pelléas* had made a lasting impact but other plays of Maeterlinck were more in the margin of Beckett's consciousness. No such reservations applied to the affinity with Charles Dickens, though of course there were still gulfs between. Beckett could never have been imagined reading his works in public as Dickens did, causing weaker souls in his audience to faint when he 'performed' the horrific murder of Nancy by Bill Sykes. Yet in more private situations like rehearsals he could impress actors with his ability to bring his characters to vivid life. 'He was the best Winnie ever', said the German actress, Eva Katharina Schultz, referring to the help he gave her when she played Winnie by reading the whole play through in German.[15] 'He would have been the perfect Nagg' was Barry McGovern's reaction to hearing him tell the 'tailor' joke. (*Sunday Independent*, 31 December 1989). I had a glimpse of this power during a conversation about *Eh Joe* in the lounge of the Hyde Park Hotel on 21 May 1979, when suddenly, in a different, rougher tone, accompanied by an expressive movement of the hands, he said, 'You know what he's really doing—strangling her.' It was the voice of Joe, the one we never hear in the play, there for a flash before he returned to his usual tone, responding to my suggestion that Joe couldn't do it, with a quiet 'He might, we can't tell. He's suffering—it's not his voice—it's in his head.'

Yet despite differences, the personalities of Beckett and Dickens often touch, in their writing rhythms. There's an extra glow when we sense these meeting-places; above all, I think, when the comic rhythm wonderfully opens up to fine shades of deeper feeling without losing a shred of its essential buoyancy. I want to dwell briefly on the incursions of Dickensian rhythm into the plays, having enjoyed them since first hearing Estragon answer Vladimir's query 'How's your foot?' with a straight-faced 'Swelling visibly.' In the French original this is simply 'Il enfle' but in English it brings in an echo from Mr Weller Senior, reflecting (at the meeting of the Grand Junction Ebenezer Temperance Association) on the members' excessive tea-drinking: 'There's a young 'ooman on the next form but two, as has drunk nine breakfast cups and a half; and she's a swellin' wisibly before my wery eyes.' That 'wisibly', for those who recall it, makes a delicious extra joke. Two ruling habits touch: Dickens's enjoyment of Mr Weller's attitude to Vs and Ws ('Quite right too, Samivel . . . put it down a we'): Beckett's enjoyment of curious games with Ms and Ws ('M' upside-down).

There are many different kinds of echo, some comic/grim, as with the Dickensian grotesques, Nagg and Nell. Popping up in their dustbins when not 'bottled', they trail memories of the Smallweeds in *Bleak House*, those querulous invalids, incapacitated in the lower regions, sitting on either side of the fireplace like battered dolls in their 'two black horse-hair porter's chairs'. The male of the pair, as in *Endgame*, is the livelier, shouting at intervals for comforts ('Shake me up, Judy!') or throwing cushions at his feebler wife. Nagg connects with him in flashes of truculence and irritating parrot cries: 'Me sugar-plum!' But he is kinder to his wife and mourns her death, something not to be imagined of Mr Smallweed.

Dickensian names find their way in: *David Copperfield* has a little Minnie, as has *All That Fall*, and a Ham, as has *Endgame* (with an extra 'm'). Many fascinating comparisons have been traced. John Pilling and H. Porter Abbott, for example, have noted the striking likeness between the master–slave relationship of *Godot* and that in *Little Dorrit* where Blandois issues commands to Cavaletto like 'Get up, pig!' and 'Sing the Refrain, pig. You could sing it once.'[16] Any reader of Dickens who knows *Footfalls* is likely to recall that other spectral, self-imprisoned being, Miss Havisham, in her once white dress, 'all yellow and withered' and the 'phantom air' upon her of 'something that had been and was changed' (a line whose rhythm could easily allow it to be taken for one of Beckett's). In both works there is a sense of characters sprung from some deep, remote source, not to be fully explained, any more than a dream can be. Dickens said his people often came to him unsought ('I thought of Pickwick') and came speaking: every word they said could be 'distinctly heard' by him. Beckett has spoken in a similar way about not knowing where his writing came from and of 'hearing' it; as the sound of a voice, perhaps, or the cartwheels, dragging steps, and panting that brought *All That Fall* to him in the dead of night.

Maddy Rooney's laborious journey to and from the railway station will surely strike readers of Dickens as having a touch of the epic quality of his many journeys: the old man and his granddaughter trudging the sinister roads of *The Old Curiosity Shop*; David Copperfield's painful struggle to haven at Betsy Trotwood's. With the last, another echo springs up: the doleful sound of Mrs Gummidge complaining. Any little thing is liable to bring a flood of tears from that 'lone lorn creetur' as she calls herself. A smoking fire can set off a bout of melancholy and when kind Mr Peggotty tries to cheer her—'Oh, it'll soon leave off'—and 'besides, you know, it's not more disagreeable to you than to us'—that's no comfort to her. 'I feel it more', she says.

Beckett's Maddy Rooney frequently falls into a similarly 'complaining' rhythm. She asks Mr Tyler to tell her blind husband that his 'poor wife' is too upset to meet him because 'it all came over me again, like a flood'. When her listener fails in sympathy she moans 'Can't you see I'm in trouble? (*With anger*.) Have you no respect for misery? (*Sobbing*.) Minnie! Little Minnie!' We never hear the full story of little Minnie, so don't know how seriously to take this lamentation. It's certainly rather absurd when she broods on Minnie's age: 'In her forties now she'd be, I don't know, fifty, girding up her lovely little loins, getting ready for the change'. Yet who knows? I guess we can take clues from Dickens here. Mrs Gummidge was a bit of a test case for Beckett, to judge from a passage in an early piece of fiction, 'A Wet Night', when a complaining Belacqua is advised sharply by his lady love not to 'put across the Mrs Gummidge [. . .] on me'.[17] He hadn't intended to, he thinks to himself: his distress is profound and 'unaffected'.

The need to make that distinction is a compelling challenge for Beckett, as for Dickens. We are invited by them both first to laugh, then to think again about the extravagances of grief: Mrs Gummidge's 'wimmicking', Maddy Rooney's cries of woe (the text of *All That Fall* is spattered with directions like '*sobbing*', '*The voice breaks*', '*brokenly*', and—surely comic—'*Handkerchief. Vehemently*'). Yet they are genuine sufferers too, as Mr Peggotty explains gently to David. People find Mrs Gummidge's crying 'peevish', but they didn't know her before the death of her husband, the 'old 'un': 'Now I *did* know the old 'un and I know'd his merits, so I unnerstan' her.'

So it is with Maddy; we listen more sympathetically when she is grieving not just for herself, nor, vastly, for the ills of the world, but for particular individuals: 'poor Dan' or the 'poor woman' listening to Schubert's music, all alone in the 'ruinous old house'.

Maddy connects briefly with another Dickensian character when she comically attempts to remember a line of verse: 'Sigh out a something something tale of things, Done long ago and ill done.' Flora Finching of *Little Dorrit* just twinkles over the horizon. But the great link here is between Flora and Winnie, prime 'scramblers' of literature, both. Flora Finching in full spate is a wonderful phenomenon: 'there was a time dear Arthur that is to say decidedly not dear nor Arthur neither but you understand me when one bright idea gilded the what's-his-name horizon of et cetera but it is darkly clouded now and all is over'. Winnie comes close on her heels, brimming over with half-remembered lines: 'something something laughing wild amid severest woe'. She keeps the beat as Flora wildly fails to do: 'such is the habit of times forever fled, and so true it is that oft in the stilly night ere slumber's chain has bound people, fond memory brings the light of other days around people'.

Winnie's superior command of scansion is one of many differences between them which make Flora more obviously a figure of fun. But she isn't only that. Like Winnie, brooding on being 'so changed from what I was', Flora touches the chord of sympathy when she anxiously greets Arthur Clennam, knowing he will find her 'fearfully changed'. She can make a heroic effort too, also like Winnie, when she braces herself with wry exaggeration: 'I am actually an old woman, it's shocking to be so found out.'

Both 'babble' away (Winnie's word) but return to certain fixed leitmotifs: the 'old way', the 'old style'. Flora can't escape her 'old habit' of calling Arthur Clennam by his Christian name—nor her new one of continually correcting herself: 'Arthur!—pray excuse me—old habit—Mr Clennam far more proper.' This gets cut down to the amusing: 'Arthur,—Mr Clennam far more proper'. Winnie's 'the old style' is a more enigmatic version of just such a mental shorthand which Flora, obligingly, always fills in: 'Oh Mr Clennam . . . you have not lost your old way of paying compliments, your old way when you used to pretend to be so sentimentally struck.'

The amused disdain some critics have felt for Winnie's disjointed rhythm is matched by Arthur Clennam's reaction at his first meeting with the 'changed' Flora. Could she really have been so silly as this, he wonders, when they were young and in love? It's certainly silly when she reminds him of the 'dear old days' before their parents 'severed the golden bowl—I mean bond but I dare say you know what I mean'. But he does come to know what she means, comes to appreciate the true feeling behind the disconnections and the 'warmth of heart' in her tone 'when she referred, however oddly, to the youthful relation in which they had stood to one another'.

Winnie has no one to speak for her; she has to do it for herself, in her changes of tone. She succeeds, I imagine, for most people. Arthur

Clennam might almost have her too in mind when he reflects on Flora's strange interweaving of the past into 'their present interview' and how, in his matured response 'his sense of the sorrowful and his sense of the comical were curiously blended'.

It is that complex rhythm of sympathy above all, I feel, which brings into the ring of fellowship both writers and those who love their work.

At the last of my meetings with Beckett, on 9 November 1989 at the *maison de retraite* in the rue Rémy Dumoncel, not very long before he died (on 22 December 1989) the Yeatsian rhythm returned like a tidal wave. I had written to tell him I planned to go via Paris to Caen to speak at a symposium on Yeats:[18] he had said he would like to see me if he were well enough. My friends, Martha Fehsenfeld and Lois Overbeck, the editors of his correspondence, kindly put me up for the night in the flat they were renting: they had found his state of health fluctuating from one day to the next so I was very happy when he rang to say he would expect me the next morning.

Others have written of the *maison de retraite*, with its quiet courtyard on to which Beckett's room opened. I will only say how, as I walked along, looking for the door, I found he'd left it open for me and when I called out how lovely it was to see him again, he called back, 'What's left of me'. It might sound grim but was somehow the opposite: a little bleak but wonderfully reassuring, said in his familiar, kindly, half-humorous tone.

In the course of a conversation that ranged rather widely, Yeats moved twice to the centre, most affectingly. Beckett wanted to know about the symposium: who would be there, what were their topics, what was mine? The answer to that last was 'The Circus Animals' Desertion', the poem in which Yeats accepts that he will need to let go the 'ladder' he has made from legends, actors, and the 'painted stage' and 'lie down where all the ladders start, | In the foul rag-and-bone shop of the heart'. Beckett took up the lines, going straight from them to the angry question that opens 'The Tower': what to do with 'Decrepit age that has been tied to me | As to a dog's tail?' It was natural to tell him then how much I'd loved his use of the closing lines from that great poem in . . . *but the clouds* . . . and for us to end by repeating them together. It was a close of sorrowful serenity, as in the poem and the play he built around it.

8
Magnetic Beckett

BECKETT was a magnet for performers and artists—actors, musicians, painters, dancers—before criticism caught up with the idea of the work's immense capacity for performance (the fiction as well as the plays proper). Reviewers were often more than a step behind. Jack MacGowran impressed them in Dublin with his one-man Beckett programme, *End of Day* (Gaiety Theatre, 5 October 1962), but *Happy Days* at the Eblana Theatre the following year drew some confused and unhappy responses. The 'astonishing virtuosity' of Marie Keane was recognized in terms not flattering to the author: it was her night, said one reviewer 'above all others (including Beckett)' (*Irish Independent*, 2 October 1963). The same reviewer praised the player but not the 'dismal attitude' of the playwright when MacGowran returned in 1965 (to the Lantern Theatre) with his compilation, by then called *Beginning to End*.

Speaking the words aloud, or hearing them spoken, has been for many a buoyant way in to Beckett's art. Just the sound can do it, whether or not completed by theatrical settings and the silent speech of face and body. Beckett encouraged 'speakings' of the work when he felt a performer was in tune with it, even sometimes when he had reservations about a particular programme, as with MacGowran's. He persuaded him to drop the mime, *Act Without Words*, as out of place, but the actor couldn't bear to lose Lucky's 'think', though it couldn't be expected to work properly stripped of dramatic context. Admittedly I have seen that happen but once only, when Jean Martin, the first Lucky, spoke it in the original French on the stage of the Olivier Theatre in 1990.[1] Under the spell of Martin's exquisite rhetorical command of a speech full of wild, disordered pain and dark wit, we became for that time the audience in the Théâtre de Babylone, all those years ago. A deeply affecting experience, made possible because in delivering an extract Martin brought the whole play with him.

MacGowran too could, of course, bring Beckett's characters, especially from the fiction, wonderfully to life, as anyone will know who saw him on stage—or in television compilations such as that made by the BBC in 1990, in which he projects exuberant passages from *Molloy* with wicked naturalness, aided by his odd idiosyncratic look of a gnarled elf, capable of anything. He makes it seem the most reasonable thing in the world to be set on transferring sixteen pebbles with ever-accelerating mad logic from one pocket of his great shapeless overcoat to another, so as to suck them 'in impeccable succession', then to throw it all away with an insouciant 'But deep down I didn't give a tinker's curse'.[2] Such inspired performances must have sent many to the books for the first time; a desirable outcome for any author and surely for Beckett, with a bitter experience behind him of the struggle to get his first novel published. Years later, another Irish actor, Barry McGovern, expressed a hope, in the programme to the Dublin premiere of *I'll Go On*, his staging of extracts from the Molloy trilogy, that it would send people to the books of 'the greatest unread author in the world'. Beckett might have been amused to know that on the strength of the first half of the show he was pronounced by a reviewer 'one of the best comic script-writers of all time' (*Irish Times*, 25 September 1985). He didn't see the production but approved the project and what he was told of it, by the actor among others (in a conversation I had with him in 1986 he remarked that McGovern had 'a real Dublin face', clearly a plus).

Those who have felt the magnetic pull of Beckett's art usually want to share it with others in some way. Theatre has offered a potent means. It took the waif-like MacGowran, trailing memories of Chaplin, though himself unique, to raise Beckett's profile in the USA, so Jordan R. Young has suggested. In its final form, *Jack MacGowran in the Works of Samuel Beckett* (Public Theater, New York, 19 November 1970), the compilation could have seemed to the uninformed a kind of play, written between actor and author (Young thinks it was so in effect, Beckett having given MacGowran so much help with it). It had huge success wherever it was played, not least in New York, where, remarks Young, in 1970 the vogue for Beckett's plays had scarcely begun.[3] This was an early proof that the fiction could speak effectively to audiences unacquainted with the books or knowing little about the author and his world.

Compilations have taken many forms, some helpfully identifying the provenance of extracts, some treating them as unidentified parts of a theatrical entity, as in Barry McGovern's readings at a Beckett symposium in Monaco in 1991, where the audience were left to fill in the sources for themselves. He was presumably still attuned to *I'll Go On*, which was just such a seamless coat.

The immense speakability of the work when transmitted by an actor in tune with it has been a potent means of illuminating and extending interest in the often difficult later fiction. The BBC and Radio Telefís Eireann have played an important part here, broadcasting readings of new works of fiction as they came out in the 1970s and later, by actors such as Magee, Ronald Pickup, and Barry McGovern. I recall a first BBC recording of *Lessness* (1970) in several voices, including Pinter's, which must have alerted many to the poetic force in Beckett's prose fiction. Beckett attended some of these recordings. Martin Esslin, who directed Magee in readings of the entire *Texts for Nothing* tells how Beckett dropped in unexpectedly to one recording session in 1974 and made a characteristic request for less emphasis: 'it should be no more than a murmur'.[4] BBC Television has contributed a few notable anthologies, and there have been some imaginative linkings of passages from the work with visual images, as in the delicately structured film biography, *Silence to Silence*, directed by Seán Ó Mórdha (Radio Telefís Éireann, 1985).

From this point in time it's possible to discern an irresistible wave carrying Beckett's fiction into performance. Barry McGovern didn't just 'read' *Stirrings Still* (1988) for the BBC: it was to be 'performed by' him, said the announcer. From that kind of performance to others on stage was to be only a step, for complete novels as well as extracts. Beckett understandably had more qualms about the former, but here again was open to such ventures when convinced of their seriousness, especially when they involved actors he knew and trusted. David Warrilow, one such, brought the cryptic novella, *The Lost Ones*, to theatrical life in a production by Lee Breuer for the Mabou Mines Company. To judge by reactions from critics who knew the work's complexity, the elliptical, ambiguous, haunting piece of fiction lost none of these qualities when staged, yet was also emotionally overwhelming. Jonathan Kalb thought that Warrilow, towering like a dispassionate Gulliver over the tiny figurines in their cylinder, was a narrator who gradually became 'more and more like a character in his story' yet kept the audience 'slightly unsure about who he really is'. In an earlier account Ruby Cohn memorably highlighted 'rending moments of performance', as when Warrilow twisted and stretched on the dark wall of the outer cylinder (surrounding the audience), expressing the rhythm of a copulation made desolate by pain and longing.[5]

An equally if not more elusive and enigmatic novella, *Ill Seen Ill Said*, was 'performed' for an academic audience of the International Federation of Theatre Research in Kent in 1998, a performance I was sorry to miss after hearing Ruby Cohn's account of it. She told of a narrator whose voice she thought had some of the whispering quality of Patrick Magee's, speaking the dream-like words against the subtly expressive, independent movements of the 'she' evoked in the narrative. This 'she', the old woman, made her way across a snow-white cloth which rolled up behind her as she made her slow moves, becoming in the end 'a character' in its own right. It is what happens for a reader too as the landscape in the novella is undone by the narrator stage by stage. John Calder thought it a vision of God undoing the world; Ruby Cohn's account made it seem a more human and touching piece. Such is the virtue of sensitive performances: not to provide 'right' or definitive answers (how could that ever be?) but to touch the chords that wake the individual imagination.[6]

A fascinating paradox lies at the heart of these transformations. The novels/novellas seem to defy or forbid adaptation to the stage and at the same time call out for it, as *Mercier et Camier* surely does, with its seductive dialogue. The laconic, witty, subtly loaded exchanges between the two old men, one tall, one short, often seem to be limbering up for *Godot*. Against dramatization, we might think, is the inescapable narrator, ever reminding us it is all illusion, defying anyone to leave him out: 'I was with them all the time.' Mercier feels him there, 'Like the presence of a third party. Enveloping us'.

Pierre Chabert met the challenge presented by this teasing narrative with what seemed to me just the right mixture of panache and restraint in his production at the Maison des Arts, Creteil (8 January 1988). It was easy to understand why Beckett, familiar with his theatre work, would have given him permission for the adaptation. Daringly he kept the two actors, Jacques Seiler and Claude Evrard, alone on stage, travelling through a world we had to piece together from their responses to it, with the aid of an offstage 'La Voix' and other occasional sound effects (the programme told us we heard the voice of Guy Jacquet and of Jean-Louis Barrault, Madeleine Renaud, and Pierre Dux). There were moments when the action seemed just on the edge of boredom: Jim Knowlson told me jokingly he longed at times for Pozzo to put in an appearance. But there was a tremendous buoyancy in the humorous sang-froid of the companions and a pervasive, melancholy poetry in the silences, emptiness, beauty of a veiled but luminous moon and the mysterious poignancy that gathered round the four objects that helped to keep the travellers going: the bicycle, the umbrella, the sack, the raincoat. When the pair abandoned the last of these, 'l'imperméable', and looked back at it, lying on the stage in a forlorn heap, it was like the moment in the medieval *Everyman* when the traveller has to take leave of everything that has made up his life, except his Good Deeds. A pure theatrical elegy. When I met Beckett just afterwards, he was curious to know if the restriction to two actors had worked and was pleased, I think, when I recounted these impressions (and rather amused by my special feeling for the misty moon).

A more debatable issue than the dramatization of the fiction has been the transference of a play from one medium to another. Here again the drive to do it has been immensely energetic. Of course it may often strike us as perverse even to think of relocating work so subtly and carefully constructed for a particular medium. It was almost unbelievable to me, when I first heard of it, that Beckett would have allowed *Cascando*, that quintessential radio play, to be performed by visible actors and musicians. The director, JoAnne Akalaitis, has said she thinks he didn't like what she told him of the production: that isn't hard to believe.[7] Yet when David Warrilow described to me the actual performance by the Mabou Mines Company, in which he took part, it became easier to imagine the adaptation casting a curiously appropriate spell. The actors were made to feel confined in a tight space by being stuck in the corner of a room, always around a table which became, in the words of the director, the 'centre of the universe' for them. Here they sat, filling in the long hours of a Nova Scotia winter, improvising a story, playing or listening to music (written by Philip Glass), one knitting, another tuning a cello; all the activities feeding into the story that gives them their 'outings'. Not the month of May, as the Opener says it is ('for me'), but a state of longing for it.

Beckett did at one time set his face against such adaptations. He refused Laurence Olivier permission to adapt *All That Fall* for the stage in 1968 and would no doubt have preferred it never to have been performed except as a radio play. Yet it had a brief television airing when an extract was included in the BBC Television anthology, *A Wake for*

Sam. It was certainly disconcerting to see the dream figures there on the screen as large as life; he in bowler hat and dark glasses, she in flowered straw, rather smart in a genteel way. Yet it would have been difficult not to become engaged with them: they created a new, more limited, but not unconvincing presence. When I showed a few seconds of the extract to an audience at University College Dublin at the start of a talk on Beckett in 1993, I was relieved to find I wasn't alone in having a sneaking interest: my hosts, Christopher Murray and Tony Roche, said they would have liked to see more of it. There is so much life and character in the plays: maybe we can afford to turn them round for different views, even at the cost of losing something, so long as part of their truth and great vitality is captured.

Of course something will be lost when a complex piece of fiction is transferred from the limitless experience of the solitary reader. The argument was put by Robert Scanlan, himself a perceptive director, in the revealing collection of interviews and letters *Directing Beckett*, edited by Lois Oppenheim. He makes careful distinctions between different success rates in free treatments of the work, but in the end opts for exact keeping to the exactness of Beckett, quoting with approval Denis Donoghue's sharp critique of the 'weightlessness' in postmodernism which frees the artist to 'do anything he chooses . . . a game without rules'. At the other end of the gamut JoAnne Akalaitis maintains that the director has an absolute right to take her or his own line: 'The script is dramatic literature. The script is not the play. The play is an event.'[8] In between there are many compromises and a feeling that times change, works need to be brought up fresh for new generations. The proof of the pudding is in the eating: if there are losses there will also be gains.

That there will be some gains we might expect. Stage adaptations of the fiction will have brought many to the work who would otherwise not have known it—and perhaps stimulated those who do know it by something unexpected, some emphasis or trick of light; or just by the relief and variety the speaking voice can provide. The fiction, however, is relatively protected from adaptation. Freebooters apart, those planning a public performance of an adaptation would expect to seek permission, which could always be refused. The real crunch comes with the plays themselves, already 'out there', waiting to be performed, needing to be performed.

How free should a director be to add touches of her or his own or recast in some way texts that are so much more than the words they contain? Perhaps with the exception of *Godot* which Beckett said he 'didn't visualize' (and *Eleutheria* which he had only started to 'see' in that way) his dramatic texts are constructed as subtle pieces of total theatre; scores for performance. The later plays create 'almost a new art-form', Martin Esslin has suggested: he sees *Footfalls* as 'essentially a picture', *A Piece of Monologue* as 'literature striving to transcend itself, trying to reach the stage of pure wordless image'.[9] This may be to under-emphasize, as I think, the subtle balancing of words and visual image, but it's a fair warning to directors against lightly taking the sort of freedoms customary with Shakespeare, who left stage arrangements to his stage manager. It's not just visual effects that come into this but the whole rhythm of the work, most obviously the pauses and silences written into the texts.

Beckett famously disapproved of JoAnne Akalaitis's 1984 setting of *Endgame* in the subway tunnel. Any production that ignored his stage directions was, he said, 'completely unacceptable' to him: 'my play requires an empty room and two small windows'. His protest was included as an insert in the theatre programme along with a denunciation of the production as a 'travesty' by Barney Rosset, his friend and publisher, on the ground that every textual specification for set, lighting, and so on was as important as the words. Robert Brustein's defence of the production, also included, argued that although Beckett's plays are among the most powerful documents of the modern age, they 'are not etched in stone'. All great works of art, he said, are open to many approaches: 'each new production uncorks new meanings'.[10]

Provocatively, Brustein drew attention to productions of the play that had got away with far worse liberties, like the Belgian production in 1983 'set in a warehouse flooded with 8,000 square feet of water'. There have been many such liberties taken, with most of the work, in many parts of the world: in Japan, according to Mariko Hori Tanaka's colourful account, there were two all-female productions of *Godot* within two years and in 1992 a performance of *Happy Days* against a black backcloth on a black floor (no mound) with Winnie pushed on stage in a wheelchair in dim light by a Willie who then left the scene. Deconstruction is much practised there, it seems, as elsewhere, with fragments of Beckett's text being woven into ingenious collages. Perhaps not to be approved, but testimony to the strong impact of Beckett's art and people's wish to absorb it into alien cultures.[11]

Compared with these go-as-you-please attitudes, the defiance by the Dutch company of Beckett's ban on an all-female *Godot* might seem negligible. Except, that is, for the effect it had on the author. He provided a rather shaky reason for not allowing a female performance—'Women don't have prostates'—but behind this, as Mary Bryden has suggested, may have been a need to keep the play his, a masculine event.[12] It hurt him to see it invaded. This has always been the strongest reason against departing from his known wishes. In a conversation with Jonathan Kalb he spoke wryly of directors' preference for dead authors and when asked why it was less important to respect an author's text after he was dead, replied, 'Well, just because then you can't hurt his feelings'.[13] For his publishers and literary executor, familiar with those wishes from long friendship, the instinct to protect them must remain. That was presumably why permission to take an all-female *Godot* to the Edinburgh Festival was refused in 1998 to the company Grimy up North. Sympathy must often be awkwardly divided in these cases.

The proof of the pudding is in the eating: it may be an adage of little practical use to those concerned with permissions, but it is surely likely to triumph in the long run. Really bad, faithless productions of any play tend to sink without trace pretty quickly and great works survive even the most idiosyncratic adaptations, as *King Lear* survived for a century altered to let Cordelia escape death and marry Edgar. If seriously thought through, even productions that miss the mark may have a part to play. In her offending production of *Endgame* Akalaitis claimed to be utterly faithful to the verbal text: 'every pause was for me almost sacred'. She never thought, she said, of telling Beckett she intended to set the play in a subway: this was a directorial choice, aimed at bringing the play closer to her audience, making it seem 'urban', 'not European'. The result, for Jonathan Kalb, not alone among critics, was to pin the play down, make it more of a 'historical allegory' and so lose the significance of Beckett's 'ambiguous time and space'. But the production generated an enormous energy of discussion, part of the nourishment a play needs for its renewals.

Perhaps we should think of productions as 'readings' of a text, in the way of critical readings which we can enjoy and be stimulated by without necessarily endorsing. Such might have been the *Happy Days* of Roula Pateraki in Athens (1990) when Winnie's mound was represented by the gigantic crinoline in which she was encased. I have been assured by well-informed friends that the performance was of high quality and the effect true to the play. The same actress did a production with Willie seated at a piano, as if really trying out different readings: the play evidently exerted a strong magnetism on her. *Happy Days* in Greek will be a different thing, in any case, and the personality of the actor must always give some individual colour (how boring if it didn't). Personality, said Yeats, when giving advice to would-be writers for the Abbey Theatre, was what stirred the Irish imagination; Wilde said something very similar.

Beckett is with them there. Despite his witty play with depersonalizing and deconstructing, he always leaves room for the expression of human personality with its deep-rooted feelings. So *Happy Days* (or *Oh les beaux jours*) can contain with equal credibility a Winnie such as Natasha Parry, delicately in control of every fine nuance, and a Rosaleen Linehan, robust, with a strong aura of the 'peasant humour' Edward Albee thought the essence of the part: she charmed the audience at Karel Reisz's buoyant production at the Almeida Theatre, London (29 October 1996). We wait nowadays for a new Didi–Gogo pair as for a new Hamlet, often astonished—and delighted—by the changes of emphasis, style, and colour that can occur within the tightly controlled scenario when a music-hall entertainer plays opposite a straight actor (Max Wall/Trevor Peacock); a renowned Shakespearian Achilles (Alan Howard) against a renowned film Gandhi (Ben Kingsley). And many more, in theatres of all nationalities.

To help the audience engage with the difficulties of a work is sometimes a motive for experiment. Edward Albee gave this as his reason for doing an extraordinary thing with *Ohio Impromptu* in 1991 (at the Alley Theater, Houston). In the belief that only a 'trained theater listener' could absorb all that was happening in the play, he ran it through three times in succession. How the audience coped with this I don't know, nor what they made of his alternating a black and a white actor in the roles of Reader and Listener. This was Albee's interpretation of the direction 'As alike in appearance as possible'. Black and white were not colours, he reasoned, but opposites and 'therefore, the same'.[14] This seems to have asked a lot of the Houston audience; but it can never be less than interesting when a major playwright brings his 'inventive feelings' to the work of a writer whom he immensely admires as Albee does Beckett.

The comment on black and white being 'not colours' tunes interestingly with the argument about 'pink' put forward by Gildas

Bourdet, in defending his much-talked-of pink set for *Endgame* which Beckett refused to allow; it was covered up in performance, though still there. Bourdet pointed out that it is not the set but the light that is described as grey in the text. But his real point was that grey, traditionally associated with Beckett's plays, has become a non-colour after over-use: it no longer disturbs, he argued, but on the contrary 'comforts' the spectator with a sense of cultural correctness. His set was to be pink and red to the point of nausea; upsetting in the manner of a painting by Francis Bacon.[15]

Here again, it is hard to know without seeing it—and no one did—how the shocking set would have worked. What we surely do know is that faithful observance of the text down to its minutest stage directions doesn't guarantee good productions; I won't be alone in having seen some worthy but dull *Endgames*, for instance. Excitement is needed, though it takes a great director to excite us with absolute simplicity. It was amusing to read the commentators in advance on Peter Brook's production of *Oh les beaux jours* in London (Riverside Studios, 27 November 1997), with Natasha Parry as Winnie, wondering what splendid new rabbit the celebrated conjuror would pull out of the hat; in what ways the play would be made new. But this was the director who wrote *The Empty Space* in which he paid tribute to simplicity. He did say in interviews that his wife was a greater purist than he, but the production showed he too could be that and still excite the imagination.

Jack MacGowran thought Beckett exceptionally kind to the 'inventive feelings' of others. True, and he stimulated those feelings by his own protean changeability; all those moves in and out of forms and genres or from English to French and vice versa. The phenomenon of the twin-language texts in the background has been a stimulus to theatrical experiment. Linda Ben-Zvi has vividly described a production of *Godot* in Israel which drew a shadow play of great local significance out of the text by using a translation divided between Arabic, spoken at first by Vladimir and Estragon, Hebrew, the 'boss' language of Pozzo, a halting version of the same for the other pair, and a literary version (for Lucky).[16] Playing the English and French texts in parallel can create unexpected effects too. *Rockaby* acquired new power for Rosemary Pountney, so she told me, when she played it in Zurich in 1996 and elsewhere, first using the recording she had made in English, then repeating the play with her recording in French. In the process she felt herself moving further into the 'white' voice denuded of inflection which Beckett often required of his actors. Her audiences too, she learned from the discussions that followed her performances, had the impression of moving 'further in' to the work as a result of the bilingual repetition (letter, 17 August 1998).

A kind of freedom—to choose between Beckett's own changes of mind—is offered by his well-charted practice of altering the texts when directing his own plays. There were some changes he wouldn't contemplate. He told the German actress Hildegarde Schmahl, when directing her in *Footfalls*, that the only way to get at the character was by locating herself in the bodily posture originally devised.[17] On other occasions, especially with the earlier plays (*Godot* had come to seem 'a mess' to him), he made many changes, some disconcertingly radical. One such, for me, was his allowing Winnie to sing a snatch of her *Merry Widow* song earlier in the play than the published text indicates. It may have related to the concept of Winnie as a 'soubrette' in this production (with Billie Whitelaw, in 1979), but it didn't strike me as a change for the better. On the other hand the amended staging of *What Where* inspired by a German televised version, gave that play a new lease of life at the Petit Rond-Point, Paris on 22 April 1986, when Pierre Chabert directed it there.

Changes to the text of *Godot* made during rehearsals of the play with Rick Cluchey's San Quentin Players in 1984 have drawn mixed reactions. In the course of interviewing Cluchey and his cast in Melbourne when they played the new version there in 1984 Colin Duckworth drew out an interesting account of how speedily, even casually, smaller textual changes seem to have been made.[18] Like him, I regretted some of these. When Pozzo rudely asks Estragon how old Vladimir is, the cheeky reply 'Eleven' seemed livelier than the 'Ageless' which took its place, though Beckett was quoted by Cluchey as saying that he had never liked the former. Pozzo no longer said 'Walk or crawl' in answer to Vladimir's question whether Lucky will be able to walk without his 'thinking' hat. The question was rephrased as 'Will he be able to orientate himself?', drawing the answer, 'I'll orientate him'; lines with much less bite. There were also cuts which distressed Duckworth by removing 'magical moments' and drove him to use the expression 'textual vandalism'. This raised hackles at the Beckett symposium in Monaco and led to claims that Beckett's alterations are almost always for the best. There was a ferment here which attested to the power of the work to release individual responses, set them really going. It is a power that can't be regretted.

Beckett was free to make changes, but should directors be obliged to follow them? Robert Brustein, supporting the Akalaitis *Endgame*, thought it appropriate for the published texts, unlike productions, to remain 'etched in stone'. It has not been exactly like this. Changes Beckett made when directing have been incorporated into 'revised texts' included in the *Theatrical Notebooks* edited by James Knowlson and S. E. Gontarski (they draw too on such materials as rehearsal notes kept by Asmus, Fehsenfeld, Michael Haerdter, and others). The original texts are still in effect the standard ones, but the revisions are also available in published form for those who wish to use them.

It is right that this should be a matter of choice; last words aren't always best ones and directors should be able to make up their own minds on the point. They may make wrong judgements sometimes, in this as in other ways, but as S. E. Gontarski has argued, apropos experimental productions, directors should be free, even to make mistakes. When the revised text of *Godot* was used by Michael Rudman in 1987 before the Production Notebook had been published, I recall the confused looks of young students sitting in the Olivier Theatre, texts and A-level guides in hand, followed by lively chat in the interval which suggested that the shock of the new had been a great stimulus. Divergences can add an extra element of interest, if only curiosity about a director's reasons for choosing one text or the other or a combination (Peter Hall followed the revisions).

A drive is under way now to devise new ways of presenting the plays, with the aim of bringing them closer to the general public. I saw it at work in Dublin during the Beckett festival of 1991 when Michael Colgan at the Gate Theatre met with panache the immense challenge of presenting the entire theatrical canon within two weeks. This meant fitting in performances at all times of day: lunchtime or near midnight for the 'shorts' or 'roughs', conventional evening slots for major productions like the *Godot* directed by Walter Asmus. This last, universally admired in Dublin, and later on its American travels, was interestingly different from Asmus's previous rather too well drilled Dublin *Godot* which kept somewhat stiffly to ideas he had followed when working with Beckett and didn't quite draw out the easy, natural quality of the Irish actors: a reminder of how a play can be reborn in many ways.

It was pleasurable to be climbing the steep, narrow stair of the Gate along with a real mix of theatre-goers, some of them 'Beckett people', in Alkalaitis's phrase, some simply responding to the theatrical excitement in the air. Excitement further intensified by controversy was generated in London in March 1994 by one twenty-minute play with Deborah Warner's *Footfalls* (Fiona Shaw as May), in the Garrick Theatre, right at the hub of London's West End.

It was an amazing experience to go into that red plush Victorian theatre, be shown to a ground-floor box (no seat cost more than £4), and look out over the stalls, or what was left of them. They had been reduced to a couple of rows, with the seats turned round, to afford a view of the circle and the platform built out from it. The biggest shock was when the figure pacing the proscenium stage in familiar mode left it and made her way (probably unseen by many in the dim light) to the built-out platform, her alternative stage, where she renewed her pacing, then returned for the final sequence to the place where she had begun.

Reactions were often emotional, even violent. May's ability to move from one place to another did undermine, some would say destroy, the central visual image of a walking woman perpetually bound to a narrow strip of light. It wasn't too surprising that the Beckett Estate should restrict performances to the one week and ban a tour abroad (there had also been technical infringement of contract in that a line was transferred from the mother's voice to the daughter's, though this was immediately put right).

For anyone who had seen the first performance directed by Beckett there were some losses, most obviously a lessening of the concentration that had gathered round the figure on the narrow strip of light—and round the light itself—and the sound of the chime, coming and going with ever-fading strength till finally, on the light's last return, it lit emptiness. The latter effect was weakened by interruption. The change of locale for the walking woman struck me at first as likely to have the same effect, then it began to seem less alien to the idea of a ghost endlessly treading the same track. On each of the places where this May walked she could only do her nine steps, over and over again, which could be said to amount to the same doom.

There was bound to be some sadness at the loss of the tenuous, poetic beauty of Beckett's vision. And yet we can't have the same experience again, just as it was. It was possible to reel with the shock of Warner's production and have reservations, as I did, yet find something in the new vision that recharged the play. The ghostliness Beckett strove for had been reduced in one way but restored in another. It was possible to believe in Fiona Shaw's May as a character in the grip of ghosts (an effect not dissimilar from the state of possession later conjured up by Deborah Warner for *The Turn of the Screw* at the Royal Opera House in 1997). Of course there was a huge contrast with Beckett's visual image, the figure with arms sadly crossed, in Jocelyn Herbert's exquisitely trailing gown of 'grey tatters'. Fiona Shaw's dowdy, short red dress, drab lisle thread type of stockings, flat Start Rite sandals summoned up a very different, less romantic, ghost.

I came to feel that this new image of a poor gawky creature, like the dismantled, odd, forlorn look of the stalls, had a light to throw on the play. The old argument about 'grey' came up in this new context when I talked immediately after the performance with actor and director. The dull red of May's dress, they suggested, so disconcerting to those with the original image in mind, might be expected in the context of the Garrick's red plush to merge; red on red, a kind of equivalent to the 'grey' of the text. In a later conversation with Fiona Shaw we talked again of 'grey' which she thought of as a non-colour, a view close to that advanced by Gildas Bourdet. I don't know whether the 'merging' worked in the way envisaged, though it may have done.

What did come through was the layer of psychological realism which is there in the text, underlying the ghostliness, giving it a human pathos. I found believable and moving the suggestion of something sadly immature and undeveloped in Fiona Shaw's movements, vocal tones, and her intonations which highlighted words like 'poor' ('your poor mind'). In recalling her girlhood she gave a big, even violent, emphasis to the unfinished word, 'dreadfully un-'. She told me in a later conversation[19] that the text had drawn from both actor and director a deep response to the awful feeling of being 'not there' suffered by the being who knows she is immature, but also a woman. Disturbingly, Shaw plucked at her skirt or clutched at the supports to the circle, the latter necessitated, I learned later, by her height, though it fitted rather well with the illusion she built up of physical awkwardness and mental desperation.

Giving a local dimension to an image doesn't necessarily blot out its universality, though in a stern review Michael Billington suggested that a timeless image had been reduced to the story of 'one doomed Irish daughter' (*Guardian*, 16 March 1994). Irishness was certainly an element. Shaw thought occasional phrases typically Irish and drew laughs when she repeated one of them, 'to put it mildly'. It was not out of key with the ironic humour that makes a subdued appearance in the text during the Mrs Winter sequence. Shaw made the most of it, her voice going high for 'Mrs Winter', as if mocking her: she gave the dialogue between Amy and her mother a more everyday, scolding quality than I had heard before, as in the mother's peevish 'you *were* there'. The emphasis fell on trauma; the benediction went for nothing. This was in tune with Warner's idea of the theatre experience as being 'about something laid bare' (*Guardian*, 12 December 1991). In our conversation of 1998 Fiona spoke of the story-telling as the narrator's 'desolate recognition' of her own experience: a telling phrase. She was alone, yet she knew she had listeners, an experience the actor sought to capture by seeing herself as a child at an Irish Feisch, being called on to tell a story, feeling equally alone and aware of the audience.

In revisiting the production in memory, I felt, as I believe she did, that we were drawn into a living experience of the play; what had caused intense controversy hadn't ceased to be provocative but lived on, a spur to the imaginative reliving of a pure piece of theatre. The ordinary, practical affairs of theatre took their place in this. They had looked, she said, for the 'hottest' place in the Garrick, the 'key' place where a ghost might choose to manifest itself. Centre stalls seemed the answer at first, but it came to be the circle, fitting with the idea of ghosts appearing high in the air. It was somehow pleasing to learn that this extraordinary staging and scheduling (afternoons, late evenings, and so on) had developed from the accident of the director being lent the theatre for rehearsals, before taking the production (as had been expected) on tour in France.

These conversations would have made clear, if the production hadn't already done so, that the spirit in which changes were made was serious, an attempt to be true to something deep in the play. Many supported the production on this ground, even if doubtful about some of its effects. Others could find no good in it: 'doodling on a Rembrandt', said Billington. Foreign visitors wrote to *The Times* expressing astonishment at such hostile reactions, arguments raged, an immense interest was raised. People (not only 'the Beckett people') flocked to this twenty-minute performance taking place not in a fringe theatre nor arts club but the centre of the West End of London. The event won a front-page headline on a leading broadsheet, a rare experience for artistic happenings. In our conversation nearly four years after the event I found that Fiona Shaw still thought of this remarkable stirring up of interest, often in unlikely quarters, as a valuable outcome of the production. This was surely so, though not the only achievement.

Another free-thinking woman director, Katie Mitchell, found an unusual way of presenting a group of 'shorts' at The Other Place, Stratford-upon-Avon (22 October 1997). How best to show these very brief plays has always been a problem. For a time directors were chary of approaching them, and actors too, some feeling, as Peggy Ashcroft did, that 'those are really Billie's'.[20] There were scheduling problems: Beckett was not pleased when *Footfalls* was shown in a triple bill.[21] That has all changed: programmes of three or more 'shorts' are now common, attracting established actors and directors and new blood, as also, in increasing numbers, enterprising semi-amateur groups and students.

Katie Mitchell's approach at The Other Place differed from any I had seen. She involved the audience physically to an unusual degree, moving us from one room to another in the building, using black drapes and lighting to create the illusion of going on journeys, some slightly hazardous, so it might have seemed from the warning posted up that 'flashing lights' would be experienced during the performance. No more than sixty were admitted at a time and it was possible to see in one day, as I did, six plays, divided between two programmes. Some of them, like *Not I*, had demanding technical requirements, so, as Juliet Stevenson said, in a conversation we had some months later,[22] it made sense to have them set up in advance and make the audience move, rather than wait for changes. But there were of course other results from being peripatetic: we had an active part to play, one with some apprehension built in to it.

There was no need to brace oneself for the opening performance by Juliet Stevenson as May. Here the atmosphere was one of deep calm and quiet. What made it so unusual, especially for those recalling the first production, was our closeness to the pacing figure in her simple, grey trailing dress. We were in the same room as her, that was clearly to be felt. Ghostliness might have been reduced a little by this closeness but, strangely, was not. In Juliet Stevenson's hauntingly quiet, level tones there was a touch of the 'white voice' Beckett used to call for, but a naturalness too which made it seem appropriate for us to be so near her. When she came to the end, she passed by us, closer than ever: a grey, dim figure in the dim light. Her wonderful, gliding ease and calm would have survived any inadvertent sound (such as had happened once or twice, she said, when, thrown by the light, she had bumped into the front row).

We weren't allowed to remain in that tenuous calm but sent on our way to another space where another actor (who had also played the mother's voice) sat in her rocking-chair, absorbed by the act of rocking. It was a space for restfulness before we were marshalled for the most demanding of the moves, along a small corridor where flashing lights and lark song conveyed different messages from the play. Mouth was there before us at our destination, already muttering into the dark. A physical toll was exacted of the audience here: they had to stand for the sixteen or so minutes' playing-time, sharing, to some slight degree, in the physical and mental ordeal the actor was undertaking on our behalf.

As it happened, I didn't stand but sat with a friend, Mary McGowan, so was unaware of the Auditor standing just behind us; this was a small hazard of a daring scenic arrangement. I had wondered whether Mouth's closeness might diminish the terrifying force the image originally had when seen far off and high in the air. But closeness induced an equivalent trepidation. Juliet Stevenson's Mouth carried us into her agony, conveying a peculiarly sharp sense of a dialogue being passionately conducted with another, hidden self.

Later, I learned from Juliet that she had formidable restrictions placed on her: darkness, clamping, a helmet (soon abandoned), the need to direct her speech at a hole cut in the black velvet of her shield. She had a hallucinatory sense of being, as she put it, 'in a queer little machine' driving along and being honked here and there by some voice which wouldn't let her keep on the track she was following. She felt anger but also a kind of relief at being able to let everything out; this she compared with the letting go induced by a therapist or counsellor who might be simply sitting there, detached, waiting.

Before the first performance, she said, she was in a state of terror such as she had never before experienced; afterwards, soaked in sweat, legs trembling, she felt only that she had been through a churning physical experience. Yet strangely it wasn't as disorientating for her as the sense of being 'not there' in *Footfalls*, sometimes feeling not quite sure where she was, in the space or in the script. It was a more variable experience than *Not I*. Yet the play had been 'exquisite' for her and she was still turning over questions about it.

Could May do the mother's voice as well as her own, for instance, perhaps a youthful voice remembered from May's youth, or would that pin it down to a voice in the head, make interpretation more limited? These were questions that would clearly go on when the production prepared for its London showing. Sites had been investigated, in the hope of finding some unexpected building such as Wilton's Theatre which had done so much for *The Waste Land* when Deborah Warner directed Fiona Shaw's performance of the poem there. But in the event a less startling venue had been arranged.

There is a special charm in new relationships with buildings and audiences and productions taken out of the normal frame: they often reach out to unaccustomed theatre-goers or those who haven't yet felt Beckett's magnetism. But whether the route is traditional or experimental doesn't matter, most would say, so long as talented people continue to infuse the plays with energies such as those I have been trying to convey, seeking in their own ways to achieve the right 'rhythmic and sonorous pattern' as Anna McMullan has called it, in an interesting comparison with the acting style of Japanese Noh.[23] There are more roads than one to Rome, though not all roads lead there.

9
Company

'THE test is company', says the narrator in *Company*, a strange saying for a novella which focuses on solitariness: it opens with a command to imagine a voice coming 'to one in the dark' and ends with a sombre reminder, 'And you as you always were. Alone.'

Yet into this silent, night-time situation a throng of company makes its way, beginning with the uncomprehended voice. It is company in itself, says the narrator, but 'not enough'. More must be conjured up out of the dark ('Voices in the Dark' was the working title at an early stage of the writing). Memories come into play, fantasies, deep thoughts and imaginings; we are let into the process by which they are shaped and sculpted till they live, become true company—for the narrator and for us. The narrator himself is part of the imaginative process: 'Devised deviser devising it all for company'. The 'test' is always the company. I think of it as a test that has in mind those outside the fable who will react to it as readers; the company must ring true for them, as for the ultimate deviser, the author.

The company summoned up from the past by the voice is dazzlingly lifelike. We see as if in the flesh before us the small boy coming out of Connolly's Stores holding his mother's hand and being inexplicably snubbed by her, the father walking the mountain roads in his old tramping rags or sitting in his summer-house, the 'rustic hexahedron', chuckling at jokes in *Punch*, his young son 'trying' to chuckle with him. These and all the many rounded, expressive figures drawn out of memory are almost artlessly vivid company.

There is another kind too, more knotty and difficult, the company offered by the relationship among the three 'persons' of the fable: narrator, voice, and silent listener or unnameable 'hearer' as the narrator dubs him. A curious embargo hangs over their intercourse. The voice speaks in the second person, intimately, though so strange and distant; the narrator in the third. The first person could be used says the narrator if the third person were able to speak 'to and of whom the voice speaks'; 'But he cannot. He shall not. You cannot. You shall not.' The element of suspense created by this embargo adds to the sense of a live, dramatic connection among the three distinct 'persons' and the shadowy authorial self implicit in the notion of a 'devised deviser'. Full entry into this complex relationship requires a good deal of effort on our part, but there is beguiling company to draw us on and a wry, humane wit to carry us through thickets of thought and self-probing. The onus is on us to become mentally agile, a condition the narrator requires of the 'hearer' he builds up within the fable, to make him better company. The mental activity need not be of a high order, he adds mischievously: 'The lower the order of mental activity the better the company. Up to a point.' That 'up to a point' is one of many little endearing turns of phrase which become hallmarks of this flowing intelligence.

In reading the novella we can't help but be stimulated into mental agility once we obey the command to imagine. We start to listen for the 'voice', wonder, along with the narrator, where it is located, when next it will be heard, what is the meaning of the 'faint light' accompanying it. We are taken over by changing rhythms as the 'you' addressed by the voice goes on a great variety of journeys into the past, one of them poignantly recurring: the country walk taken 'With at your elbow for long years your father's shade in his old tramping rags and then for long years alone'. We travel in a boy's mind from complacent illusion to horrid reality when he finds the dead hedgehog he had pitied and neglected ('You are on your back in the dark and have never forgotten what you found then. The mush. The stench'). We wait nervously with the young man for the 'She' who is late at their rendezvous ('Bloom of adulthood. Imagine a whiff of that'). The challenge raised by these distant scenes is to see into them 'As you could not at the time'.

In the turbulent space where the fable is being constructed we are plunged into a creative process that is always on the move, full of energy and invention. Rhythms change with the mercurial moods. A sense of huge effort comes through the set-piece 'crawls' which mimic in terms of the body at full stretch the arduous poetic act of evocation. The narrator makes the connection with dry humour when he comments, apropos the problematic limits on the 'crawling creator', that 'many crawls were necessary and the like number of prostrations before he could finally make up his imagination on this score'. In more relaxed, meditative mood, the narrator plays with the notion of the 'hearer', that creature he can't do without but which remains always mysterious, the 'Unnamable'. He has some fun with the shaping of him: 'Let the hearer be named H. Aspirate. Haitch' (an Irish pronunciation joke). But the rhythm turns melancholy as he muses on how the hearer's physical senses must be imagined: 'Taste? The taste in his mouth? Long since dulled. Touch? The thrust of the ground against his bones.' Death comes closer with these reminders of old age corroding the senses: the novella ends with an apocalyptic vision of the body parts stiffening 'Till from the occasional relief it was supineness becomes habitual and finally the rule.' Yet the effect is not depressing. Too much has been gained by then; deep insights and an overwhelming sense of human tenderness as well as sardonic awareness of human absurdities. Wit enlivens it all: the dark thought of old bones leads into a playful flourish of erudition, 'All the way from calcaneum to bump of philoprogenitiveness'. The best company in the novella is the personality behind the complex twists and turns of the imaginings.

It is not a great step from being actively involved as a reader to imagining the text in performance, its subtle music being spoken by a fine, resonant voice. This has always been a familiar response to the fiction, as the previous chapter indicated, and many have felt an especially strong pull to *Company*. In the year of its publication, by John Calder in 1980, a reading by Patrick Magee was broadcast in July by the BBC and a staged reading directed by John Russell Brown for a platform performance in September at the National Theatre. In 1983 Mabou Mines staged a version and the next year a full-scale performance of the French version, *Compagnie*, was presented in Paris by Pierre Chabert, with Pierre Dux in the solo role (Théâtre du Rond-Point, 15 November 1984). From this developed S. E. Gontarski's English-language version of the Chabert adaptation which was given at the Actors' Theater's Half-stage, Los Angeles, in February of the following year.

I missed the first readings and had no chance to see Chabert's production (nor the American ones), but the wish to hear the novella spoken stayed in mind. Chance took a hand with two meetings, both at Beckett conferences, the place where academic and theatrical interests have often run together into production projects. First, at the University of Texas at Austin in 1984, I met Julian Curry, who was there to give a performance of *Krapp's Last Tape* in which he had been directed by Tim Pigott-Smith. We kept in touch and I learned that he was on the look-out for some other solo role in a Beckett work. At another great gathering, Beckett dans le Siècle, held in Paris in 1986 to honour Beckett's eightieth birthday, I talked to Pierre Chabert who kindly offered me the script/scenario he had used in his staging of *Compagnie* two years before. I could have it translated into English if I wished and use his stage directions. He had already made a similar arrangement with Gontarski, referred to above.

Chabert's generosity was a stimulus to thoughts of a full-scale production. I sent Julian a copy of *Company* which he hadn't read but instantly liked, then moved to a first shot at performance, having told Beckett I would like to try this. The occasion would be small and informal: a weekend seminar in one of the University of London's Bloomsbury houses. Having attended conferences at Paris and Stirling in 1986 I thought my own university should make a contribution to birthday celebrations for Beckett before the year was out. Colleagues and postgraduates in London were invited, together with any 'Beckett people' I knew to be around at the time (by good fortune, Ruby Cohn was one thus able to join us).

Preparation for the occasion had included readings and discussions with Julian and the hard task of cutting the delicately structured piece to fit into about an hour (Beckett had been agreeable to my doing this). There were losses, of course; some I especially regretted, like the boy's encounter with the old beggar-woman and her archaic leave-taking, 'God save you little master'. But cutting was needed, I felt sure, to allow the audience (any audience) to respond with full, unflagging attention to the demanding, intricate work. If it went beyond the natural attention span, its impact would be diminished, I feared, and some of its fine shades of feeling lost. Julian as an actor knew the importance of right timing and how easy it would be to stretch an audience too far for a complete response. In the event, I cut nearly a third of the novella, preserving, I hoped, its structural balance and proportions. We used this script in the performances to follow, beginning with the Bloomsbury reading.

There were other choices to be made before the novella could take shape for performance, even as a reading. How, for instance, should the 'voice' be done? The script Pierre Chabert gave me showed the pains he had taken to avoid using the actor's recorded voice; the most obvious way of expressing the mysterious phenomenon, a voice that is the speaker's own and yet strangely separate from him. Beckett had been to some extent involved in Chabert's adaptation: he had wanted a recorded voice, but Chabert had worked out a way of lighting the actor's face which disguised the fact that it was he who spoke the voice's lines. It would be much simpler to use a recorded voice, he had agreed, when I confessed to being daunted by his approach. I had no doubt that we would go for the simpler technique (which developed its own complications) and follow Beckett's preference. There was insufficient time to prepare a recording for the reading in Bedford Square so Julian simply emphasized at the start the distinction there was to be made between the third and second persons by cupping his hand round his mouth for the latter's opening lines. In performance later the recorded voice was similarly restricted to openings, the actor then taking over almost as if from a prompt.

Lighting effects could only be hinted at in the reading but a black-out for the start and finish seemed essential, and this was set up by a student crew organized by Nick Firth, the technical stage director in my department at Royal Holloway College. A full performance seemed not too far away when the voice that commands 'Imagine' emerged from the dark and the last line was spoken out of darkness.

Julian sat throughout, with a script, relying on his impressive vocal flexibility to bring into the scene a sense of the restless bodily activity evoked in the novella, the long walks of memory, the exhausting crawls expressing the stops and starts of the creative imagination punctuated by endless questioning: 'Can the crawling creator crawling in the same create dark as his creature create while crawling?' Any staging, even the first attempt at it, had somehow to capture this spirit of movement and intense bodily effort, as I believe Julian's did.

It was at the Bloomsbury event that I first met Tim Pigott-Smith who had, I knew, been hearing Julian read: he came to offer help and later to discuss the possibility of a full-scale production. This was not long in coming about. Although during 1987 Tim was heavily committed to Peter Hall's productions of three of Shakespeare's late romances at the National Theatre (playing Leontes and Iachimo and relaxing, piquantly, with Trinculo), he found time to rehearse Julian in *Company*, moving it much nearer to being a play, one involving a good deal of physical movement. Importantly, he devised a complex synchronization of sound and lighting which Nick Firth helped to realize in detail in our Studio Theatre at Royal Holloway College, Egham, where final rehearsals were held. Julian gave two performances there on 2 and 3 June; it was the first step *en route* for the Edinburgh Festival, London, and a variety of locales, including New York.

The script didn't change during rehearsals, though at one time Tim had doubts about the long, elaborate meditation on the hands of a watch which comes towards the end and might, he thought, check the flow. He tried cutting it but it refused to be cut, partly because Julian had made such a virtuoso performance of it. A mesmeric interest developed, I thought, as he reflected, in only part-quizzical tones on that commonplace thing, the movement of the second hand and its 'shadow' round the dial of a watch ('At 60 seconds and 30 seconds shadow hidden by hand' and so on). I was glad of his enjoyment of it, for I took the episode to be not only a fine flight of fancy but an affecting revelation of the homely grain of realism at the core of the whole work: the narrator's insomnia. Painful in itself as a common phenomenon, it had added poignancy for those who knew of Beckett's own suffering from the miserable affliction. But for anyone, I thought, there would be an uplifting sense of relief and release in the lyrical close of the night-time reverie when dawn comes and the low sun shining through the eastern window 'flings all along the floor your shadow and that of the lamp left lit above you'. Julian made a trip to Paris to meet Beckett (having previously met him only once, in an accidental way at the Riverside Studios): he found himself, somewhat to his embarrassment, reciting the watch sequence to its author at his request. I assumed it went well; at any rate Beckett told me that he'd had 'an agreeable meeting with Julian Curry' (letter, 9 November 1987).

As on later occasions, the try-out at Egham showed how Beckett's fiction when staged could attract the interest and often devotion of all sorts of people, not just those already addicts. The mix began with the production team, where well-known, highly experienced, professional actors were backed by a student crew, albeit a well trained one, and a complex sound and light system was carried through by a technical stage director in an academic department (he had, however, professional theatre lighting experience behind his expertise). The mix continued when two of the students, Will Scarnell and Jonathan Ratty, accompanied the production to Edinburgh, assuming responsibility for the stage management, lighting, and sound. The audience at Egham was also pleasingly mixed; people from the neighbourhood, academics and students with a wide range of subject interests, leading Beckett scholars, theatre agents, actors (one of whom, Fiona Shaw, was, as I have described in the last chapter, later to make a great stir in a Beckett production).

In watching the earliest rehearsals I had wondered if the solitary figure of the 'devised deviser' was too mobile, but mobility was what we wanted, and by the time of the try-out in June it had come to seem a natural expression of the energies in the text. So long as the sitting, walking, lying, and so on wasn't in crude parallel with the narrative, there were potent resonances to be gained from changes of movement. The figure lying prone, arms crossed on his chest, in fading light at the end, took on a monumental look, like an effigy on some crusader's tomb.

In tune with the keynote for any Beckett staging, 'less is more', the set for this one was bare—black drapes—and the only furniture a solid wooden chair with arms and high back. As I told Beckett when keeping him informed of developments, the chair allowed Julian a variety of postures: sitting on or resting against it, or standing behind and looking over, as when he conjured up the sinister 'eye'. Once he stood on it, as if poised for the dive called for by the father's voice, 'Be a brave boy'. The chair underwent sea-changes according to venue; normally rather humble, even battered, it became in Monaco, where it was borrowed from the opera house, magnificently ornate. Sitting in it, Julian Curry had a look of Hamm, lording it in a wheelchair elevated to imperial proportions (it made problems for the stage staff in not providing enough room for the loudspeaker usually placed there).

Apart from the pair of boots placed downstage, a whimsical directorial touch, the only other object on stage was an effigy created (with the aid of a tailor's dummy) out of a shabby, long-skirted, greenish coat, broad-brimmed hat, and stick. I assured Beckett that this figure, which he had evidently heard of from someone who saw the production at Edinburgh, was discreetly used. It was a dim shape, only just visible in the background for most of the time; then once or twice lit so as to become a suggestive shadowy 'other'. In the lyrical meditation that begins 'A strand. Evening. Light dying', stage light falling on the figure's stick created a path of faintest, ethereal light on the stage floor. It hovered there, then slowly faded as the actor evoked and finally took leave of the dream figure leaning on his staff: 'the skirt of your greatcoat and the uppers of your boots emerging from the sand. Then and it alone till it vanishes the shadow of the staff on the sand.' This lighting effect devised by Tim Pigott-Smith was for me a moment of pure theatre and a fitting accompaniment to the delicacy of the words.

The effigy acquired an offstage life of its own, and a name, Flynn; Julian used to include it in his bow at the end and take charge of the precious stick when the production travelled. The first of its journeys was to the Edinburgh Festival, to play at the Demarco Gallery Theatre, 9–29 August 1987. We had our tripartite collaboration on a firm footing by then, with Curry in the solo role, Pigott-Smith as director, myself as adapter, responsible to Beckett for the text and what happened to it in performance. The business and publicity which also fell to my share had many surprises to spring, as when we arrived at Edinburgh to find the tiny new theatre and its lighting/sound equipment far from finished. Technical effects loomed up as a potentially nightmarish problem: when Tim arrived from London to set up for the opening, it was still touch and go whether we could make it on time, and guests invited by Demarco to an informal reception which should have led into the preview found themselves, to their amusement, invited to the technical rehearsal instead.

Yet the atmosphere in the theatre carved out of his gallery space by the adventurous Richard Demarco was wonderfully favourable to the performance. Julian preferred it, I believe, to all others where we gave *Company*. The small numbers it could accommodate (forty-seven) and the actor's closeness to them in the open space allowed for a low-toned style that suited the piece and made more startling those moments when the actor let loose some of the pent-up passions in the text, the explosion of feeling, for instance, at the thought of being born on a Good Friday: 'You first saw the light and cried at the close of the day when in darkness Christ at the ninth hour cried and died.' This was delivered with tremendous brio, causing a shock in the quiet room. Telling too were the little throwaway remarks, one of the novella's great charms, which in this intimate space could be spoken in a voice dropped almost to nothingness. That was the voice used for the narrator's responses to his own sad question: 'What kind of imagination is this so reason-ridden?' The pause that followed gave haunting force to the quiet answer: 'A kind of its own.'

Audiences were diverse as always at this festival where people had the habit of dropping in to shows out of general curiosity. There were Beckett lovers in our audiences too, of course, an exhilarating mix of friends and strangers, actors and scholars. One of the last-named, Robert Scanlan, reported on the production to Beckett (who told me of this later; news of productions always filtered back to him). I knew Scanlan didn't really approve of adaptations but he had apparently referred favourably to such things as the handling of structural divisions in the narrative. This was encouraging, as were the enthusiastic reviews we received, and the Fringe First awarded by *The Scotsman*.[1] Our thoughts turned to fresh fields and, after appearing at the Belfast Festival (23–8 November 1987), the production made its way to London, to play at the Donmar Warehouse, Covent Garden, for three weeks (18 January–6 February 1988) in a double bill with another solo performer from Edinburgh.[2] Here the theatre, though still an open space, was much bigger (seating 240), and the audience even more various. Billie Whitelaw came, as did many other actors and theatre people; John Calder's staff managed to see it (as publisher of the English text he had been immensely supportive from the start of the venture). There were casual visitors to London along with regular Donmar supporters, television people, scholars, and students: a total mix. I felt more keenly than ever the power Beckett's art had once people were exposed to it, to draw them under its spell. Those already familiar with the work, so my own experience suggested, would be likely to find new lights cast on it from the new angle. 'Company' became a word with extra meaning, there was a sense of fellowship in sharing the novella with audiences and working on it, as we did at the Donmar, with heroically devoted theatre people such as Nica Burns and her colleagues.[3]

At the Donmar, as in the smaller studio spaces previously experienced, the figure in the open-necked shirt and dark grey corduroy trousers was never just a man recalling in solitude the phases of his life. The voice that said 'You' was quite tightly enclosed in the wry, questioning of the other, third-person voice: irony and sadness were always seeping through from it. One reviewer, Irving Wardle, was more struck by the mental wrestlings than the vignettes of memory; for him the dramatic temperature took a 'decided dip during this anecdotal material. It becomes riveting when there is no escape into the past' (*Times*, 21 January 1988). Though myself fond of the memory sequences and their refreshing variety, I was glad the reviewer had been gripped by our presentation of the imagining self and our focus on an 'intelligence' which was not to be pinned down as a person. This had certainly been our aim. 'There is no him', Beckett had told me during one conversation about *Company*; he made the same remark to Julian when they met, as he had to others.

Though some critics thought *Company* should always be a 'silent, readerly, solitary' experience,[4] the reactions of our audiences suggested that the physicality of performance often sharpened the mental interest and poetic force of the novella. The dispersal of the unpredictable voice among artfully placed speakers drew them into the puzzlement and slight shock experienced by the protagonist, and kept the long reverie dynamic for them. The quizzical humour never far off in the novella found expression in one or two little extra, silent touches as when, after musing on the habits of the voice such as its way of changing place and tone in the course of a sentence, the actor stopped and remained silent; long enough to cause unease (had he dried?). Then he resumed: 'Another trait its long silences when he dare almost hope it is at an end.' The gentle sympathetic laughter at the little joke expressed a kind of relief, I thought, and eased the way into the intent, apprehensive listening called for when the voice was spoken of in a darker vein.

I had sent Beckett a marked copy of the script showing this sort of detail. He didn't quarrel with our treatment and took a benevolent interest in the production, conveying pleasure in its favourable reception and good wishes for different venues. Julian Curry and I (Tim Pigott-Smith was kept in London by theatre commitments) learned a good deal from our travels with it abroad, especially how vital it was to stress in writing well in advance of our arrival the complications of the sound/lighting set-up. Lulled by the simplicity of the set and a production lasting only an hour, stage staff tended to underestimate the time needed for technical preparation. It was often a shock when they came to grapple with thirty sound and sixty lighting cues, the placing of the five loudspeakers, and the need for total black-outs at start and finish (technicians were usually reluctant to blot out lighted exit signs, as ideally required).

Different patterns of response from audiences emerged too, though what came through to us overwhelmingly was the exhilarating sense of the novella's power to affect a great diversity of people. There was usually a strand of Beckett scholars, but apart from this audiences varied greatly, as did the theatres. At Dublin, in the Beckett Festival of 1991, it was a familiar, open-space, studio type (the Samuel Beckett Theatre in Trinity College). There was an international flavour about the audience here and a sense of liveliness stimulated by the conference fizz in the city background and the fact that all Beckett's plays were on show at the Gate Theatre. Earlier that same year in the Principality of Monaco (18 May 1991) the venue was the Princess Grace Theatre, with its large proscenium stage: a bonus here was the sound of sea gently lapping outside, a real-life descant to the faint sea-sound effect the performance began and ended with. I had been invited to take the production there as part of the symposium, 'Beckett and Beyond', organized for the Princess Grace Library by C. George Sandulescu but the audience included invited guests and members of the public: in the theatre's elegant foyer there was a piquant mix of Beckett scholars and fashionable residents of the neighbourhood. Its proscenium stage was one of the few things Monaco had in common with a previous venue, at the Lehman College Center for the Performing Arts of the City University of New York in April 1988. There the theatre (also large) filled up with an audience drawn mainly from the neighbourhood, the Bronx; many were black and Hispanic, some had never seen live theatre till then. Beckett was very sympathetic to this last event. When its organizer, my friend, Alice Griffin, wrote to him about it, hoping for his good wishes, he sent her a letter of great friendliness.[5]

Wherever we took the performance there were reminders of how differently it was possible to view the text, how it positively stimulated individualism and difference. One of the critics who thought the novella shouldn't be staged, Carla Locatelli, was a participant at the Monaco symposium. Not wishing to upset our friendly agreement to disagree on this point, I didn't risk asking her whether after seeing the production she changed her view that 'Unless the part is played by a ventriloquist' one cannot indicate the co-existence and yet distinction of 'voice' and 'hearer'.[6] Also at Monaco, at the other extreme of the critical argument, was S. E. Gontarski, who leant to the view that *Company* 'works equally well on stage and page'.[7]

In his 'English language version' of Chabert's adaptation of *Compagnie* Gontarski had shown his own individualism. He diverged from Chabert in using a recorded voice, but that of course was what Beckett had wanted. Much more unexpected were his shock tactics for drawing the audience into the lonely situation of the protagonist. These included shrinking their numbers from a possible sixty to thirty, and intensifying the 'black box' effect of the Chabert production by draping the seats in black floor-length crepe. They were arranged in an irregular pattern which refused people 'the comfort of sitting next to anyone' and bolted to the floor in that position to prevent any (surely natural) inclination to move them closer together.[8]

This was a long way from my idea of the work as a source and nourishment of company. I had quaked a little at the all-black scenario in Chabert's script and been relieved to learn from Gontarski that Beckett had softened it by changing the black costume originally intended for Pierre Dux to a homely pair of grey pyjamas. Though blackness was part of the effect in our production, Pigott-Smith's lighting had a colour range to tune with changes of mood and memory in the monologue: the merest hint of palest green shadows on the stage, for instance, to suggest the 'trembling shade' of an aspen, when the love scene moves from ironic into lyrical mode. Stan Gontarski floated the intriguing idea that we might have a back-to-back production of our two so-different versions; it would certainly have brought out the novella's power to stimulate individual responses, but, alas, perhaps unsurprisingly, this was not to be.

Company seemed likely to take a new turn when in New York Julian Curry and I met D. A. Pennebaker, renowned for his filming of Bob Dylan on tour. He saw the production and invited us to dinner in his apartment, after a visit to his studio where we saw the videotape of Jack MacGowran's extraordinary performance in *Krapp's Last Tape* which Pennebaker had been responsible for restoring to usability after its long years of neglect in an attic.[9] We discussed the possibility of televising my adaptation, an idea that I had been contemplating and had mentioned to Beckett, who had received it sympathetically. Turning over possibilities with Penny, as he liked to be called, brought the idea into sharper focus. It would have been exciting to work with someone so experienced in documentary television and also in Beckett matters.

The possibility didn't develop, but later in the year came alive again, oddly enough, through Yeats, when at the International Yeats Summer School, Sligo, in August I met Ann Mann, there to record interviews for a BBC programme to be broadcast the following year to mark the half-century since Yeats's death.[10] We talked of Beckett, she asked to see the script of *Company*, then passed it on to Chris Hunt who ran the independent television company, Iambic Productions.[11] He saw possibilities for a televised version and took up the project; it proved a long commitment for him, as for Ann and others involved.

In shaping the screenplay, as I began to do in 1990, I kept to the structural divisions of the narrative in the stage script and to the length of one hour. Changes had to come in, however; what had worked in the theatre would have been flat if simply transferred to screen. These changes raised queries from the Literary Executor, Jérôme Lindon, but in the light of discussion, through correspondence, and at a meeting Chris Hunt had with him in Paris, he accepted that the permission Beckett had given me to make a television version of the adaptation could extend to some divergences from the stage script. He made the proviso that we should include on the screen at the start a rider to the effect that Beckett had not seen the adaptation; it seemed reasonable and was accurate, though of course my hope was that if he had seen it he would have approved. I did feel sure that, whatever he might have thought of specific changes, he would have known some would be needed, to fit the stage script to another medium. There was a precedent in his own work for this. I was grateful to Lindon for accepting my good faith in this matter as also to Edward Beckett for his benevolent concern, then and throughout the long-drawn-out saga that followed.

The changes made for the screen didn't upset the primary situation: the man alone in the dark, listening to a voice he can't control and which he both dreads and longs to hear. On screen he would begin and end in a real room, stylized so as to have some affinity with the 'familiar chamber' of Beckett's later plays. With him in the room would be a mute figure, the 'hearer', the 'Unnamable. You'. The figure would lie prone, change places with the narrator, be projected into landscapes of the mind, take the 'outings' called for by the off-screen voice. Like the room, the landscapes seen by the viewer would be both real and abstracted, at times 'composed', near-surreal, at times closer to reality. In one style a figure might be seen in outline, trudging a recognizable country road; in the other, hands would appear, holding a dark shape (the hedgehog) from which darkness would spread across the screen. Ethereal blue would fill a blank screen to suggest the boy's visionary experience of distant mountains which he re-experiences lying in bed at night: 'Fall asleep in that sunless cloudless light'.

There would be some touches of the solid reality that is deep in the text, and essential to it: if real-life material were likely to be the most visually telling, it would be used. The scenery of Beckett's life had already been made familiar, by *The Beckett Country* in 1986, and by TV documentaries such as *Silence to Silence* which interwove the more obvious autobiographical allusions in *Company* with shots of places like the Ballyogan road ('That dear old back road') and the house where the 'you' of the narrative first saw the light.

These were incidentals, though valuable. The purpose must remain what it had always been: to convey as effectively as possible the complexity and strangeness of the experience; the mental struggles, the anxieties as well as the ecstasies of the imagination at work, the ingenuities of the wit. It seemed appropriate to bring into the screenplay visual heightenings of certain inner events, for instance the narrator's intuition of following a 'beeline' and the shock of perceiving it take a great swerve, 'withershins'. A blur of figures on a sheet of white paper would figure as an emblem of the narrator's delight in mathematical calculations: 'Even still in the timeless dark you find figures a comfort. You assume a certain heart rate and reckon how many thumps a day.' The white sheet of paper—suggesting the activity of writing as well as fondness for figures—would dissolve into the white snowy fields and these give place, with the same magical suddenness as in the text, to the same fields in spring, startlingly strewn with sheep's red placentas. There seemed room here for an artist, to serve Beckett's words on a screen in the way that Avigdor Arikha and others had done in paintings and drawings.

I started work on the screenplay with the expectation that Julian Curry would continue in the solo role and Tim Pigott-Smith co-direct with Chris Hunt, but the broadcasting companies had their own ideas on such things. It was from the commercial sector that the first show of real commitment emerged and there the project would only be considered if it had what was regarded by them as a star name, preferably with world-wide celebrity, to carry it. With a completed screenplay and after a huge investment of time and effort by Chris Hunt and colleagues, we had to face this inescapable fact. A deep disappointment to Julian and Tim, it was taken by them, professionals as they were, with a good grace when it became clear that the situation wouldn't change. Yorkshire Television were prepared to back the production if Paul Scofield played in it and this for a time seemed a possibility. Chris and I had a congenial meeting with him when he was enthusiastic about the project, calling it 'an actor's dream'. But circumstances later obliged him to withdraw, and Yorkshire Television's disastrous encounter with the Thatcher 'franchise' operation put a brake on their readiness to take chances elsewhere.

We were left, after various other flurries of possible commitment, by the BBC, for instance, in the tantalizing situation of having a screenplay that had excited much interest, permission to use it, a television company to produce it, but no network to show it. A familiar situation in television, I was often reminded by my battle-hardened collaborators. And so it remains.

It's on another note that I want to end however, one of gratitude for the experience of knowing *Company* as I came to know it during the decade of working on it with such talented and committed collaborators, with stage crews, television staff, and with the help of many generous supporters and backers, not all of whom I've been able to name, though they are thankfully remembered. Gratitude above all to Samuel Beckett for giving us a work of such poetic beauty and human vitality that it will always attract people to its complexities and inspire new ways of conveying its ever-resonating words. Worlds of the mind opened up for us involved in the staging (and the moves towards televising) the novella, as I hope they did for the audiences who joined us in the company of *Company*.

Notes

INTRODUCTION

1. Letter to the author, 16 Apr. 1975.
2. The 'Whoroscope' Notebook (MS 3000) is in the Beckett Archive of the Beckett International Foundation at the University of Reading, as also the Johnson material donated by Ruby Cohn. Material relating to Pierre Chabert's productions may be found here.
3. James Knowlson, *Damned to Fame: The Life of Samuel Beckett* (London: Bloomsbury, 1996).
4. H. Porter Abbott, *Beckett Writing Beckett* (Ithaca and London: Cornell University Press, 1996), p. x.
5. Anthony Cronin, *Samuel Beckett: The Last Modernist* (London: HarperCollins, 1996), 384.
6. Billie Whitelaw, *Billie Whitelaw . . . Who He?* (London: Hodder & Stoughton, 1995), 148.
7. Maria Irene Fornes is quoted by Toby S. Zinman in Enoch Brater and R. Cohn (eds.), *Around the Absurd* (Ann Arbor: University of Michigan Press, 1990), 206.
8. Enoch Brater, *Why Beckett* (London: Thames & Hudson, 1989), 68.
9. Interview with Tom Driver (Columbia University Forum, Summer 1961), in Lawrence Graver and R. Federman (eds.), *Samuel Beckett: The Critical Heritage* (London, Henley, and Boston, Mass.: Routledge & Kegan Paul, 1979), 220.
10. Christopher Ricks, *Beckett's Dying Words* (Oxford: Clarendon Press, 1993), 1.
11. Paul Foster, *Beckett and Zen* (London and Boston, Mass.: Wisdom Publications, 1989), 243.
12. Interview with Tom Driver, in Graver and Federman, *Samuel Beckett*, 220.
13. Richard N. Coe, *Beckett* (Edinburgh: Oliver & Boyd, 1964), 5.
14. Knowlson, *Damned to Fame*, 684.
15. Andrew Kennedy, *Samuel Beckett* (Cambridge: Cambridge University Press, 1989), 63.
16. Martin Esslin, *The Theatre of the Absurd* (Harmondsworth: Penguin Books, rev. edn., 1968).
17. See *TN* iii, p. xvii.
18. Barbara Hardy, *Tellers and Listeners* (London: Athlone Press, 1975), p. ix.
19. Brenda Maddox, *Nora* (London: Hamish Hamilton, 1988), 524.
20. S. E. Gontarski, *The Intent of Undoing in Samuel Beckett's Dramatic Texts* (Bloomington: Indiana University Press, 1985).
21. Deirdre Bair, *Samuel Beckett* (London: Cape, 1978). This biography appeared two years after the first production of *Footfalls* and made explicit the connection between the play and Beckett's life.
22. Eoin O'Brien, *The Beckett Country* (Dublin: Black Cat Press, in association with Faber & Faber, 1986), p. xix.
23. Quoted in Knowlson, *Damned to Fame*, 481.

24. John Peter, *Vladimir's Carrot: Modern Drama and the Modern Imagination* (London: André Deutsch, 1987), 17.
25. Quoted in Kathleen Tynan, *The Life of Kenneth Tynan* (London: Weidenfeld & Nicolson, 1987), 121–2.
26. Mel Gussow, *Conversations with (and about) Beckett* (London: Nick Hern Books, 1996), 139.
27. Jordan R. Young, *The Beckett Actor* (Beverly Hills, Ca.: Moonstone Press, 1987), 14.

CHAPTER 1

1. Doubt has been expressed about connections with Strindberg's Glazier though Knowlson records that at some stage *A Dream Play* was known to Beckett. See Knowlson, *Damned to Fame: the Life of Samuel Beckett* (London: Bloomsbury, 1996), 379.
2. Ruby Cohn confirmed to James Knowlson that she was told this by Beckett: ibid. 378.
3. Letter to Nancy Cunard, 5 July 1956.
4. 'The long crooked straight is laborious but not without excitement'. Letter to George Tabori, 23 July 1983.
5. He wrote to Tom MacGreevy in 1936 that he had been studying Geulincx's *Ethics*: instinct told him it was worthwhile because of the text's 'saturation in the conviction that the *sub specie aeternitatis* vision is the only excuse for remaining alive'. Letter to Tom MacGreevy, 5 Mar. 1936, quoted in Knowlson, *Damned to Fame*.
6. Following the success of *Waiting for Godot*, Beckett withdrew *Eleutheria*, refusing requests to publish or produce it. After his death, to great controversy, it was published in 1995 in the original French (Paris: Les Éditions de Minuit), and in an English translation, *Eleuthéria*, by Michael Brodsky (New York: Foxrock Inc.). Quotations are taken from the latter edition: the title is given in the original, unaccented, form.
7. 'The Tragical in Daily Life' ('Le Tragique quotidien') is a seminal essay on modern theatre in *The Treasure of the Humble* (London: George Allen, 1897).
8. Letter to the author, 12 July 1973.
9. *TN* ii. [3].
10. MF 218–20.
11. In 1988, for the University of London, then for the Yeats International Summer School at Sligo. Robert Gordon played Speaker.
12. Alan Schneider's article 'On Directing *Film*', in *Film by Samuel Beckett* (London: Faber & Faber, 1972). Scenario, illustrations, and production shots included.
13. Our production of *Eh Joe* was made in 1972 by the University of London Audio-Visual Centre, with David Clark directing and myself as producer (Sandra Clark worked on voice with Elvi Hale: she was given a credit as co-producer).
14. Jocelyn Herbert, *Jocelyn Herbert: A Theatre Workbook* (London: Art Books International, 1993), 98.
15. *Billie Whitelaw . . . Who He?* (London: Hodder & Stoughton, 1995), 80.
16. See Herbert, *Jocelyn Herbert*, 92, for an illustrative sketch.

17. Keir Elam, 'Dead Heads: Damnation—Narration in the "Dramaticules" ', in John Pilling (ed.), *The Cambridge Companion to Beckett* (Cambridge: Cambridge University Press, 1994).
18. *TN* iii.

CHAPTER 2

1. John Gruen, 'Beckett Talks about Beckett', *Vogue* (London, Feb. 1970); Beckett is said to have described 'an existence where no voice, no possible movement could free me from the agony and darkness I was subjected to.'
2. 'Dante... Bruno. Vico.. Joyce', in *Disjecta*, ed. Ruby Cohn (London: John Calder, 1983), 33.
3. See Jocelyn Herbert, *Jocelyn Herbert: A Theatre Workbook* (London: Art Books International, 1993), 89. For fuller detail see also Billie Whitelaw, *Billie Whitelaw . . . Who He?* (London: Hodder & Stoughton, 1995), 116–33.
4. Deirdre Bair, *Samuel Beckett* (London: Cape, 1978), 94.
5. See Mary Bryden (ed.), *Samuel Beckett and Music* (Oxford: Oxford University Press, 1998), 95.
6. Kay Boyle, 'All Mankind is Us', in Ruby Cohn (ed.), *Samuel Beckett: Waiting for Godot. A Casebook* (Basingstoke and London: Macmillan, 1987), 177.
7. MF 229.
8. Letter to the author, 7 Dec. 1997.
9. 'Dante... Bruno. Vico.. Joyce'.
10. 'Dame Peggy Ashcroft interviewed by Katharine Worth', in Linda Ben-Zvi (ed.), *Women in Beckett* (Urbana and Chicago: University of Illinois Press, 1990), 14.
11. Keir Elam, 'Dead Heads: Damnation–Narration in the "Dramaticules" ', in John Pilling (ed.), *The Cambridge Companion to Beckett* (Cambridge: Cambridge University Press, 1994), 153–5.
12. MF 29–58.
13. My conversation with John Beckett took place at a conference on Beckett at Goldsmith's, University of London, in 1996.
14. James Acheson, *Samuel Beckett's Artistic Theory and Practice* (Houndmills, Basingstoke and London: Macmillan, 1997), 206. Kipling figures suggestively in Acheson's discussion of Bam's preoccupation with 'what' and 'where'.

CHAPTER 3

1. Peter Bull, *I Know The Face But . . .* (London: Peter Davies, 1959), 69, 70.
2. Wall's piano-playing professor used to call 'Albert, where's the stool?', drawing out 'stool' as Krapp does 'spool'. This turn was included in the programme on Max Wall made by BBC TV (Television South) for Channel 4 in 1983.
3. Deirdre Bair, *Samuel Beckett* (London: Cape, 1978), 385, 483.
4. See *Happy Days: Oh Les Beaux Jours*, ed. James Knowlson (London, Faber & Faber, 1978), 134.
5. Held in the Beckett Archive, University of Reading, MS 1396–4–10.
6. Samuel Beckett, *Dream of Fair to Middling Women*, ed. Eoin O'Brien and E. Fournier (London and Paris: Calder, 1993), 48.

7. See e.g. Bair, *Samuel Beckett*, 472; Beckett, *Dream*, 113 ('in the thick of the popular belief').
8. Peter Davison, *Songs of the British Music Hall* (New York and London: Oak Publications, 1971), 29.

CHAPTER 4

1. *Mercier et Camier* was published in French in 1970, and in English in 1974.
2. Julie Campbell, 'Pilgrim's Progress/Regress/Stasis: Some Thoughts on the Treatment of the Quest in Bunyan's *Pilgrim's Progress* and Beckett's *Mercier and Camier*', *Comparative Literature Studies*, 30/2 (1993), 137–52.
3. For further detail on the productions made by the University of London Audio-Visual Centre, with myself as producer and David Clark as director, see Ch. 7.
4. Beckett heard the recordings in 1976. An account of the occasion is given in Ch. 7.
5. Everett Frost directed five of the radio plays, including *Cascando* (with Alvin Epstein as Voice) for the Beckett Festival of Radio Plays, National Public Radio, Washington, DC, 1989. New music by Morton Feldman for *Words and Music*, and by William Kraft for *Cascando*.
6. For a fuller account of Humphrey Searle's music for these plays, see Katharine Worth, 'Words for Music Perhaps', in Mary Bryden (ed.), *Samuel Beckett and Music* (Oxford: Clarendon Press, 1998), 9–20.
7. Billie Whitelaw, *Billie Whitelaw . . . Who He?* (London: Hodder & Stoughton, 1995), 153.
8. For Beckett's list of the objects in Winnie's bag, see *Happy Days: The Production Notebook of Samuel Beckett*, ed. James Knowlson (London: Faber & Faber, 1985), [41].
9. Comments recorded by Martha Fehsenfeld in the rehearsal diary she kept during Beckett's 1979 production of *Happy Days*. Quoted in *Happy Days: Production Notebook*, ed. Knowlson, [17].
10. Ibid. 54.
11. Deirdre Bair, *Samuel Beckett* (London: Cape, 1978), 17.
12. Walter D. Asmus, 'Rehearsal Notes for the German Première of Beckett's *That Time* and *Footfalls* at the Schiller-Theater Werkstatt, Berlin', *Journal of Beckett Studies*, 2 (Summer 1977), 82–95.
13. Enoch Brater, *Beyond Minimalism: Beckett's Late Style in the Theater* (New York and Oxford: Oxford University Press, 1987).
14. Letter to Tom MacGreevy, 2 July 1933 (Trinity College Library, Dublin).
15. Both are small towns in Kent: the improbable Snodland is a real name: as 'Esnodiland' it figured in the Domesday Book (1086).

CHAPTER 5

1. Samuel Beckett's *Proust* was first published in 1931 (London: Chatto & Windus).
2. Beckett quotations are from *Proust and Three Dialogues: Beckett and Georges Duthuit* (London: Calder, 1965), 30–1.

3. Barbara Hardy, *Shakespeare's Story Tellers* (London and Chester Springs: Peter Owen, 1997), 127.
4. James Knowlson, *Damned to Fame: The Life of Samuel Beckett* (London: Bloomsbury, 1996), 352. 'Make that clear once and for all', Beckett told him.
5. Martin Dodsworth, '*Film* and the Religion of Art', in Katharine Worth (ed.), *Beckett the Shape Changer* (London: Routledge & Kegan Paul, 1975), 180.
6. More detail is given on this production which was made in 1972, in Ch. 7.
7. Yasunari Takahashi, 'The Theatre of Mind: Samuel Beckett and the Noh', *Encounter*, 58 (Apr. 1982), 72.
8. My account of this production, '*The Words upon the Window-pane*: A Female Tragedy', is in Warwick Gould (ed.), *Yeats Annual 10* (Basingstoke and London: Macmillan, 1993), 135–58.
9. Beryl S. Fletcher and John Fletcher, *A Student's Guide to the Plays of Samuel Beckett* (London: Faber & Faber, rev. edn., 1985), 234.

CHAPTER 6

1. *Happy Days: The Production Notebook of Samuel Beckett*, ed. James Knowlson (London: Faber & Faber, 1985), [99]. The lines from which Winnie quotes run: 'I say confusedly what comes uppermost; | But there are times when patience proves at fault, | As now: this morning's strange encounter—you | Beside me once again'.
2. *Othello*, v. ii. 145–7; *TN* iii. [30].
3. 'I have tried too in my time to be a philosopher; but I don't know how, cheerfulness was always breaking in': Oliver Edwards to Dr Johnson, quoted in *Boswell's Life of Johnson*. James Knowlson records that the edition used by Beckett was that of George Birkbeck Hill (1887).
4. Thomas Gray, 'Ode on a Distant Prospect of Eton College'. See S. E. Gontarski, Beckett's *Happy Days: A Manuscript Study* (Columbus, Oh.: Ohio State University Libraries, 1977), 68.
5. Charles Wolfe, 'Song', in *The Burial of Sir John Moore and Other Poems*: 'Go, forget me—why should sorrow | O'er that brow a shadow fling? | Go, forget me—and tomorrow | Brightly smile and sweetly sing.'
6. Antonia Rodríguez-Gago, 'Molly's "Happy Nights" and Winnie's "Happy Days" ', in Enoch Brater (ed.), *The Theatrical Gamut* (Ann Arbor: University of Michigan Press, 1995), 29–40.
7. See *Happy Days; Oh Les Beaux Jours: A Bilingual Edition*, ed. James Knowlson (London: Faber & Faber, 1978); *En attendant Godot*, ed. Colin Duckworth; Harry Cockerham, 'Bilingual Playwright', in Katharine Worth (ed.), *Beckett the Shape Changer* (London: Routledge & Kegan Paul, 1975).
8. W. B. Yeats, 'Gods and Fighting Men', in *Explorations* (London: Macmillan, 1962), 20.
9. J. Knowlson 'Beckett's Production Notebooks', in Ruby Cohn (ed.), *Samuel Beckett: Waiting for Godot, A Casebook* (Basingstoke and London: Macmillan, 1987), 52.
10. P. J. Murphy discusses Job quotations in 'On first looking into Beckett's *The Voice*', in John Pilling and M. Bryden (eds.), *The Ideal Core of the Onion: Reading Beckett Archives* (Reading: Beckett International Foundation, 1992), 63–78.

11. Verna Foster, 'Beckett's Winter's Tale: Tragicomic Transformation in *Ohio Impromptu*', *Journal of Beckett Studies*, 1 (1992), 67–75.

CHAPTER 7

1. The Yeats productions directed by Niema Ash were performed at the Howff Theatre Café, Regent's Park, and recorded by the University of London Audio-Visual Centre in 1973.
2. In Shaw Centenary programme, Gaiety Theatre, Dublin, 1956. Quoted in *Samuel Beckett: An Exhibition held at Reading University Library May to July 1971*, catalogue by J. Knowlson.
3. The oblique allusion to Hesione Hushabye in *Heartbreak House* occurs in 'A Wet Night', in *More Pricks than Kicks* (London: Chatto & Windus, 1934). See also n. 17 below.
4. Samuel Beckett, 'The Essential and the Incidental', *The Bookman*, 86 (1934), 111.
5. *'Dancing a Jig in the Bed': The Music in Sean O'Casey's Life*, compiled and presented by Ann Mann, produced by Piers Plowright (BBC Radio 3, 12 Jan. 1997).
6. See for instance 'Beckett and the Radio Medium', in John Drakakis (ed.), *British Radio Drama* (Cambridge: Cambridge University Press, 1981), 191–217; 'Journal de Cascando', *Revue d'Esthétique* Samuel Beckett special number (Jan. 1986).
7. *Eh Joe* was filmed in 1972 and the radio plays recorded on the following dates: *Words and Music*, 18 Dec. 1973; *Embers*, 30 Jan. 1976; *Cascando*, 8 Sept. 1984.
8. Richard Allen Cave, *New British Drama in Performance on the London Stage 1970–1985* (Gerrards Cross, Bucks.: Colin Smythe, 1987), 118.
9. Royal Holloway College, as it was in the period referred to in Chs. 7 and 9, later changed its name to Royal Holloway, University of London.
10. Clas Zilliacus, *Beckett and Broadcasting* (Åbo: Åbo Akademi, 1976), 103. The most comprehensive and searching study of the topic.
11. For further detail on Searle's music for the two plays see Katharine Worth, 'Words for Music Perhaps', in Mary Bryden (ed.), *Samuel Beckett and Music* (Oxford: Oxford University Press, 1998).
12. The Beckett productions by the Harold Clurman Theatre, New York, in which David was playing, moved from Edinburgh (where we first discussed our *Cascando* plans with him) to the Donmar Warehouse Theatre, London (28 Aug. 1984).
13. *Maeterlinck's Plays in Performance* (Cambridge: Chadwyck-Healey, 1985), in the Theatre in Focus series, gen. ed. Richard Allen Cave.
14. Despite encouragement from Brussels and elsewhere, the project was not realized at that time, though the idea has been revived since.
15. Eva Katharina Schultz quoted in Linda Ben-Zvi (ed.), *Women in Beckett* (Urbana and Chicago: University of Illinois Press, 1990), 22.
16. John Pilling, *Samuel Beckett* (London, Henley, and Boston, Mass.: Routledge & Kegan Paul, 1976). H. Porter Abbott, *Beckett Writing Beckett* (Ithaca and London: Cornell University Press, 1996).
17. The allusion to Mrs Gummidge in 'A Wet Night' includes the enigmatic phrase 'before the coverture'; this replaces 'before the coucherie', in the equivalent pas-

sage in the novel *Dream of Fair to Middling Women*, ed. Eoin O'Brien and E. Fournier, published only after Beckett's death (London and Paris: Calder, 1993).

18. The Colloque International at Caen, Normandy, organized by Jacqueline Genet, took place on 10–11 November 1989. I conveyed to the small group of invited participants Beckett's greetings and sympathetic interest, as he had asked me to do; and drew a few comparisons between his own art and Yeats's poem in my talk. It was published in Jacqueline Genet (ed.), *Studies on W. B. Yeats* (Caen: Groupe de Recherches d'Études Anglo-Irlandaises du C.N.R.S. (GO929), 1989).

CHAPTER 8

1. The programme at the Royal National Theatre's Olivier Theatre, a tribute to Beckett after his death, included many leading performers and readers of Beckett's work, including Billie Whitelaw and Harold Pinter. The National Theatre became the Royal National Theatre in 1988.
2. 'A Wake for Sam' (BBC2, 27 Jan. 1990).
3. Jordan R. Young, *The Beckett Actor* (Beverly Hills: Moonstone Press, 1987).
4. Martin Esslin's account is quoted in James Knowlson, *Damned to Fame: The Life of Samuel Beckett* (London: Bloomsbury, 1996), 604–5.
5. Ruby Cohn, *Just Play: Beckett's Theater* (Princeton, NJ: Princeton University Press, 1980), 228. Jonathan Kalb, *Beckett in Performance* (Cambridge: Cambridge University Press, 1989), 137–9.
6. Conversation with Ruby Cohn, 12 Aug. 1998. The director was Laura Jones, 'Voice' Eric Prince, 'She' Wendy Ishi, designer Robert Braddy.
7. JoAnne Akalaitis has spoken of her production of *Cascando* in interviews in Kalb, *Beckett in Performance*, and Lois Oppenheim (ed.), *Directing Beckett* (Ann Arbor: University of Michigan Press, 1994).
8. Interview in Oppenheim, *Directing Beckett*, 137.
9. Martin Esslin, 'Visions of Absence: Beckett's *Footfalls, Ghost Trio* and . . . *but the clouds* . . .', in Ian Donaldson (ed.), *Transformations in Modern European Drama* (London and Basingstoke: Macmillan, 1983).
10. Theatre programme for production of *Endgame*, directed by JoAnne Akalaitis for the American Repertory Theatre, 1984–5 season.
11. Mariko Hori Tanaka, 'Special Features of Beckett Performances in Japan', in Lois Oppenheim and M. Buning (eds.), *Beckett On and On* . . . (Madison and London: Associated University Presses, 1996).
12. Mary Bryden, *Women in Samuel Beckett's Prose and Drama* (London: Macmillan, 1993), 82 ff.
13. Beckett's remark to Kalb is recorded in *Beckett in Performance*, 78–9 and 152.
14. Edward Albee interviewed: see Oppenheim, *Directing Beckett*, 80–91.
15. Gil*das* Bourdet, 'Fizzle', in Oppenheim, *Directing Beckett*, 155–60.
16. Linda Ben-Zvi, 'All Mankind is Us: Godot in Israel 1985', in Ruby Cohn (ed.), *Samuel Beckett: Waiting for Godot. A Casebook* (Basingstoke and London: Macmillan, 1987).
17. Kalb, *Beckett in Performance*.
18. Colin Duckworth, 'Beckett's new *Godot*', in James Acheson and Kateryna Arthur (eds.), *Beckett's Later Fiction and Drama* (Basingstoke and London: Macmillan, 1987).

19. Conversation with Fiona Shaw, 3 Aug. 1998.
20. Peggy Ashcroft used these words to me in the interview recorded in Linda Ben-Zvi (ed.), *Women in Beckett* (Urbana and Chicago: University of Illinois Press, 1990).
21. In a conversation of 1976 Beckett told me of his dislike for the grouping of *Play*, *That Time*, and *Footfalls*.
22. Conversation with Juliet Stevenson, 3 July 1998.
23. Audrey (later Anna) McMullan, 'The Disciplined Body: Samuel Beckett's Late Drama', in Yasunari Takada (ed.), *Surprised by Scenes* (Tokyo: KenKyusha, 1994), 395–6.

CHAPTER 9

1. Reviews were consistently appreciative: 'And richly deserved it was', said Owen Dudley Edwards of the Fringe First Award to my adaptation (*Irish Times*, 7 Sept. 1987); John Peter praised Julian Curry's 'brilliant solo performance of a Beckett text' (*Sunday Times*, 30 Aug. 1987); Tim Pigott-Smith was admired for directing with 'equal delicacy and precision' (*The Scotsman*, 11 Aug. 1987). When transferred to London the production was included in the *Sunday Times*' Critics Choice (24 Jan. 1988).
2. *Company* at 7.15 p.m. was followed at 8.45 p.m. by Julie Forsyth in *Kid's Stuff (Enfantillages)* by Raymond Cousse, by coincidence a playwright said to be admired by Beckett. Quite a number of the audience attended both performances.
3. Nica Burns, as Artistic Director, had a vision of theatre which she followed courageously at the Donmar, making it one of the liveliest venues in London for new work and experiment.
4. Eileen Fisher, ' "Company": A Mabou Mines Production at the Public Theater, New York City', *Journal of Beckett Studies*, 10 (1985), 165.
5. Beckett's letter to Professor Alice Griffin (14 Mar. 1988) thanked her for the forthcoming festival to remember his birthday (lectures, symposium, and exhibition in addition to the production) and sent best wishes for the success of *Company*, 'so strikingly adapted by our friend Katharine Worth, and performed by Julian Curry'.
6. Carla Locatelli, *Unwording the World* (Philadelphia: University of Pennsylvania Press, 1990), 171.
7. S. E. Gontarski, '*Company* for Company: Androgyny and Theatricality in Samuel Beckett's Prose', in James Acheson and Kateryna Arthur (eds.), *Beckett's Later Fiction and Drama* (Houndmills, Basingstoke and London: Macmillan, 1987), 194.
8. Ibid. 197.
9. MacGowran's performance, directed by Alan Schneider, had been taped in a New York studio in 1971, then lost sight of.
10. The programme on Yeats, *Ceremony and Innocence*, was compiled and presented by Ann Mann and produced by Piers Plowright (BBC Radio 3, 1989). Ann Mann was at this time writing and presenting programmes for radio and television, often on writers with a strong interest in music such as Yeats and Synge.

11. Chris Hunt was at that time already building up his reputation as an accomplished producer and director of television programmes on artistic subjects. These have ranged from the dramatic and literary—Shakespeare (1987–9), Shaw (1988), Aldous Huxley (1994)—to the musical: José Carreras (1992), Puccini (1998), and the feature-film version of Trevor Nunn's production of *Oklahoma*, directed by Hunt in 1998.

Index

Selected references to Beckett's plays are listed alphabetically; adaptations and other works by Beckett appear as subentries under 'Beckett, Samuel'. Page references to productions of his plays and to major adaptations of his work are in bold.